W9-CPK-491

Comp City

A Guide To Free Las Vegas Vacations

Other Huntington Press titles:

Bargain City: Booking, Betting, and Beating the New Las Vegas
by Anthony Curtis

The Theory of Blackjack: The Compleat Card Counter's Guide to the Casino Game of 21
by Peter Griffin

Extra Stuff: Gambling Ramblings
by Peter Griffin

Comp City

A Guide To Free Las Vegas Vacations

Max Rubin

Huntington Press

Comp City: A Guide To Free Las Vegas Vacations

Published by
Huntington Press
5280 S. Valley View Blvd., Suite B
Las Vegas, NV 89118
(702) 597-1884 Vox
(702) 597-5208 Fax

ISBN 0-929712-35-8

Editor: Deke Castleman

Production & Design: Bethany Coffey

Jacket Design: Scot Briscoe

Jacket Photo: Greg Preston

Printing History
1st edition—May 1994

To Mom—for giving me life

To Joann—for giving me love

To Megan and Joe—for giving me hope

To Doc—for giving me a bunch of money

Acknowledgements

Learning to be a comp wizard was a non-stop hoot. Turning what I learned into a book was a never-ending chore. If these people hadn't helped me out, cheered me on, and held my hand through the drudgery, I never would have finished. Thanks to Alice, Bethany, Bill, Billy, Blair, Bobby, Boobie, Bozo, Bucky, Bunkie, Buzz, Chuckster, Cindy, Donnie, Eric, Filthy Phil, Froggy, Gary, George, Grandma, Hazel, Jack, Jessica, Jim, J.J., Joe, J. T., June, Katie, Karol, Kimmy, Laura, Lee, Lefty, Leslie, Lester, Lloydo, Marvy, Mike, Moochie, Munchkin, Patricia, Rickley, Ron, Steve, Tom, Vickers, Virginia, and to all the unsung chums who so bravely spilled their guts to me about casino marketing.

I am indebted to Stanford Wong and Peter Griffin, who unselfishly gave their time and generously lent their brains to this book.

We are all indebted to the Las Vegas resorts which have handed over their leadership to callow CFOs and MBAs who live in a world of numbers alone.

Finally, to Anthony Curtis, the tough, precise, and honor-bound publisher who kept me honest, and Deke Castleman, the patient, articulate, and inspiring editor who let me soar. Thank you for sharing my dream.

Table of Contents

Introduction

Imagine you're on "Wheel of Fortune." I know, as far as anyone other than your close friends or family is concerned, you don't even know who Pat Sajak is, right? But let's face it, watching "Wheel" is one of those mindless pleasures that even the slickest of us have found ourselves doing at one time or another. Okay. You're on the show. A new superprize goes on the wheel. It's "Free Las Vegas Vacations for Life." The announcer does a gushing voice-over for a video of a happy couple flying first class, cruising to a luxury hotel in a limo, checking into a deluxe suite, watching star-studded shows, dining on gourmet meals, and gambling the nights away.

The category is "Clue." You spin. The wheel lands on $400. You say "T."

Pat says, "Yes. There are six T's."

You spin again. The wheel clicks onto $500. You say "R."

Vanna starts turning letters—four R's.

Yeehaw! You're on the right trail. You spin again. The wheel lands on the superprize, Las Vegas. You say "F!"

Pat cries, "Yes! Two F's."

You're sweating now. You buy a vowel. "O."

"Yes! Five O's." Now you look at the board. You study it hard.

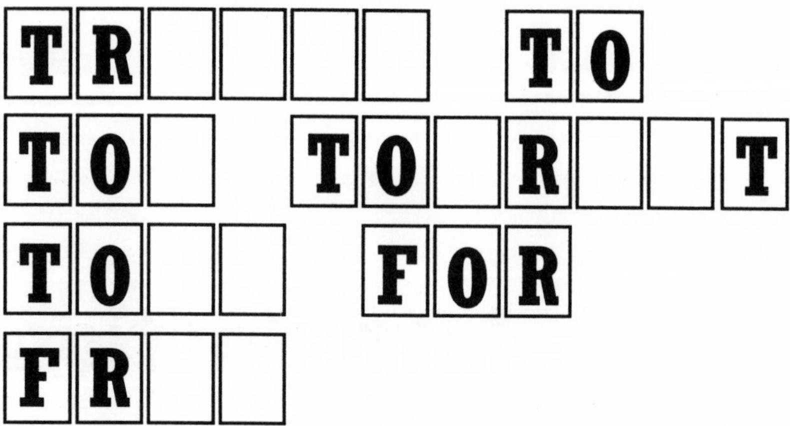

Your knees buckle as you tell Pat you're going to solve the puzzle. "Travel To Top Tourist Town For Free?"

"That's right!" Sajak screams over the roar of the crowd. "You've just won the cash and a lifetime of romping in the city that never sleeps."

You? Winning a lifetime's worth of vacations on a game show? Farfetched? Not at all. *Impossible* is more like it. No one's ever done it and no one ever will, because no one could ever afford to let the likes of you and me loose in Las Vegas for the rest of our lives—on their nickel.

What's not impossible, farfetched, or even improbable, however, is going to Las Vegas for the rest of your life as the guest of the casinos. What's more, you can live that life for less than the taxes you'd pay if you won your new lifestyle as a prize. Las Vegas vacations. Freer than free.

How? The answers are in these pages, revealed for the first time ever, and you won't have to wait long to learn them.

The premise is simple. Until now, the casinos dangled comps to lure your bankroll. After reading *Comp City*, you'll know how to dangle your bankroll to lure the casinos' comps.

Here's why it works. In all but the most primitively managed gambling operations, impersonal computers determine a player's comp rating. The computers are programmed by the casino's marketing and auditing departments, the number crunchers upstairs who decide what comps a customer is entitled to. The front-line casino personnel—floormen—have little, if any, decision-making authority concerning a casino's comp policies. But it's the floormen who compile the *data* which the computers analyze. That creates flaws in the system. First, it's easy to pull the wool over the eyes of the floormen who evaluate you. Second, it's even easier to trick the mavens in casino marketing who interpret the information the floormen send upstairs. Casino marketing knows that, over time, the house advantage, versus players with poor to average skills, will grind out about 2% of the money wagered on a blackjack table. And most casinos will return 35%-50% of the player's expected losses in comps. In other words, a $25 blackjack bettor will give the casino $1,500 (sixty $25 bets) in action an hour, from which the casino expects to win about 2%, or $30 for the hour, and return you $12-$15 in comps. Your actual loss, if you play an informed game of blackjack, will be 0.1% to 0.5%, or between $1.50 and $7.50 per hour that you play. In short, they expect you to lose $30. You only lose $3. But you still get back $12-$15 in comps. Are you getting this? You earn up to $15 for every hour that you play $25 blackjack. (I'll get into the complexities of *expected* losses versus *possible* losses and the ramifications of high-stakes play later in the book.)

So far so good. But it gets better. The trick is to make it appear that you're betting more, playing longer, and playing worse than you really are. I told you you wouldn't have to wait long to discover the method that'll provide you with unlimited vacations, but we should slow down a little to make sure we all understand just what a comp is and who gets them.

Comps occur on two levels: the comps that anyone can get and the comps that are only given to qualified players. We'll begin with what I refer to as the "comp classics." The classics include free parking (garage and valet), free cocktails, free tobacco, and casino funbooks, coupons, souvenirs, and other low-end giveaways. These comps are offered by most casinos to everyone who gambles (and some who don't), and it requires no special skills or knowledge on the part of the customer to take advantage of their availability. There are virtually no qualifying criteria for getting them, except for showing up.

The comps we're most concerned with include meals (from buffet to gourmet), rooms, shows, airfare, limo rides, golf, and invitations to special events. The only people who get this kind of stuff are players from whom the casinos think they will win a lot of money. Hustling the casino for these comps understandably involves financial risk on the part of the hustlers, but the risk can be minimized by knowledgeable "comp wizards."

What's a comp wizard? A comp wizard is someone who has a consciousness of comps and plays with the intention of taking advantage of the incentives and rewards that casinos offer gamblers. This doesn't imply that they're skilled at playing the games or even know how the comp systems work. But all comp wizards know how to throw the switch on the great comp-providing machine. How? In a word, they *ask*. The first objective of *Comp City* is to teach you how to become a comp wizard.

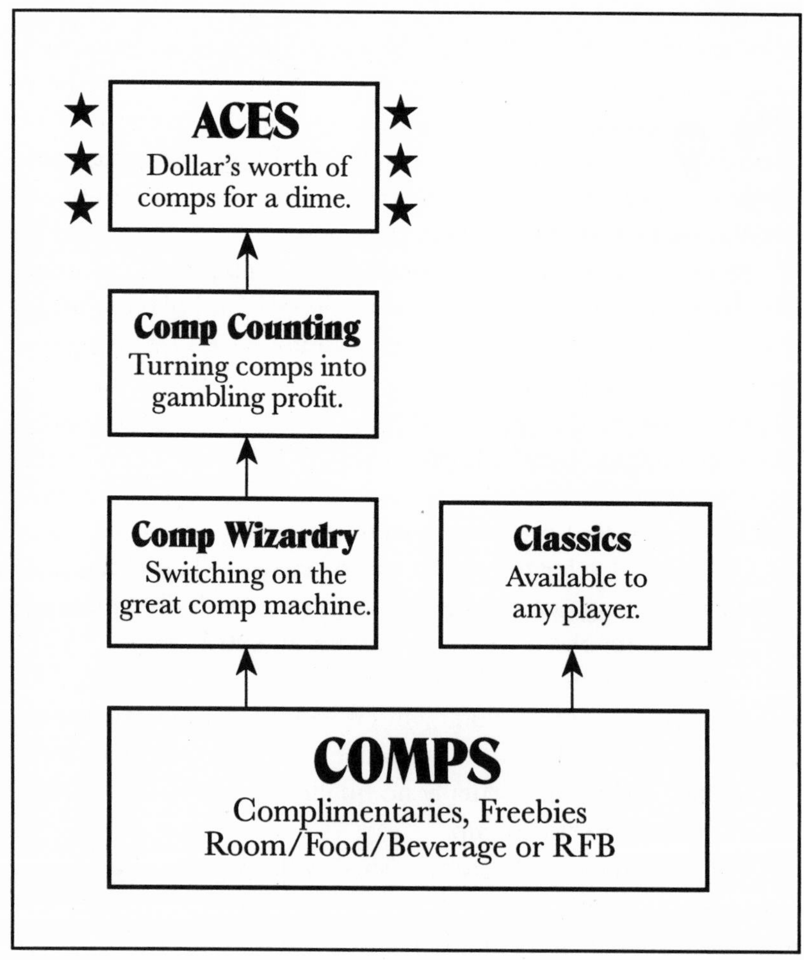

Once you've mastered the technique of asking for comps, you'll begin your apprenticeship to become a "comp counter." Comp counters have a specific and direct understanding of how to profit from the comp game. They know how to factor in the house advantage on table games versus what they earn in comps so that they always have a substantial advantage over the house when they gamble. Not to be confused with "*card* counting," which requires having everything but a good time, *comp* counting is an easy and fun way to beat the joints at their own game. Comp counting also works with special promotions and slot-club memberships and we'll cover these topics as well. Scores of comp counters today capitalize on the comp system, but they never quite seem to sink their hooks in deep enough to draw blood.

The highest form of comp counting is employed by the practitioners of "ACES" (Advanced Comp Equivalency Strategy). Teaching you ACES is the ultimate goal of this book. When you're done, you'll be able to develop your own unique, original, and artistic modus operandi for beating the casinos at their own game by getting a dollar's worth of comps for every *dime* you lose.

By the time you finish *Comp City*, you'll be thanking the casino owners for building these sparkling monuments where you can set up your own little free-vacation business. And the most laughable thing is they'll treat you like royalty while they're paying you to play! Heh heh heh.

It's taken me 25 years of banging around the industry as an amateur gambler (sucker), dealer, pit boss, casino owner, and eventually professional player to develop ACES. This system is quick and easy to learn, fast and fun to perfect, and best of all, it too is free. *Comp City* is the only gambling book ever written that will pay for itself with your first two hours of play after only a single reading.

Guaranteed!

Welcome to a lifetime's worth of Las Vegas vacations that are freer than free.

My Life as a Comp Wizard

I sat back, took a deep breath, and watched the Las Vegas Strip whir by as the airplane rumbled down the runway and eased to a stop. Halfway down the escalator to baggage claim, my guest saw a uniformed driver standing next to the luggage carousel holding a sign with my name on it. She squeezed my arm and whispered, "This is like a dream."

"No dream, darlin'," I laughed, "this is the real deal." The driver, Horatio, recognized me and hustled over. I was feeling pretty smug, but being a classy guy, I tried not to show it. Horatio hoisted our luggage and ushered us to a white stretch limo parked curbside. Iced cocktail glasses awaited on a burnished wooden table. Automatic dispensers holding call-brand liquors beckoned. I poured two stiff ones and we slipped back into the plush velour cushions as the headliner at our casino crooned on the stereo.

We pulled underneath the hotel's porte cochere. A snappy doorman assisted us out of the limo and directed us to VIP Services. We bypassed the jammed hotel lobby. A VIP hostess approached and handed me our keys.

We went upstairs to a lavish suite. Our host Artie, had been kind enough to send up a fruit basket. He even remembered my favorite champagne. I popped the cork and pulled back the curtains. The Strip glittered and hummed. We had three nights of this ahead of us and all it was going to cost—well, we'll get to that later. Suffice it to say, I'd already won and hadn't even played yet.

Sipping the bubbly, we reviewed the menus from the hotel's many restaurants, and decided on Northern Italian. I called VIP Services and was told that a table would be ready in twenty minutes. Upon entering the restaurant, the maitre d' warmly shook my hand and the waiter welcomed me by name. After three appetizers, Caesar salad, and a light pasta dinner washed down with three different wines, I signed the tab and left a nice tip. Maybe it gets better than this somewhere. If you ever find out where, let me know.

After dinner it was off to the blackjack tables. I spotted my favorite floorman. He welcomed me as I handed him a small gift. Then I settled in for a couple hours of comp wizardry and we finished the evening with a jacuzzi, more champagne, and sleep.

The next afternoon, after a double bloody Mary and steak-and-eggs brunch in bed, I spent a few more leisurely hours playing blackjack while my guest got pampered, powdered, and poodled in the spa. A French gourmet dinner followed, then it was showtime.

Artie the host escorted us past the 600 people waiting in line and introduced us to the showroom captain, who gave us the best seats in the house (at least that's what he said when he stuck out his mitt). After the performance it was off to the lounge show, where drinks, of course, were free.

This gluttony went on until it all became a blur. On our last morning, just before checkout time, I called Artie to ask how much I owed for the weekend. He laughed and said it was all on the house. No surprises there.

While the limo took us back to the airport, I tried to recall the whole 72-hour cholesterol and champagne slugfest. As we pulled to the curb and the driver handed our luggage to a skycap, I looked back at the Las Vegas skyline and marveled to my guest that we'd just had a ridiculously opulent weekend for what a single gourmet meal would have cost in any other big city.

We got on the plane, and just as we were taking off she asked me when I was coming back. "Next week," I said, matter-of-factly.

"You do this every week," she asked?

"Yeah."

"How can you live like this every weekend?"

"Easy. It's free."

"You're addicted to those comps, aren't you?"

"Yeah," I admitted. "I'm a regular comp junkie."

She was right. I *was* addicted. I was hooked on free suites, free food, free booze, free limos, and free cross-country airplane rides. What's more, I was even addicted to bellmen, waiters, dealers, and bosses groveling before me every time I walked into a casino.

Am I in recovery? Recover this, chucko! I'm still one of the world's foremost comp junkies, and proud of it. Comps are my life. I eat 'em, I sleep 'em, and I drink 'em. Hell, I even ride around in 'em.

Don't get me wrong. Gambling is hard work if you have to

win to pay the mortgage. I've done that too. But that's not what this is about. This is about going first class, and not breaking a sweat getting there. This is about comps—wizardry, counting, ACES. This is about sitting down at a blackjack table or in front of a slot machine, games that more and more people are playing as a form of entertainment and recreation, and grabbing the share of amenities that you're entitled to simply for being there. All I'm going to do is show you how to claim what's rightfully yours.

1

The Evolution of Comps

An Irreverent and Original History of the Rating Game

Before we delve into the preparations for and practice of comp hustling, it's instructive to review just how the gambling business has come to define and embrace the concept of giving away comps to entice gamblers to give away their money.

Grind Stores and Google

In the early part of this century, illegal gambling flourished in Kansas City, New Orleans, Miami, Newport (Kentucky), Hot Springs (Arkansas), Steubenville (Ohio), Saratoga (New York) and, to a lesser but significant degree, almost every other major city in the U.S. It was controlled by a loose-knit band of organized criminals, and protected by crooked cops, corrupt judges, and winking attorneys general. Despite its illegality, gambling was so far-reaching that at its peak, Al Capone's live wire broadcasts of horse racing results (even when the races themselves were wired) from scores of tracks around the country had roughly 1,000 off-track bookmaking subscribers. Las Vegas gambling (also illegal) was minuscule then, and barely noticed on the American gambling scene.

Gambling was legalized in Nevada in 1931, and when Hoover Dam was completed in 1935, the region was assured an unlimited supply of water and electricity. The Las Vegas boom was inevitable, but the first gambling entrepreneurs were mostly small-time back-room crap and bingo operators from Southern California. They took over some of the downtown clubs and brought their best customers with them. A few big-time offshore gambling-ship owners followed, and Las Vegas began to become known as a place to go to gamble.

Still, Las Vegas was considered the stepchild of Reno, where most of the state's money and power, and almost all of its notoriety, had been firmly entrenched since the early 1900s. Las Vegas city boosters were desperate to build an economic base that would allow them to compete with Reno. But up until the mid-1940s, the only gambling attractions of which Las Vegas could boast were the downtown grind stores, and the El Rancho Vegas and Last Frontier Hotel, two hacienda-style casino playgrounds-of-the-stars on the edge of town.

Enter Bugsy Siegel, in 1944. Bugsy had been dispatched to Southern California by his East Coast partners to organize the underworld (and, incidentally, to evade a murder rap). That accomplished, he turned his attention to moving in on the legal gambling in Nevada. Reno, his first choice, was controlled by Raymond and Harold Smith, Bill Harrah, and several established ranching families. They all had bedrock political alliances, plenty of money, and at that time, the toughest bunch of fist-fighting, sharpshooting security guards in the country. Bugsy and his hoods showed up flashing their bankrolls and .38s, but after a couple of nasty nose-to-nose skirmishes, organized crime's advance guard wisely decided that southern Nevada would be a softer spot to set up shop.

When Siegel's Fabulous Flamingo opened in the middle of the desert in 1946, it was Las Vegas' first joint designed to cater to the criminally chic. Employing what came to be known as "Google" or glorified coffee shop architecture, the Flamingo was a casino that everyone, especially old-time gamblers, could identify with, only bigger and brighter. There was one problem. The concept didn't work. Southern Nevada was simply too far away, too obscure, and too hot and dusty to attract the wise guys. Someone had to figure out a way to get gamblers to Las Vegas.

The Feds to the Rescue

You've read stories about Benny Binion, Howard Hughes, Kirk Kerkorian, and the other so-called fathers of Las Vegas gambling who are credited with making Las Vegas what it is. But their impact pales in comparison to another man who, though reviled by the old-time gamblers and feared by the Las Vegas establishment, was most responsible for making Las Vegas the gambling capital of the world. If this city ever erects a monument to the real Father of Las Vegas, it would have to honor a rabble-rousing U.S. Senator from Tennessee named Estes Kefauver.

What did E.K. do to deserve such a lofty place in Las Vegas' history? In the late '40s and early '50s Kefauver's Senate Committee to Investigate Organized Crime brought so much heat on the illegal gambling trade that it managed to shut down virtually all the casinos across the United States. After that, dozens of smart, tough, rich crooks were looking for a place to muscle (with cash and firepower) back into action. Las Vegas was the only place to go.

The timing was right because Las Vegas was welcoming any and all comers. Moe Dalitz showed up in 1950 with his Cleveland partners and built the Desert Inn. Houston gambler Jake Freedman built the Sands in 1952, and sold limited points in the club, but only to other illegal gamblers who had connections to gamblers in areas of the country not already covered by his staff. In order to qualify as a Sands point holder, you had to be willing to work at the property, you had to know a lot of high rollers, and you had to be responsible for collecting unpaid markers. As evidenced by the enormous success of the Sands (until Howard Hughes bought it in 1968), the formula worked and it was copied again and again at new properties that were opening up and down the Strip.

Freedman's system at the Sands was the first effort at organized casino marketing. Remember, this was a time when the club operators relied little on advertising, preferring instead to foster one-on-one relationships with their customers. But even with the buddy system, the concept of grand-scale giveaways (full comps) was not familiar to gamblers, since the operators relied more on loyalty than bribery. Up until this time, the only comps that even the sportiest of the early Las Vegas casinos offered were cheap whiskey and bad cigars. Then, as the postwar migration of wiseguy money to the desert got underway in earnest, the newer and classier joints began giving customers better perks, such as cigarettes, meals, and hookers. Incredibly, a lot of clubs still had selective policies that limited free cocktails to only their better bettors, while penny-ante players paid for drinks. (It wasn't until the late '50s that the Las Vegas casino managers finally figured out that alcohol promotes reckless gambling, and then every gambler in town was treated to free booze.)

Sin City Steps Up Its Play

While Senator Kefauver's committee was inadvertently concentrating the criminals in Las Vegas in the early '50s, the Las Vegas Chamber of Commerce was working to attract the general public. First, they commissioned the Las Vegas News Bureau to take pictures of any and all events around Las Vegas. Then they distributed the photos with press releases on a regular basis to all but the smallest newspapers. One winter day an editor in Amarillo would get a photo of busty bikini-clad showgirls shooting dice on a floating crap game in the Sands pool. (Floating crap game, get it?) The next week the editor would open his mail and see a shot of an atomic bomb's mushroom cloud rising above Fremont Street. A week later the editor would receive a press release about Frank Sinatra punching a gangster casino boss in the nose.

Cheesecake, A-bombs, and the mob. Not a lot of other cities had that kind of public-relations trail mix. Nosiree. In addition to enhancing a slightly sinful image, the Chamber of Commerce took a step in a different direction, in an attempt to bring legitimacy to Las Vegas. In the mid-'50s, they created the Convention Authority and started wooing conventioneers. They imposed a room tax to build the Convention Center and to finance a full-bore, nationwide, marketing assault. They sent reps on the road and engineered huge, quick-hitting media blitzes aimed at travel agents and convention coordinators.

While the Convention Authority was pumping up the overall Las Vegas visitor volume, each hotel was targeting its own marketing niche. Since the volume was increasing, the hotel's comp policies weren't budging. Then it happened (trumpets please)—the best month ever in the evolution of comps. April 1955. In these four glorious weeks, the Riviera, Dunes, and New Frontier all opened. As the new joints and the old joints tried to steal each other's customers, the floodgates of comps were released. Food, booze, shows and, for the first time, rooms were lathered on all but the worst slugs.

It got better. In 1956 the Hacienda and Fremont opened, the Tropicana and Stardust were being built, and if you couldn't get a free meal, it meant you weren't in Las Vegas.

I'm telling you, it was hog heaven, and I mean hog. A player would check into a hotel, put a thousand or two on deposit, and hit the town with his hands out. In those days, there was no player tracking, no ratings, no auditing, and if you wanted to see a show across the street, any pit boss in your joint would "make a call" and you'd be all set up. When the bosses across the street called your boss for the same favor, he'd reciprocate. It was hunky dory. And speaking of hunky, there were some other "fringies" that came with the deal.

Showgirls. Cocktail waitresses. House hookers. This was not Gloria Steinem's kind of town. If you put up, say, $2,500 and bet $50 to $100 a hand for an hour or two, all you had to do was call over your pit boss and the joint would send a live one up to your room for your entertainment pleasure. The house picked up the tab, and if you were lucky, you didn't pick up something to take back home to the missus.

Junkets and the First Comp Wizards

In 1961, a new Flamingo stockholder threw a party and flew in a plane-load of wealthy friends from Florida to show off the hotel. While his guests were there, the hotel recorded its biggest "drop" (buy-ins at the tables) ever and decided to pick up the tab (room, food, entertainment, even the chartered jet) for the whole group.

This inaugurated the era of the junket—a plane-load of gamblers who qualified for free airfare, room, food, and beverage by putting up a required amount of front money. The junkets were run by junket masters, who were paid by the casinos for every gambler they brought in.

The first customers to come out on these junkets were mostly criminals. We're back to crooks again, but you've got to remember, Las Vegas wasn't only built *by* criminals, it was also built *for* criminals. Not just mobsters, but also small-time bookies, numbers runners, knee breakers, con men, land swindlers, and the usual assortment of all-around bad guys. But by far the most common type of "criminals" were good-guy legitimate businessmen who were deft at handling cash-register receipts, but somewhat lax in their civic duty when it came time to remember their silent partner, the IRS. With a delicious twist, the businessmen would snag the money the government had earmarked for something incredibly brilliant like tobacco subsidies, and blow it on the table

Whacking Out . . .

While it wasn't exactly Marquis of Queensbury marketing, the casinos had another way of making payroll. They cheated. In the bad old days, when the owners were former bootleggers, gangsters, and cheaters from all walks of life, most of the joints had a "chopper" in the blackjack pit, a smooth-as-silk card sharp who would whack out drunks making a run at the house's bankroll, and a boxman or two on the dice games who were adept at switching in loaded dice under the high rollers' noses.

A lot of times the house wasn't even aware that they were cheating the customers. It worked like this. Mr. E.Z. Mark would come in and put $5,000 in the cage. He'd get liquored up, the choppers would whack him out of his money, and then "dump off" about 80% of what they'd stolen from the mark to their own outside agents, who'd "win big" on the tables (long before video cameras taped all the action), go to the cage, cash out, and vanish.

while getting free cigarettes.

The Flamingo owners soon began experimenting with chartered junkets from cities around the country and before long the four-day group freebie was a mainstay at Bugsy's former joint. The Dunes soon followed suit, then the other premium Strip hotels. Junkets flourished through the 1960s.

Up until 1962, women were not especially welcome on junkets. But the wives, being wives, still wanted to come along. When the Dunes installed a topless show, they started insisting on it. Dunes management capitulated and amazingly, the women started going to the topless shows, too. Imagine, going to a strip joint and *taking your wife...* because she *wants* to go. What possessed these wives to go along with their husbands while they stared at six-foot-tall, 22-year-old showgirls is beyond me. But it worked. Sin was in. Maybe it was because after seeing all those leggy tomatoes wiggling on stage, the old men turned into horndog casino-love-gods and actually paid a little attention to the

. . . and Dumping Off

When the unsuspecting (or otherwise) casino manager reviewed the night's take, the joint had made a healthy 20% return on the $5,000 cash drop, the poor slob got entertained by a showgirl or two, and the chopper and his agents cut up the rest of the money, which was nearly always spent wisely on booze, broads, and dice as soon as they got off work.

A couple of those mechanics became casino managers at the most prestigious hotels. Others continued to ply their trade against the house and became wealthy landowners. Sadly, a few wound up as cactus fertilizer when they finally got caught practicing their lifelong professions.

A smattering of the old-time crossroaders are still playing against the house from the outside, which is probably safer now than it ever has been, because the new-guard, college-grad staffs in the casinos are as woefully ignorant of cheating scams as they are of comp wizardry.

women that came out with them on the airplane.

It was hands-on back then. The Tropicana had a golf course. They had dealers. In order to deal at the Trop, you had to play golf. With the customers. On your own time. The dealers kept their own tips and were allowed to eat and drink and golf on the comps of the customers they played with. It was a country club with a casino inside. The Desert Inn, Dunes, and Stardust operated the same way. Dealers doubled as hosts and business boomed.

About three hours after the first junket hit town, the first comp wizards started plying their trade. They were known as "riders," guys who put up front money, but never really had gambling in mind, only revelry. And oh man, those were the days for revelry! There was no marketing paper trail, no auditing of average bets. In fact, for six or seven years of junketeering, those original comp wizards got an entirely free ride, because nobody in accounting had the guts to confront the old-time casino managers or junket masters about the freeloading.

It wasn't until the late 1960s, after Howard Hughes showed up with his MBA bean counters, that Las Vegas finally witnessed the first casino countermeasures designed to stop the riders. What do you suppose these geniuses did when they discovered the freeloaders? With typical Las Vegas knee-jerk mentality, they killed junkets. Revenues fell. So they reinstated junkets. Then the riders hopped on the charters again. What to do?

In the late 1960s, Caesars made the first move, by reimbursing individual airfares instead of chartering junkets, but it didn't work; since individual travel costs were much higher, these gamblers were required to deposit about twice as much front money as traditional junket gamblers. When faced with this proposition, the players just went to the other casinos where they could get a better deal.

So the casinos tried something else, equally futile. The organizers informed each customer, before the junket left for Las Vegas, that the hotel reserved the right to charge him for the RFB bill and airfare if his gambling action didn't warrant the comps. While it did discourage many riders from getting on the planes, the disclaimers were virtually worthless once the persistent riders landed, for two reasons. First, federal law prohibited charging a person airfare on a hosted charter. Second (you're gonna love this one), the Nevada Gaming Control Board, in order to prevent the appearance of its licensees engaging in deceptive advertising, expressly prohibited hotels from charging *invited* guests unless they had been issued, in writing, clearly defined comp-qualification criteria. The house's only fail-safe method of ensuring that a customer paid his bill if his play didn't warrant a comp was to have each customer sign a statement prior to checking in that he had read the established comp criteria. Nice try. A better system was needed.

Playing To Your Line

The first attempt at creating an efficient, all-encompassing comp formula was made by Hughes' auditors who, being auditors, had a terrible aversion to simply giving away so much in comps to junket participants, especially with no concrete policies and procedures. So they came up with a means for evaluating players that took into consideration two pieces of the comp jigsaw puzzle: the size of a credit line (or front money), and the number of markers taken. This early formula was primitive; the auditors didn't need to know how long you played or how much you bet. All they cared about was how high your line went and if you played to it. The better junkets required a $5,000 minimum credit line. To qualify for the free room, food, and beverage to which the junket entitled you, you had to take markers (draw money against your credit line at the tables) for the whole $5,000. That's all. Nothing more. Your whole job, in the three or four days of the junket, was to take ten markers for $500 each. What? Make a few bets? Sure! What the hell.

Actually, the few bets did come into play. Every time you took a marker against your line, the pit boss would write down your first few wagers on the back of the marker. And that was *really* it. Ten markers, ten or fifteen bets, and the rest was free—free room, probably some free food, maybe some free entertainment, and definitely plenty of free time. Did I mention that the minimum bet was $25? Good God.

All the auditors cared about was that the comp recipient take a lot of markers, and they installed a simple rating system based on it. After each junket, the junket master received a report based on the value (A to D) to the house of each player. "A" players were the first to be invited back, then "B" players. If the plane still wasn't full, "C" players were contacted, as well as the friends of "A" and "B" players. "D" players were taken off the list entirely.

It was in the junket master's best interest to make sure that all his players understood, and exploited, the system, so the fix was in on virtually every junket that came to Las Vegas. It happened every hour of every day for many years. A junket participant took a marker for $500 worth of chips, made a few token bets (losing, say, $50), and cashed out the remaining $450 in chips at the cage. Then he sat down in another pit on another shift with a new boss, took another marker, played a little more blackjack, and traded the rest of the chips for cash. If the player had put up actual front money, at the end of the junket he'd turn in his markers and get a little of the remaining cash back or just zero out his account. If, as was usual, the junketeer was gambling off of a line of credit, he'd turn in the cash and have his markers ripped up. The casinos referred to this practice as "marker churning," and it caused all kinds of problems, as we'll see.

A few of the joints tried to limit marker churning by stopping people from cashing out large amounts of chips at the cage if they owed markers. How? Someone wanting to cash out, say, $450 in chips, was asked by the cashier, "Do you have any outstanding markers?" Some unscrupulous souls, to sidestep this annoyance, probably lied. Others just cashed out chips for a hundred or two at a time. Many wives cashed chips; strangers were even paid to exchange chips at the cage. I know it's a bit hard to imagine that anyone could be so deceitful, but trust me, they were.

False Drops and Marker Welshing

The system should have worked, at least according to the way the auditors figured it. First, they assumed that the players would play to their lines. That is, the players would draw down all their credit or money on deposit and gamble with it. Again, it didn't matter how high they bet or how long they played, just that they took out all their money. Second, they figured that the casino would hold about 20% of the drop. They either didn't understand, or just didn't consider the fact, that a high hold percentage requires extended play on the part of gamblers—play they weren't getting. Based on these erroneous assumptions, the casino would give the players comps worth up to 50% of their expected loss, which under this system came to 10% of their credit lines. Far too much.

This archaic system created a three-way rift among auditors, junket reps, and casino managers. Most auditors didn't even understand the nuts and bolts of gambling, let alone the mentality of the comp wizard, and they simply couldn't grasp the idea that a player might win enough chips in his first or second session that he wouldn't need additional markers. They didn't understand that if a gambler won $5,000 on Friday playing off his first marker, he wouldn't take another marker on Saturday or Sunday. Thus, the auditors came down on the junket reps for their players who "weren't gambling," because no distinction was made among players who won, who gambled conservatively, or who were freeloading. Meanwhile, because the riders were scamming the casino by churning all their markers, they were establishing a "false drop" (making it appear as if the table action was much higher than it really was). A false drop, in turn, created a lower "hold percentage" (the money won by the casino divided by the buy-ins of the gamblers). The churned markers were negatively affecting the auditors' almighty profit indicator.

This situation drove the auditors to rat out the casino managers to the corporation executives, who came down on the bosses because they couldn't achieve the win percentages that the weenies upstairs thought they should. That put the bosses in the middle of a squeeze play that they couldn't escape: if a boss wanted to ensure a higher hold percentage to protect his butt on one side, he had to stop all the marker churning. But if he wanted to make sure that the comps he was okaying for his players (to comply with the house's marketing policies) weren't out of line, he had to have a lot of markers churned.

In a nutshell, everybody was pissed at everybody.

Another interesting spin-off from this comp conundrum was that it substantially increased the percentage of unpaid credit. Here's why. The casino told a player he had to draw down the full

$5,000 of his line or deposit. While churning the markers, he played a little, making $25 bets, while getting plied with free booze. By the time he was well lubricated, he headed over to the joint next door—with five grand in his pocket. He jumped into a crap game and got busted. So now he'd lost the money at a casino other than the one he borrowed it from. Or, he skipped the craps and spent it at the hotel jewelry store on a woman he met in the bar. Or he used it to make payroll on a faltering business back home. Keep in mind that Nevada gambling debts were not legally collectable until 1983.

Who got the grief for the unpaid markers? The junket reps. Not the executives. Not even the bosses in this instance. And certainly not the bean counters. Accountants were (and are) adroit at pointing fingers at everybody else. It's never their fault when something goes wrong and they've got the statistics to prove it. God bless their calculating hearts.

The End of the Beginning

Something had to give. By the late '70s, we see the first stirrings of the system that has become prevalent in the casino industry today. Though the actual moments and characters are lost in the mists of history, what probably happened was this. An old-time accountant at, say, the Desert Inn, who'd survived the owner transition from Moe Dalitz to Howard Hughes, is playing golf with a shift boss from Caesars and a junket master from Brooklyn. Now they're at the nineteenth hole, tossing back a few comped scotches and laughing at the accountant for missing a game-losing three-footer (still common among accountants). The junket master starts in on the shift boss, complaining about how the casino has been really busting his chops over freeloaders. Then the shift boss shoots back that by now he can spot a marker churner at 100 yards—without his distance glasses. Not to be outdone, the accountant describes how his chief financial officer boss, another of Howard Hughes' Harvard MBAs, is calling him on the carpet about comps.

Accountant (Count): This jerk, who wouldn't know a snake eyes if it was sitting on his head, calls me in and starts asking me,

'What the hell are all these comps being slathered around town without so much as a receipt?' Can you believe it? He's been in the rackets for all of two months, and he's bustin' my chops about comps!

Junket Master (Junk)—pursuing his freeloader agenda: Hey, I can see why he doesn't understand it. You know, I've been trying for years to get you number geeks with brown shoes to forget about this playing-to-the-line crap. What you guys need to do is have the floormen watch the players a little more, and put down their average bet, not just the minimum, and how long they play. Then you'd have a much better idea of how much you're supposed to win and you could give them back half of that in comps and get off my case about the fleas.

Shift Boss (Boss): Get off *your* case? What about me? I get heat from you. I get heat from the president. I get heat from the auditors. For what? Trying to do my job! (He pauses, considering what the junket master is proposing.) Well, wait a minute now. Average bet times hours played. I think you might have something there. Yeah. That'd let us cut out the riders who take all those markers and don't bet squat, and my hold would—hell, I bet it'd double. And I could still take care of the guys that deserve getting comped.

Count (smiling): Yeah. We're on to something here. So I go to my boss and tell him we'll make everyone play, say, four hours a day and bet, maybe fifty dollars a hand. What's a guy like that worth to us?

Boss (calculating): Well, let's say we're dealing a round a minute, 60 hands an hour. Four hours. Um, that's 240 hands, times fifty bucks, that's...

Count: Twelve thousand dollars. Now, you casino guys generally expect to hold twenty percent, right? Twenty percent of twelve thousand dollars is two thousand four hundred. And you junket guys expect us to give back half of that in comps. So your player is entitled to twelve hundred in comps for four hours play?

Junk (smiling): Yeah!

Boss: Whoa, whoa, whoa! That's terrible!

Count: Of course it is! Because the twenty-four hundred isn't what we're *winning*! Why? Because the twelve large isn't the *drop*, it's the *action*. You guys don't expect to win twenty percent of the action, do you?

Boss: No. It's twenty percent of the drop.

Count: Yeah but, a drop of $500 can produce twelve grand worth of action, right? Hell, a drop of twelve grand could give us only $500 in action if a guy's blatantly churning markers.

Junk (frothing): Wait a minute! You can't tell me a guy with twelve large ain't worth twelve grand in action—

Count (interrupting): Yes I can! All these years not one wise-guy in the entire casino business has ever figured out that the expected win from a gambler is *not* directly related to his line or how much he drops. What it is related to is… uh… give me a second here... what it is related to is the average bet times the house advantage.

The junket rep and shift boss don't quite get it.

Count: What's the edge on a blackjack game?

Junk: Gotta be at least ten percent—

Boss: Not a chance! Scarne puts it at about five percent. Two, three percent we'd be safe.

Junk: Safe?! What are you, nuts? You think I'm gonna fill up a plane with gamblers if you're giving comps based on a lousy three percent?

Count: Maybe, maybe not. But let's figure it out. Three percent of twelve grand is three-sixty. Half of that is one-eighty in comps.

Junk: One-eighty! For a guy with a twelve-thousand-dollar line? Jesus H—

Count: Don't you get it? A player's *line* doesn't prove a thing! The *markers* a guy takes don't prove a thing. What matters is how much he bets and for how long. Hey—you were the one that suggested it in the first place!

The accountant and the shift boss pat each other on the back, laughing. They look over at the junket rep who, knowing his days are now numbered, has suddenly gone pale.

Count (to Junk): What are the odds a junket rep would come up with a way to keep the freeloaders from beating us up on comps? Wait till my boss hears this one. Even he's gonna understand. Thanks.

Junk (keeling over): Urk!

Bingo! The old-time comp wizards were finished.

The New Formula

In the early '80s, Caesars became the first casino to change its comp policy from a drop-based to a win-estimate formula. Caesars already required a junket gambler to make $50 minimum bets at blackjack and $100 at craps, and now they added a four-hour-daily minimum-playing-time requirement for a three-day stay. Hilton, the Desert Inn, and other premium joints quickly followed suit.

The new procedures changed everything. The floormen's and pit bosses' clerical responsibilities increased dramatically. But they only collected the data and sent it upstairs, where marketing had the chore of determining a player's comp equivalency (value). The equivalency was double-checked by auditing to see that it matched the formula. This took a lot of comping discretion out of the hands of the pit bosses, which hurt the players.

The first hotels to implement the new system lost customers who, used to the old way of doing things, didn't want to be called on the carpet for their play (or lack thereof). Also, bosses who tried to toe the company line had to say no to their old customers, who walked across the street where the comp criteria were still exploitable. On the other hand, the real gamblers were finally being evaluated by a system that was (ostensibly) more accurate in terms of establishing the true worth of a customer. It turned out that many gamblers with smaller budgets had always been ignored, though the amount of action they supplied actually warranted the big comps. Meanwhile, a lot of the so-called high rollers who received the big comps hardly gave the house a shot at their bankroll. Now, guys who only had $1,000 to risk were getting their just comp desserts, while the old-time big shots were getting invited not to come back at all.

Initially, table-game revenues dropped as the comp criteria were tightened, but by 1986, table-game revenues had recovered and comps were up, too. Most of the clubs by then had gone over to the new comping formula, which ferreted out the freeloaders and rewarded their truly valuable customers with great comps.

Another trend that emerged in the mid-'80s that also affected the comp situation was the growth of slot machines as a dominant force in the casino, and hence slot players as a new group deserving of comps. By now, slots had become the main revenue producers, and the joints were marketing slots more and more.

But all was not perfect in Compville, because the system had one very weak link. The inherent weakness in the system was (and is) that someone—the floorman—had to observe the play and accurately record the data that the marketing people used to determine comps. The original player-tracking methods were cumbersome and time-consuming, and since a sizable percentage of the floormen in Las Vegas at that time were functionally illiterate and couldn't make heads or tails of the paperwork, it didn't get done properly. Even if the paperwork didn't pose a problem, at best a very limited sampling of play occurred. Maybe one out of every fifty hands played in a three-hour session was (and still is) notated as the average bet. Not only that, but an even bigger flaw was the compromised integrity of the bosses. The casinos encouraged the floormen to become familiar with the customers (both to promote good relations and to rate them more accurately). These acquaintances and friendships quickly resulted in the players extending gifts (and outright bribes) to the bosses in return for favorable ratings. This tactic has been raised to an art form over the last ten years, which is part of what this book is about.

VIPs On Their Own

The new comp system pretty much killed junkets, by successfully ferreting out the old-time comp wizards, along with the non-gamblers with whom unscrupulous junket masters filled up their planes. (Needless to say, this also put an end to a whole lot of other money scams that the loose junket system inspired, such as loan sharking, kickbacks for credit, marker welshing, and out-and-out thievery). Many junket gamblers abandoned Las Vegas altogether and headed for the Caribbean islands; junkets flourished in the Bahamas. In addition, the real VIPs wanted the freedom to travel according to their own schedules, not the junkets'. Finally, larger aircraft were quickly replacing the smaller outdated planes and though they were cheaper to operate, they were harder to fill.

Today, old-style junkets (other than international charters from the Orient) have gone the way of the single-coin slot machine. Some of the premium clubs still offer what they call "junkets," but they're really weekend trips for small groups of players from the same part of the country, which the hotel blocks in advance in order to get discounts from the airlines, not the old-guard groups of friends and mob associates who gave early Las Vegas so much of its flavor and reputation.

The Way It Is

Over the course of the '80s, rating systems became more sophisticated and bosses became more proficient at the paperwork. Computer-generated player tracking was instituted up and down the Strip and before long there were fewer old-time freeloaders than Milton Berle fans. But while the original comp wizards were dying off, a very select breed of hustlers began to recognize that, for all of the casinos' newfound sophistication, they still went through reactionary comp cycles, similar to the progression of shutting down junkets to get rid of the riders, then starting them up again to restimulate the sudden drop in business. Casinos clenched when comps got out of hand, then loosened up when, invariably, the table drop began to fall. A few masters of the comp game learned to catch the right casinos at the right point in their cycles, and old-time comp wizardry metamorphosed into new-age comp counting.

As we slid out of the '80s, the casinos came to believe that it was almost impossible for a player to get a comp for nothing. So they relaxed, secure in the knowledge that their magical comping formulas, pencil-pushing pit bosses, and high-tech tracking systems were virtually fail-safe.

Wrong again.

Crime Plays

Now that you know Las Vegas was built by and for criminals, the question remains: do Las Vegas casinos still cater to criminals? Gimme a break. Unless it's someone with a serious death wish, who the hell *else* is going to play blackjack, craps, or baccarat at $25,000 a throw? It sure ain't gonna be someone who's *earned* his money. Let me tell you about a couple of former customers who topped the Las Vegas list.

Two of the biggest "whales" (guys who bet $200,000 a hand for days at a time) in Sin City history increased the bottom line at some Las Vegas properties by as much as thirty million a year in their heyday. Sadly (for the casinos and themselves) they both had some bad luck in 1992.

Have you ever heard about those golf country clubs in Japan that cost a million dollars to join? One of these legendary Las Vegas high rollers built a beautiful new Japanese golf course and sold memberships at the unheard-of low, low price of $15,500. He claimed he was selling only 1,830 memberships, so his golf-crazy Japanese customers rushed to snap up the "limited" supply. In fact, the developer foisted over 52,000 of these "exclusive" beauties and made, well, let's see—52,000 memberships times $15,500 comes to eight hundred million dollars. Now, what's a guy going to do with that much ill-gotten gain? He's going to give a lot of it away. And he did. To Caesars, Mirage, Hilton, Tropicana. This whale tipped the dealers at one hotel alone over four million dollars in his two-year run there before the Nipponese gendarmes put the hooks on him. He's now serving a 12-year sentence and isn't expected to be paroled anytime soon, as he committed what is considered the most heinous crime of all in Japan: messing with someone's tee time.

The other whale? He was in, shall we say, the loan business. He'd blow five mil during a single play and pay the casino with cash. Cash cash. Bills. Duffle bags stuffed with greenbacks. He played all over the world, against the Tong in Asia, against the Donald in Atlantic City, against the Steve at the

Mirage, and all points north, south, east, and west.

From 1990 to 1992, his worldwide gambling losses were reported to be over one hundred million dollars. He started playing for credit. His reputation was going bad all over the world. Rumors flew that he was losing control of his street people in Tokyo and Osaka. And he was putting serious heat on his Yakuza (Japanese Mafia) colleagues.

Late one evening when returning home in Japan, he was met in his kitchen by several gents sporting missing pinkies. They introduced him to the miracles of ginzu magic and he was found chopped up into over 40 pieces on his kitchen floor (and the knives never lost their edge).

Funny thing, too. After he died, not one of the casinos he owed money to ever sent a credit representative to Japan to talk to his associates about collecting the unpaid debt.

So much for the whales. On a lower tier the bookies and drug dealers still keep Las Vegas the world's number-one fight venue and sports-betting capital, while seemingly respectable businessmen of all ilk continue to dump their untaxed, stolen, and otherwise funny money into the ever-swelling coffers at the tables. The casinos don't ask where the sports get the money and most of them aren't volunteering any information, either.

What does this mean to us? Other than the fact that the crooks keep the bottom lines pumped up for the likes of you and me, not much really, because these modern-day miscreants really have no interest in comp wizardry, which relies on wits and charm instead of the cold-blooded avarice they practice every day. I just thought you'd like to know.

2

Today's Comp System

Ratings, Formulas, Equivalencies

Comps are now based on ratings. Ratings are now based on a formula that predicts the casino's potential to win a gambler's money. All casinos follow some version of the same formula: the average bet times the hours played times the house advantage. The house then gives back (in comps) about 40% of what it expects to win. The amount of comps a player has earned is called his "equivalency."

If you're a rated player, the casino gives you a VIP card. You hand it to the floorman when you sit down. On a rating slip, the floorman writes down your name, how much you buy in for, and how much you're betting per hand. When you leave, he logs your playing time. This information goes to marketing, where it's de-

How the Casino Thinks

Average Bet	Hands Played (blackjack)	Casino's Expected Advantage	Casino's Expected Win	Equivalency Ratio	Equiv-alency
$100	60 (1 hour)	2%	$120	40%	$48

cided what kind of goodies you get. It works like this.

In the chart on page 21, the gambler receives about $48 in casino comps for each hour he plays, because he's rated for a $120-per-hour expected loss. But this is where you can beat 'em. If you play a perfect game of blackjack, your expected loss is only about one-tenth of what the house thinks it is. So, instead of $120, you lose $12, and still get your $48 worth of stuff. Take a look at this.

What a Comp Wizard Knows

Average Bet	Hands Played	*Known Disadvantage*	*Expected Loss*	*Equivalency Ratio*	Equivalency
$100	60 (1 hour)	*0.2%*	*$12*	*400%*	$48

That's not too bad—$48 worth of stuff for only $12. But it's not even close to what happens once you learn to play the ACES game. Let's take another look. This time, the casino still thinks you're betting $100 a hand 60 times an hour, when in fact you're only betting $50 a rattle for about 45 hands.

What an ACES Player Reaps

Average Bet	Hands Played	*Known Disadvantage*	*Expected Loss*	*Equivalency Ratio*	Equivalency
$50	45 (1 hour)	*0.2%*	*$4.50*	*1,067%*	$48

Now you're only losing $4.50 an hour and the house is still giving you back almost $50 an hour for the same play.

This, of course, is a simplified example. Qualifying standards for the more valuable comps are very precise. In most casinos, a gambler who bets $50 a hand and plays for four hours can get a room ("R") on the house. If the same player steps up to $75 a hand, the casino picks up his food, too ("R, F"). When he starts betting $100 a hand at all but the premium clubs, he'll be entitled to room, food, and beverage ("RFB"). Now he gets to ride around town in a limo and slurp champagne like he's some kind of sheik or something.

What does all this mean? It means that all of you who scrimp and chisel and wring every last cent out of every dollar you spend in Las Vegas have still been paying too much! You can get twice as much for half the money. The only catch is you have to play. Still, once you master comp counting and learn when to play, how to play, where to play, and how you can make your bets look bigger than they really are, your vacations will cost you as little as a dime on the dollar, and *you'll* be the sheik. Would you spend $50-$100 to ride in a limo, stay in a suite, eat gourmet meals, see a show, and gamble for two days? Of course you would. Is comp counting for everybody? Read on.

The Comp Hierarchy

Comp	**Qualifying Play**	**Expected Comp Cost**
Free parking validation	Anyone (must go to cage)	$0
Two Cocktails & Tobacco	$2/hand (5 minutes)	0.02
Two Buffets	$10/hand (1 hour)	1.20
Two Coffee Shop-*Downtown*	$15/hand (1 hour)	1.80
Two Coffee Shop-*Strip*	$25/hand (1 hour)	3.00
Two Nights Casino Room Rate-*Downtown*	$15/hand (8 hours)	14.40
Two Nights Casino Room Rate-*Strip*	$25/hand (8 hours)	24.00
Two Nights Free Room-*Downtown*	$25/hand (8 hours)	24.00
Two Nights RFB-*Downtown-Low Strip*	$75/hand (8 hours)	72.00
Two Nights RFB-*Mid Strip*	$100/hand (8 hours)	96.00
Two Nights RFB & Golf-*Premium Strip*	$150/hand (8 hours)	144.00
Two Nights RFB & Airfare-*Premium Strip*	$200/hand (8 hours)	192.00
Two Nights RFB (Deluxe Suite) & Golf	$200/hand (8 hours)	192.00
Premium Lanai suite with the works	$500/hand (8 hours)	480.00 *
Private Jet, Penthouse suite, Private gaming	$5,000/hand (8 hours)	4,800.00 *
727, RFB for 20, Driver, Chef, Big suite	$100,000/hand (8 hours-Baccarat)	1,000,000.00 **

* Comp wizardry at this level is impossible to disguise, but comps still run about 25¢ on the dollar.

** Lily livers need not apply.

A Comp For Every Budget

Not everyone has the bankroll or the heart to play high-stakes blackjack. That hardly precludes you from exploiting the system. With only a few hundred dollars you can still have a big edge every time you sit down. Let's say your choke point is $10-$15 a hand. All you have to do is pick out a nice place downtown with good blackjack rules and play an hour or two. Then get a comp to the coffee shop, run up as large a bill as you can (often $40+), and you'll be a big winner.

Las Vegas touts its vacation values worldwide. And when you're in town, you're bombarded with food specials trumpeting prices that harken back to the '60s. Let's take an example from the chart on the previous page. Have you ever heard or seen anything about unlimited food for two in a first-class coffee shop for less than two dollars? No, and you never will. Why not? Because the casinos don't even know they're offering it to the masses and wouldn't tell them if they did!

It can't be that easy, you're thinking. I'm telling you it is. The weakness in the casino comping system has been one of the best kept secrets in Las Vegas (even casino executives don't really understand it). Until now.

Key Words

For you grammarians, PC people, nitpickers, and Anglophiles, I know what the King's English is supposed to look like. But *Comp City* is written from the gut (which, in my case, is where most of me's wound up over the past ten years, learning everything you're about to read). This book is deliberately styled to ooze the sights, sounds, and flavor of Las Vegas casinos—bosses and dealers, gamblers and hustlers, wizards and suckers, slicksters and whacksters. This might be a new language to some of you, so here are a few hints to help your reading along.

As far as gender identification is concerned, throughout the book the word "wizard" is assigned to both males and females. (Words in the same family—lizard, gizzard, blizzard—don't seem to have any inherent gender assignment. Well, in Las Vegas, lizard might.) Similarly, the word "floorman" is used for both men and women. Casino pits are not politically correct; if you asked, for example, to speak to a "floorperson," no one would know what you were talking about, and if you asked for a "floorwoman," there's no telling who they'd think you were looking for. Also, I've used "floorman" and "boss" interchangeably to denote any executive who observes play in the pit. The distinction between pit boss and floorman is made when necessary.

This book gets a little technical at times. Whenever you run across an unfamiliar word, simply look it up in "The Lingo" section. A few terms are critical to the understanding of ACES. "Expected result" refers to the win or loss you can expect from gambling, based on the size and number of your wagers multiplied by the "house edge" (the casino's mathematical advantage on a given game). A "rated player" is a gambler whose play is monitored for the purpose of issuing comps.

3
Bracing for ACES

For as long as casinos have been chewing them up and spitting them out, gamblers have been moaning, "You can't beat these joints." They've been right, too. But that's about to end. As soon as you understand the ideas in this chapter, you'll forge ahead of 99% of the poor suckers who ever attempted to beat a casino at its own game. You'll depart the ranks of casino prey and assume the role of predator, feasting on comps like a jackal on an old warthog (with apologies to a couple of Vegas World pit bosses who immediately come to mind).

"Bracing For ACES" prepares you for your comp assault on the casino, covering all the preliminary considerations up until the moment you sit down at a blackjack table. This chapter begins with a discussion on learning to play a perfect game of blackjack, because blackjack is the vehicle you'll use to navigate through the comp system. Blackjack is the only table game offered by Las Vegas casinos where skillful players can obtain an advantage, not only as card counters, but now as comp counters. Card counters make money by increasing their bets when the deck is rich in tens and aces. The casino staffs are trained to catch them and card counters try not to bet big when they're being watched. Comp counters only increase their bets when the bosses *are* watching, and the staffs aren't even aware that they exist.

This chapter also shows you how to determine your place on the comp roadmap, relative to your bankroll—a crucial concept. If blackjack is the vehicle, your bankroll is the fuel that powers it. Whether you can afford to risk $250 or $25,000, whether you're a $10 or $1,000 bettor, you'll learn how to use your bankroll to get the comps that you so richly deserve.

Finally, I'll show you how to scout a casino in which to ply your trade. The casino is the avenue you cruise to reach your comp destination. Knowing who is who in the casino (from a host to a relief dealer), and how to deal with them, is crucial for reaching your goal: ACES.

But First, A Word About Asking

The very first concept that you must embrace is that it's important to ask. Throughout your career as a comp counter, you'll be continuously asking for things. If you don't ask, they can't say yes. If you do ask, they might say no. But not asking all but guarantees that you'll get nothing.

Many people, amazingly enough, think that asking a boss for a comp is degrading. That's okay with me, and it should be okay with you, too. Let those people go hungry, or pay retail like all the other ill-informed sheep that Las Vegas leads to the slaughter. We're here to play blackjack and get paid for it in food and drink and other amenities.

Like everything else in ACES, you'll have to develop your own style of soliciting comps. I can, and will, repeat how important it is to ask, and I'll even suggest a few creative approaches. But the more creative *you* are—along a range of techniques from reticent to brazen—the more you'll get in return.

It's as simple as that. You have to ask if you shall receive.

Blackjack is Your Vehicle

ACES *is* blackjack. Repeat it. Blackjack. It doesn't roll off the tongue. It leaps out. Two short syllables that say everything there is to say about 1990s' culture. Though the Spanish, French, and Italians all claim to have invented the game of "twenty-one," the nickname "blackjack" was originated right here, back in the turn-of-the-century gambling dens of Indiana, America's heartland. In a variation of twenty-one played at a racetrack in Evansville, a player was paid an extra five bucks if he was dealt an ace and the jack of spades or clubs. Hence, blackjack. It's the only table game in Las Vegas that's guaranteed to win you comps time after time.

How about the other table games? Let's take craps. Pardon my French, but it sounds like shit to me. Speaking of French, what about roulette. Roulette? I've lived out west for nearly 30 years and any game that ends in "ette," I ain't playing. Keno? Bingo? Lotto? Those games only keep about 25¢-50¢ out of every dollar you bet on 'em. Why don't they just call them all dumbo? And what about all those new games like Caribbean stud and Chinese pai gow poker and super pan 9 and chuck-a-luck. Chuck my lunch! They're all a bunch of trumped-up, high-house-edge games played by suckers who haven't got the sense to get in the cellar with a tornado on the way.

Nope, it's blackjack. Why are you even thinking about playing some sissy game like baccarat? Hell, you can't even pronounce it the way they do in casinos without sounding like William F. Buckley or worse. If they said it right, like maybe if it rhymed with "pack-a-rat," I might take a look at it. But no, to say it the "right way," you've gotta raise one eyebrow, make your lips all pouty, drop your voice way down and say "Bach-o-rah," like you're doing some kind of prissy cheer for an 18th-century German Baroque composer or something. Besides, the percentages for baccarat are about eight times worse than a good blackjack game. And you have to sit next to all these snooty suckers who drink espresso with their pinkies stuck out like they're trying to impress the owner of the joint (who's probably laughing his head off while he guzzles his Maxwell House with both hands and wipes the drool on his sleeve).

Gamblers everywhere else in the world are suckers. It's Americans who figured out how to play blackjack to win. Who do you think were the forefathers of basic strategy? That's right. And who was the first card-counting revolutionary? Ditto. And the strategist who came up with card-counting teams? Yep. And the foot-controlled blackjack computer? Uh huh. And comp counting? Yours truly—a God-fearin' Texan.

"So," you ask, "why do Americans love blackjack so much?" Because it *can be beaten.* Period. Probably not by 99.9% of the people who play it, but by a few, and that's enough to keep the hope alive. Comp wizards love blackjack too, but for another reason. Blackjack is the only mainstream casino game for which the house advantage versus a particular player can not be readily determined. That's because the magnitude of the casino's advantage depends on the skill of the player, and players' skills vary widely. Still, the house assigns the same expected loss to every player, usually somewhere around 2%, because that's what the casino wins on average. Bottom line? Once you become a good blackjack player, your (comp) gains will be subsidized by the losses of the bad players.

If you want to win the comp game, it's essential that you hone your blackjack skills. Dedicated students of the game can become very good. So good, in fact, that they actually have an advantage

The Play of the Public

In 1987, Peter Griffin handicapped the play of the public in a conference paper entitled *Mathematical Expectation for the Public's Play in Casino Blackjack.* Griffin concluded that the public misplays "about one hand in six or seven," and plays at a losing rate that's about 1.4% higher than that of a perfect basic-strategy player. This means that the average player loses at a rate just under 2%, assuming a starting casino edge of 0.5%. (According to Griffin's study, Las Vegas gamblers play at a rate that is about 0.25% worse than the overall average, fixing their expected losses at more than 2% and providing an even greater level of subsidization for comp counters.)

over the casinos. You've all heard about card counting. It really works. But it's also relatively difficult and time-consuming to master. Don't worry; you won't have to become a card counter to make blackjack work for you. You do, however, have to be able to play *basic strategy*. Basic strategy is the set of guidelines that delineates the best way to play any hand versus each of the 13 possible dealer up cards. The action specified by basic strategy (hit, split, stand, double) is always optimal, and once you've mastered it, there'll be no guessing, no vacillating, and no hunch-playing involved in your decisions.

It's important to understand that learning basic strategy will not make you a winning blackjack player. You will still lose money over time. But you'll lose at a rate that's so minimal, the comps you receive will make you a big net winner. Let's take a look.

Here's a breakdown of what a basic-strategy player faces playing blackjack in a typical Strip game. (This is the long-term expected result. For a look at what can happen in the short-run, see "Play to Your Bankroll".)

Average Bet	$100
House Percentage	0.2 %
House win per hand	20 ¢
Hands an hour	60
House win per hour	$12.00

The bottom line, $12, is the amount you expect to lose betting $100 a hand for an hour. Now I'll show you how much the house will give you back in comps. Remember, casino marketing makes no provision for your ability to play basic strategy and this is what they *think* they'll win from you.

Average Bet	$ 100
House Expected Win	2.0 %
House win per hand	$ 2
Hands an hour	60
House Expected win per hour	$ 120
% House Returns	40 %
Comps Earned (Equivalency)	$ 48

That's not too bad—$48 worth of stuff for only $12. Sound hard to do? It would be if you were on your own. But you're not. You're riding with the Maxster now. Saddle 'em up.

Learning Basic Strategy

Learning the complete basic strategy will take a little work. If you make a diligent effort, you should be able to memorize the entire strategy (see "Complete Basic Strategy" in "Appendix") after four to eight hours of study.

If you just can't bring yourself to learn the complete basic strategy, you won't have as high a profit margin as is portrayed throughout this book. However, every little degree of improvement helps. Simply playing blackjack according to the six rules in the abbreviated basic strategy below will chop the casino edge down to about 1%. Rules #3 and #4 are the most important to learn. A soft 17 is a total containing an ace, i.e., (A,6) or (A,2,4).

Abbreviated Basic Strategy

1) Always split eights and aces.
2) Double 10 & 11 against dealer's 2-9.
3) You hold 12-16; dealer shows 2-6 — Stand.
4) You hold 12-16; dealer shows 7,8,9,T,A — Hit.
5) Stand on 17-21, except always hit on soft 17.
6) Never take insurance.

Computer Learning

You can study the charts if you like, but a much easier way to learn basic strategy is to use a computer program. You practice by playing blackjack against computer-generated hands displayed on your monitor. When you make a strategy error, the program alerts you. Since it's more like playing a game than doing a chore, you learn faster and more completely. I like Stanford Wong's *Blackjack Analyzer.*

The Rules Affect the Edge

After you've improved your playing skills, your next concern is choosing the best blackjack games. All blackjack games are not created equal, and the casino advantage versus basic strategy players can vary from zero up to more than 2% on some double-exposure games (both dealer cards dealt face up) and a few of the newfangled blackjack variations that are surfacing. If you don't mess with these high-edge mutants, you can keep the casino advantage confined to a range from 0% (single deck, dealer stands on soft 17) to about 0.8% (six decks, dealer hits soft 17). How important is it to play the better games? Very important in the long run. Here's a look at the difference in expected losses (for a $25 average bet) in a blackjack game with a casino edge of 0.2% versus a game with a casino edge of 0.7%.

$25 bet for	Expected loss at -0.2%	Expected loss at -0.7%
1 hour	($3)	($11)
10 hours	($30)	($105)
50 hours	($150)	($525)
100 hours	($300)	($1,050)
1,000 hours	($3,000)	($10,500)

There are two ways to determine a casino's advantage on its blackjack game. The easiest is to let an expert do the work for you. Stanford Wong's newsletter, *Current Blackjack News*, updates the casino advantage for all blackjack games in Nevada (and other parts of the country) on a monthly basis. If you subscribe to the newsletter, you'll have the up-to-date casino advantages at your fingertips.

If you don't want to pay for CBJN (currently $95), you can figure out the edge on your own. You need to know the number of decks being dealt and whether or not certain options are allowed. Look at the chart on the next page. Start with the base percentage that corresponds to the number of decks being used, then add or subtract the value of any of the five "options" listed here that the casino employs on its game. (There are many other possible options, but these are the most common.)

Variables for Determining Player Edge

Number of Decks (edge in %)

Decks	Edge
1 deck	0.00
2 decks	-0.30
4, 6 decks	-0.50
8 decks	-0.60

(The base percentages assume: dealer stands on soft 17; split and resplit any pair except aces which may be split only once; double down on any two cards but not after splitting; no surrender.)

Effect of Options (in %)

	Single Deck	Multiple Decks
dealer hits soft 17	-0.19	-0.21
double 10, 11 only	-0.26	-0.17
double after split	+0.14	+0.14
late surrender	+0.03	+0.08
resplit aces	+0.03	+0.07

Here's an example. Let's say you're playing a double-deck game, with the following departures from the two-deck base percentage game: dealer hits soft 17, and double after split is allowed. The calculation goes like this:

2 decks	-.30
dealer hits soft 17	-.21
double after split	+.14
Total	-.37 (round to -.4%)

Adding the values in this way yields a good approximation of the casino advantage. Remember, if you wind up with a "-" sign preceding the number, the casino has the edge. On the rare occasion that you get a "+" sign (single deck, dealer stands on soft 17, double after split), the player has the edge.

One more thing. You won't benefit from the good rules on a blackjack game (double after split, late surrender, and resplit aces) if you don't know how to take advantage of them (see the "Appendix" for "Basic Strategy for Favorable Blackjack Options").

Why Casinos Don't Know If You Play Basic Strategy

Caesars Palace has a spot on its blackjack rating slips which can be marked to indicate that a player knows basic strategy. If a subordinate suspects that a player is good, he has to notify his superior boss. That boss has to watch the player for a minimum of ten minutes (and that's usually not enough time) to verify that the player, indeed, plays basic strategy. The result? Rating slips at Caesars almost never indicate that a player uses basic strategy.

Why not? How would you feel if you called your boss over and had him watch a game and you were wrong? There is no upside in the casino business for making a mistake. An employee is much better off not swinging than batting .500. It's one of the quirks of the industry. It doesn't matter if you're right. Just don't be wrong. Mistakes are cumulative in casinos. They stay with you for life. Errors of omission go unnoticed. To stick your neck out in a casino is to flirt with the executioner who, even in this age of "enlightened management," still swings a mean axe.

In this fashion, casinos are like governments. It is death for a junior executive to show any initiative. You do your eight hours and go home. If you do a good job and you're lucky enough to pal around with a few big shots, you *might* have a nice spot someday. If you're stupid, rude, and lazy but your wife's uncle runs the joint, you *will* have a nice spot someday. If you pester your boss and make him watch every player you suspect of knowing basic strategy, you'll *never* have a nice spot. Human nature. It's what makes casinos bog down and comp wizardry work.

More Help

The most complete and accurate basic strategy for any number of decks and combination of rules is contained in *The Theory of Blackjack* by Peter Griffin. The most comprehensive overall treatment of basic strategy is contained in the book *Basic Blackjack* by Stanford Wong. You should get them both (see "Resources" for information on obtaining these and other recommended books on blackjack).

Bankroll is Your Fuel

The size of your bankroll will determine several things: how much you should bet, how long you can play, and most importantly, what level of comps you can expect.

By now you probably want to know where you fit into the comp hierarchy, and how you can formulate a strategy that's optimal for your level of play. In short, what kind of comps are you entitled to if you're a $5 bettor, or a $50 bettor, or a $500 bettor?

Anyone with a few nickels to slip into a slot machine can easily score the comp classics—souvenirs, funbooks, free parking, tobacco, and alcohol. These are not unimportant freebies. But if you want to survive the natural swings of wins and losses long enough to qualify for some kind of meal or room comp, you'll need the gumption to bet at least $5-$20 a hand, and a bankroll of at least $100 to $1,000. At this level, you'll still be more concerned with protecting your limited bankroll than scoring a major comp. Look at it this way. A free meal in a town where you can get a 10-ounce steak dinner for $2 is hardly worth the agony that going broke can cause you. You're far better off taking advantage of the great deals in food and rooms that are synonymous with a Las Vegas vacation (best described in *Bargain City*; see "Resources") and practicing a more judicious brand of comp counting. Also, at this level of wizardry, where you play is just as important as how much you bet and how long you play.

Serious comp counting begins with bankrolls of about $2,500. At $5,000, you'll have the ammunition necessary to go for RFB at some of the lower-level casinos. Many more ACES moves are available to high rollers than to medium and low rollers. Larger bankrolls are necessary for advanced techniques; the larger the bankroll, the higher the octane for cruising. I consider the lower boundary of true high-roller status to be a bankroll of $10,000. Obviously, this is a somewhat sparsely inhabited universe; people who are able and want to deposit ten grand in a casino cage and make hundreds of $50 to $100 wagers are few and far between in the real world.

The proper assessment and handling of your bankroll is important. Refer to "Play to Your Bankroll" to determine where your bankroll puts you on the comp map. Once you know how big your playing stash will be, you can use the unique "Bankroll Index" in the back of the book ("Appendix") to guide you to the comps within your means.

The Casino is the Avenue–Scouting the Joints

When you're ready to enter the realm of advanced comp counting, you'll need to know how to interact not only with hosts, but also with the room reservation agents and casino bosses. For most of you, this initial foray into the bowels of casino marketing will be your first real-life incursion into the comp system. If you're nervous about calling strangers and asking the wrong questions or making a mistake, phone a couple of joints you're not interested in and practice a time or two. You'll find the best time to call is between 8:00 a.m. and 11:00 a.m. (Vegas time), during the week, when it's not too busy.

Here's how it works. Refer to the scouting checklist (see "Appendix") and have a copy of it by your side before you call the casinos. The phone numbers are in the back of the book under "Vital Stats." Have the PBX operator connect you with Room Reservations. Ask the reservations agent what the weekend rate is for a room. She'll ask, "Which weekend?" Name one, but don't be surprised if you have to offer a couple of alternative weekends before you find one that isn't sold out. When you finally get a price, jot it down. Then ask her how much for the cheapest suite.

She may go back into her "For when?" routine. When she quotes you a price, enter it on the "Weekend Suite Rate" slot on your checklist and ask her to transfer you back to the PBX operator. Sometimes they can't make the transfer, so you'll have to call back.

When you connect with the operator again, ask to speak to a table games host. When the host comes on, tell him that you're a blackjack player, you visited his casino on your last trip, and would like to stay there your next trip out. Be prepared to make a little small talk, then ask him what it takes to get a room comp. He'll usually quote you a number right away, something like "$50 a hand for four hours a day." Make sure that it's the requirement for room only, then ask him how much for RFB. It will usually be two to five times what a room-only comp is. Then ask him how much more for airfare. Be polite, but be direct. He won't be offended (you wouldn't believe some of the calls he gets from professional grinders). By using the checklist, even if it's your first call, you'll sound like you know what you're talking about.

Important. The host will often ask when you were there and what time you played. He's fishing to find out if you were rated, because if you were, he can extend you privileges right away. Tell him it was late at night and you didn't bother getting rated, because you were staying somewhere else. He'll understand.

Once the questions get around to airfare, a lot of hosts will tell you they don't pay airfare or that you'll have to establish credit or deposit front money (and don't be surprised if it's a lot.) The rule of thumb for airfare is 5% of your line, or 10% of your losses, providing you played within their guidelines. If the host offers to book a room for you, politely decline. (You'll want to compare the information you get from the hosts at other casinos before committing.) If he presses you, tell him you'll call him back after you've decided when you can make the time to come out.

When you decide where you want to stay, call the host back. If it's 30 days or more in advance, you've got a real good chance of getting a room in the hotel you want, particularly if you agree to apply for credit or put money up front. If you're the spur-of-the-moment type, you may have to shop around at a couple of joints to get what you're looking for.

If you've posted all of the information you've accumulated from the room agent and the host, you'll know exactly how much and how long you have to play to get the comps you want. Now you need to know what kind of blackjack game they deal to see if they offer real comp value.

If you don't already know the casino's blackjack rules, have the host transfer you back to the hotel operator. Ask for a blackjack pit. No matter who answers, ask to speak to a floorman. They come in all shapes and sizes, so don't be surprised if the floorman sounds like a snot-nosed kid or a Teamster bill collector. Whoever it is will (sometimes grudgingly) tell you the house blackjack rules. Write them down. If the floorman is friendly, or at least talkative, you can ask him about the guidelines for comps for buffets, coffee shops, and shows. The reason that you want to ask the floorman (and not the host) about these comps is that floormen can issue "limited" comps, but they have to adhere to strict guidelines. So he'll give you the exact requirements, while a host might tell you to "go ahead and gamble and we'll evaluate you at the end of the play" for the lower-end comps, to get you out of his hair. Even if the floormen can't write the comps, they speak to the hosts often enough to know exactly what's expected to get a comp request approved.

Once you know the casino's blackjack rules and low-level comp requirements, you can refer back to the "Variables for Determining Player Edge" to figure out what the casino's advantage is. And now, at long last, you have everything you need to determine exactly what your expected costs will be, and if the casino is ripe for a plucking.

Establishing Your Worth

Comp policies for high-end play are based on a casino's perception of its ability to relieve you of your bankroll—they have to believe they have a shot at a score. By applying for credit or depositing cash up-front, you enhance that perception. The bottom line is: the higher your credit line or cash deposit, the easier it is for you to get comped.

High-end play, as far as credit is concerned, is generally considered to be a bankroll more than $2,500. If your bankroll is less than that, you should simply bring cash—or personal checks, travelers checks, cashier's checks, or government checks. Don't put your money on deposit. You'll look a lot more sporty when you buy in for cash ($300-$500 depending on how much you're going to bet) and hand them your VIP card, than if they pulled your computer profile and saw that all you came with is a puny $1,500.

Credit

Most people have the notion that casinos give gamblers revolving lines of credit. They're wrong. Casinos rarely loan players bankrolls, so the word "credit" itself is a misnomer. What they do is extend check-cashing privileges.

When a first-time customer asks for credit, he fills out an application that gives the casino access to the particulars of his bank account. This can be done through the mail before the trip. Simply call VIP Services at your casino of choice and ask for a credit application; it'll take two to three weeks to process. Establishing your account beforehand is a must if you plan to arrive at the hotel on a weekend or holiday when the banks are closed. But you can apply in person if the banks are open when you check in.

Another way to establish credit is to phone a host and give him the information. The joint will contact your bank and call you back with the approvals. This usually takes about a week.

Whenever you apply, a casino representative contacts your bank, tells someone at the bank that you've applied for check-cashing privileges, and asks for your six-month average bank balance. The bank responds with a universal one-digit, one-word banking code that represents the balance.

The number represents the digits of dollars in the account.

"1" = $1-$9
"2" = $10-$99
"3" = $100-$999
"4" = $1,000-$9,999
"5" = $10,000-$99,999
"6" = $100,000-$999,999

The words "low," "medium," and "high" represent the range in the balance. "Low" means the average balance is 1 to less than 4 units, "medium" represents 4 to less than 7 units, and "high" is 7 to less than 10 units. Confused yet? Look at these examples and you'll understand.

• A "low 3" falls between $100-$399. Get it? A low three-digit account.

• A "medium 4" represents a balance of $4,000-$6,999. Now we're in the middle of the 4-digit range.

• A "high 5" tells the casino that you've got $70,000-$99,999 to squander and that they'd better give you some skin right now, because they've got a live one.

After they've gathered the information concerning your financial condition, the casino sets your credit limit. Always aiming to please, they generously extend check-cashing privileges for up to 100% of the six-months' balance. Pretty darned nice, if you ask me.

Once the casino knows how much it can nick you for, it sets up your account and gives you a VIP card that's good all around the casino. Now you get to walk up to any blackjack, roulette, or dice table like a big-time high roller and say, "Gimme five hundred." You toss out your VIP card. A floorman slithers up and hands you a "marker," which you sign. Then the floorman tells the dealer to hand you a mess of chips.

What do you do then? You play. If you win, you give them back the chips (just the ones they gave you, not the ones you win) and they tear up your markers. If you lose and you're using casino credit, you pay up before you check out.

Credit Criteria

Casino credit is much easier to get than traditional revolving charge accounts or loans. The casino doesn't care if TRW says you're a flake, and it doesn't give a hoot about your salary, job history, business acumen, or health. All it wants to know is that you've got some money in a bank account, that it's been there a while, and that you don't have a history of hanging bad paper in casinos. That's it.

A guy who keeps $20,000 in the bank but just got out of Chapter 7 bankruptcy last year can get a big advance from the casino, while a guy who has a 20-year history of paying off his debts on time, but only has $500 in the bank, won't get spit. The chart on the next page illustrates the difference in applying for a revolving charge account (from a bank) and applying for casino credit.

Applying for Credit

What a Bank Wants To Know	What a Casino Wants to Know
How long have you been employed?	You got any money?
Where?	Where is it?
What is your position?	You ever stiffed a casino?
What is your salary?	
Why did you leave your last job?	
What was your salary there?	
Do you have a checking account?	
What is the balance?	
Do you have a savings account?	
What is the balance?	
Do you own your own home?	
How long?	
What is your mortgage balance?	
Do you have any credit cards?	
How much do you owe?	
Who else do you owe?	
Who else?	
Have you ever been in prison?	
Do you really think we're going to loan you any money?	

Paying Up

For most first-time credit customers, the terms are simple. You write a check covering the amount of your losses before you leave.

If you don't pay up before you leave, you won't get away with much, because the markers you sign at the tables in exchange for chips are actually magnetically encoded checks that will go right through your bank account if you try to weasel out of paying what you owe.

After one trip with no hitches, you're considered an established player. On your second visit, most (of the larger) casinos will give you up to 30 days to pay off your markers. After your second play, it goes something like this. Casino collections sends you a bill within a week. If they don't get their payment in full by the end of the following week, they send a nice letter. Most places take you through a series of about six dunning letters (which get a taste testier each time) before they resort to sending the markers through your bank. If you're trying to pay up, but your wife has locked up your bank account after discovering that your "business trip" was really a fling in Las Vegas, the joints will understand and let you pay off 20%-30% a month—but they won't be happy about it. If you stiff them completely, it gets ugly. Fast. Does the thought of two knee-breakers banging on your door at midnight scare you? Wrong movie. This is the '90s. It's much worse. They use attorneys now. Knees heal. Bad credit ratings don't, and with the spread of casinos nationwide, gambling debts are collectable almost everywhere.

Front Money

Let's say you've played in a casino a few times, you're known there, and this time you lose your entire credit limit. Most casinos will gladly extend your credit 25%-50% over what you had in the bank just for the asking. It's a good thing that very few gamblers lose their heads and chase good money with bad when their luck runs out. As it is, the joints only wind up extending credit limits for, oh, maybe half of their customers in a given year. How can a guy pay off a check for 50% more than he has in the bank? What, you've never heard of pension plans or the kid's college funds? Get real. If a guy's got the gambling fever, he'll find the cure.

Considering the effects that alcohol and adrenaline can have on your judgment during the heat of battle, it's a much safer bet to deposit "front money" in the cage when you come to town and avoid giving the casino access to your bank accounts. Why? Because at some point in your comp-hustling career, you might find yourself losing control. Front money is the world's most effective method of damage control in a casino.

It's real easy, too. All you do is call ahead and tell them you're coming. Then show up at the cage with the amount of cash that you want to "play against." They'll have you sign a signature verification card so that no one can forge your name on the tables. Then they'll hand you the VIP card with your name and account number on it and away you go. Before you leap into action, though, call a host over when you're putting up the money to make sure he knows how much you're good for. Since you've extensively researched the club, you'll know how much and how long you'll have to play to get your comps, but it's important for the casino execs to connect a face with the account in case you need special favors.

The Cash Player

The cash player in a casino embodies all that's good about the rapidly vanishing Wild West ethic. He has freedom, he has choice, and he eats or starves by his own hand (or hands). He has privacy, he often looks a whole lot richer than he really is, and he gets comped. Almost everyone likes someone who acts like he wants to throw away a pocketful of money, and the joints thrive on these people. Indeed, the sharpshooters upstairs love cash players, as long as they think they can keep 'em in the crosshairs, because not only are most of them suckers, they save a world of paperwork.

To play cash or not to play cash? The choice is yours. To earn your rewards, you can join the pedestrian fold, play by the rules, and tell the casino everything they want to know about you. Does this sound like big brother is watching? Well, little brother, you *are* being watched. And not only from the surveillance cameras, but also from the floor with the help of the computers. A casino can track and keep a record of a player's every step, from the time he sets foot inside the casino to the time he checks out of the hotel. Nowhere else in the world is the public so closely watched 24 hours a day.

You can subtly step off the tracking track by playing for cash. Cash play can get you any level of comps that credit or front money can. There are four reasons you should play cash: first, you can't lose more than you brought; second, privacy; third, if you don't have enough bankroll to get the casino's attention with a big deposit or credit line; and fourth, if you want to appear to have more money than you really do.

As a cash player, you don't even have to give them your name if you don't want to. If you don't give a boss information, you can still get low-limit comps, but anything more than what a floorman can give you is out of the question. Why? Because the floorman has to defer decisions on comps more valuable than coffee shop and buffets up to his boss. The only way his boss can evaluate your worthiness is to either peruse your rating slip or pull your file up on the computer. If there's nothing there, that's what you'll get.

Credit

Advantages	**Disadvantages**
Up to 30 days to pay	Your banker learns you're a gambler
Safety	Casino knows how much you have
Always rated	Casino will extend more money
Shows casino they can win a lot	

Use if you want a float or to get biggest comps.

Front Money

Advantages	**Disadvantages**
Shows casino they can win a lot	Casino may require bigger deposit than you have to get comps you want.
Safety	
Always rated	
Can't go "on tilt" and borrow more	

Always use if you have enough up front to qualify for the level of comps needed.

Cash

Advantages	**Disadvantages**
Churn, Churn, Churn	Reporting Requirements
Freedom to play anywhere	Possibility of loss or theft
Get to mind your own business	Might forget to get rated

Use whenever you have less than $2,500 or you want the casino to believe you have a bigger bankroll in order to qualify for higher comps.

Special Tips For Establishing Your Worth

• If you ever become "bad pay" (fail to pay your marker or bounce a check), your record goes to an outfit known as Central Credit. Central Credit then wire-transfers reports to all of Las Vegas' casino credit offices. Not only will the casino you stiffed stop giving you check-cashing privileges, but you'll also be known all over town as an "NG" (no good). Every Las Vegas casino, big and small, will know who you stiffed, when you stiffed 'em, and how much you stiffed 'em for; the info goes in your permanent records.

• If you just "fall through the door" (which means you're not staying in the casino's hotel) on a weekend and ask for credit, you'll be asked if you're established anywhere else. If you are, the joint will check with Central Credit and run an "In-Transit Check." Central Credit will call all of the other casinos you've played in and if you've been good pay, the casino you're at will usually give you 30-day check-cashing privileges right away.

• If you've used credit and you're "walking" with the casino's chips (that is, not paying off your credit markers at the table when you're an obvious winner), the casino will insist that you redeem your markers upon departure. (They really don't want to be in the "no-interest loan" business.)

• Casinos will honor money-market accounts with check-writing privileges. Don't be surprised if they someday say it's okay to pledge your IRAs, too.

• If you don't have enough in your account to cover the check, inform the casino of it before the checks are processed. Bouncing a check on a casino will ruin your comp-counting career forever.

• It's not in a casino's best interest to embarrass you and they're masters of discretion for their best customers. If you run into credit problems, work with your host or the credit department to avoid the numerous hassles that a casino can cause you.

• If you lose your entire credit line but can only pay off a portion each month, when it is paid off the casino will reduce your credit line to the amount that you were able to pay each month. Say you lost $10,000 and sent only $2,500 a month for four months. When the bill gets paid off, the casino will only extend you $2,500 in credit.

• Some clubs have a nifty custom of taking a guy's credit limit up until he crashes and burns. Known as "shooting stars," these players come in and lose, say $10,000. They pay right away. They ask for $20,000 the next time. No problem. Pretty soon, they've got $100,000 lines, but they've lost so much that their net worth's not even close to that. What happens? On their last loss they're through, but as far as the casino's concerned, so what? They got everything the guy had anyway. (A couple of years ago, a crooked Canadian bank teller lit up the Atlantic City sky for millions before his luster faded.)

• Other clubs have a policy of protecting the customer. If he's drunk, they won't extend his credit at all and they'll never go over 25% of his established line even if he requests it in a lucid moment away from the tables. These customers, over time, have a lot more value to the casinos than the "shooting stars"—although they're not near as much fun to watch!

• Casinos will settle debts for long-term top players without ruining their credit ratings at home. If a guy blows $200,000 over two or three years and gets to a point that he can't pay his last $10,000, sometimes they'll settle the debt by zeroing out his account and inviting him back as a cash-only player.

• If you owe the casino money and try to put up front money without negotiating the terms, they have the right to snatch the money from the account, and they will. While not that great for customer relations, it does have an interesting way of getting the player's attention the first time he asks for a marker on a game.

• If you want to cash a large out-of-town check, but don't have casino credit, the casino can only call your bank during business hours to see if it's good. If it's after hours, you'll have to go to a cash machine.

Know Your Host

You've learned to play basic strategy perfectly, determined the size of your bankroll, selected a hotel, and opened your account. You travel to Las Vegas and check in. Your next step is to meet the host who's set everything up, and become his new best friend. Before you meet him, though, it's good to know what he's about and why he's important to you.

In the old days, hosts were the colorful, cantankerous, and brutal icons of the Las Vegas Strip. They had roots in illegal gambling and were often called upon to personally collect debts. Only a handful of these old-time hosts remain in all of Nevada. Today, you'll find (mostly) college-educated, well-dressed, manicured, marketing executives. They are clearly at the top of the comp pecking order, and you should never try to go over their heads to their superiors. As far as your comps are concerned, they don't have any superiors. The buck definitely stops with them.

A host's value to the casino is based on a number of factors. He's responsible for approving markers and assisting with collections (through entirely legal means), hosting special events, handling established customers, and introducing new customers to the property. One of his top priorities is the cultivation of new customers (make them regular casino customers). Good news for us comp cribbers.

A host's most important asset is his "book," that is, his customers. It's as important for him to have you as his customer as it is for you to have him as your host. Hosts will go to great lengths to claim you as one of theirs, both to ensure job security at their present casino and to increase their value to other casino marketing departments when they decide to shop their services to rival employers.

Whose Was That High Roller?

To give you an idea about the "great lengths" to which a host (and his bosses) will go in order to claim you—the qualified gambler—as a personal customer, let me regale you with one of the funniest things to happen to a casino in the '80s. A Strip hotel had just changed hands. The neophyte owners were trying to understand the complicated casino business, which they'd just jumped into with blinders on. There wasn't a lot of good news in this joint until a distinguished-looking gentleman from Saudi Arabia, along with an entourage of about 10 hangers-on and semi-starlet types, approached the baccarat pit early one Sunday morning, plopped about $30,000 cash on the table, and started firing it up.

Host A introduced himself to the new customer and found

out that he was staying at Caesars Palace. He immediately called the day-shift boss to tell him about "his" new customer. The shift boss was delighted. He introduced himself to the gentleman and, after offering him a floor of vacant luxury suites, became fast friends when the wealthy Arab agreed to move in. The day shift boss called the casino manager at home and told him about "his" new customer.

The casino manager hopped in his Cadillac and hustled down to the property to watch the action. The high roller proceeded to lose about $20,000 before the shift changed. Host B then came on shift and offered to treat "his" new guest's party to a gala private dinner. Invitation accepted, they took on the gourmet room and ran up a $6,000 bill, including two bottles of Louis XIII brandy.

Host B then introduced the new customer to the swing shift boss, who immediately took him under "his" wing and explained the hotel's liberal credit policy.

The Saudi then put up a $500,000 cashier's check drawn on a Saudi bank. The casino manager called overseas. The check was good. The table limits were raised to $25,000 a hand (a huge bet in those days) and by the time Host A came back to work 12 hours later, the Saudi had lost damn-near half a million more.

So now the sheik wanted credit. Host A followed all normal procedures. He called the guy's bank for a customary credit approval. He was told that not only was this guy the brother of some big-shot prince over there, he had a "high-9" ($70-$99 million) checking account and was good for more if he needed it. The host smugly forwarded the information to the casino manager. They raised the limits to $50,000 a hand and gave the guy $2 million in credit. He kept losing, but during the play, dished off about $500,000 to his paramours, who would belly dance over to the cage and cash out the chips. The bosses grimaced when the ladies took the money, knowing from experience that harem girls' tips never went back into action, but they knew they were still going to mash this guy and they weren't about to piss him off by telling his concubines that they couldn't have a little spending money.

Now the guy was stuck $2.5 million, including his cashier's check, and his girls had about half a million tucked away. A two million net loser in two days. Not bad, not bad at all, the casino boys chortled. Now the Saudi wanted another $3 million. The casino manager conferred with the president. They gave it to him.

He kept losing, but he kept giving the three beauties handfuls of chips, which they kept redeeming for cash. At the end of the three-day play, the Arab had lost over $5.5 million. Minus about a million he'd given his girls, the hotel had whipped this guy for over $4,000,000 after comps (which reportedly ran over $100,000, including a chartered 727 to the Near East).

So whose customer was it? Host A, Host B, the day-shift boss, or the swing-shift boss? None of the above. The casino manager, being top dog on the property, proudly took full credit for the Arab's play and made sure the president of the hotel knew what a swell job he'd done stealing this guy away from Caesars.

Now Host A and Host B were both pissed at the casino manager. They had gotten this guy to play here, they had treated him like royalty, they were responsible for the house winning over $4 million during the last 72 hours, and they wanted credit for it. The shift bosses, old hands at playing the political game, knew that there was no upside in sniveling and wisely backed away from the controversy, humbly deferring to their boss.

The hosts didn't give up. They demanded a meeting with the hotel president to state their cases and to ask for a bonus because they'd done such a jam-up job. The president heard them out and agreed that they were indeed responsible for the Arab's play. The matter of the bonus would be discussed with the board of directors, who were meeting the following week, but the president assured them that they would get their just desserts.

The two hosts and the casino manager were ecstatic. They went shopping for cars, bought new wardrobes, and crowed up and down the Strip about their coup.

They crowed too soon. See, there was this one tiny little problem. When the cashier's check was presented to the Saudi bank, there *was no bank.* This guy had set up an elaborate wire-fraud scheme with a phony Arab bank and the casino soon found out that the name the player had given them was phony too. They'd been skinned for over a million dollars! Every major boss in the joint was in on the conspiracy and didn't even know it.

You should have heard whose customer it was then. "All I did was offer him a room," squealed Host A. "It wasn't me who extended him the credit."

"Who you looking at?" bleated Host B. "So I had dinner with the guy, that's my job, right? That's all any host can do, right?"

"I knew I shouldn't have listened to these jerks," the casino manager grumbled to the president as they put out an APB on the slicksters from Meccaville.

And so it was left to the president to explain to the board of directors that they had been hoodwinked by a team of professionals and that the hotel was out over $1 million in actual costs, with another $4 million in uncollectable markers on the books. But it wasn't his fault, either.

When the carnage had cleared and the dust had settled, the management massacre was still to come. Needless to say, it was not a pretty sight, as hosts and bosses had to answer for the customer who suddenly belonged to them all.

Sad story? That depends on whose side you're on. I've always had a hard time feeling sorry for casinos, but this tale of casino woe underscores the mentality of the people that you're going to be dealing with. If you want your host to want you, you've got to paint as pretty a picture of yourself as you can stand without throwing up.

Hosting the Host

After you check into the casino, go to the cage and tell the cashier you'd like to talk to the host who set you up. If he's not on duty, meet another one (no harm in having them fight over you). Whoever shows up, introduce yourself and ask him if he can help you set up an account. He'll pull your name up on the computer and see that no one's laid claim to you, then he'll step right in and help you with anything you need. Once you're established, shake his hand and say goodbye. Don't bug him again for little stuff like reservations for dinner and shows—that's what the hostesses at VIP Services are for. Only talk to him if you need something VIP Services can't give you (upgrade to a suite, show tickets, golf, airfare, etc.).

In most cases, you won't see the host again, unless there's a problem. If he's on duty when you're checking out, make sure to thank him and tell him what a great time you've had. Give him your card and let him know he's your one and only host. Once you're in his magic computer, you'll go on his personal mailing list and you'll be invited to every special event, from slot tournaments to prize fights to New Year's Eve extravaganzas. Now, if you behave and don't make an obvious swine of yourself, whenever there's a dispute, he'll be in your corner because you're "his" customer. If he ever leaves the property for another Las Vegas resort, he'll invite you in RFB just to try out his new joint. At worst it's a free vacation. At best you'll get a new host at the old property and have the old host at a new property, which translates to two RFB weekends that are yours for the asking.

In some hotels, if you have an account but haven't made contact with a host, one might "cut into" you while you gamble. Hosts know that gamblers don't like to be bothered, especially when they're getting stomped, so he'll only spend a minute or two on the game with you. Use this time to take a break. Make a big bet in front of him, then stand up and engage him in idle chit chat. He'll like that and will probably talk to you for at least a couple of minutes or until his beeper goes off, telling him somebody else wants something for free. Once you're his pal, if he's good at his job, he'll periodically stop by your table to say hello and ask how you're doing.

If a host does stop by to say hello, take the opportunity to find out your score in the rating game. Ask him if you've been playing enough to qualify for the comps you want. He'll pull up your record on one of the pit computers and scan your file. Oftentimes, he'll nod and say you've played enough for the weekend. You can soft peddle the question by claiming you'd like to go out and look at Hoover Dam, check out the Luxor, or something, and want to know how much longer you need to play. If he tells you you're looking good, quit as soon as he walks away. If he tells you that you need to put in a couple more hours, put in a couple more hours.

The host will often give you a lengthy questionnaire when you meet. He'll want to know what events (boxing, golf, shows, etc.) you like, when your birthday and anniversary are, and such. Unless you're hiding something, fill it out, because all of the data on your questionnaire will be entered into a computer and you'll be "remembered" every time something you're interested in is on the horizon. And he'll sometimes send you a gift out of the blue.

People like people who do things for them. Don't forget it. Do something for your host, even if it's trivial, like a compliment in front of his boss or a nice letter to the president of the hotel—it doesn't really matter, as long as you do something. He'll like you. And you'll learn to love him, because he'll do plenty for you.

Last but not least, be aware that all premium customers not only expect comps, they demand them. And remember that casinos have to buy their players by offering the best comp deals and the best service. Don't be afraid to ask for what you want. All the veterans do. The worst that can happen is a host will say "no."

VIP Services Staff

I've been telling you to call VIP Services, but haven't really told you who you'll be speaking to. Ladies. Nice ladies who are trained to cater to gamblers' urgent needs and off-the-wall requests.

The operative word in VIP Services is "services." The ladies in the office are not hosts. They are *hostesses.* Both for the hosts and for you (and they do fix coffee). Think of them as your "girls-Friday" anytime you're on the property. They'll make your airline reservations, show arrangements, and do anything else a concierge at an exclusive hotel might do.

Use them, but don't abuse them. They're generally cordial women and pleasantly attractive. It's too bad they're used to dealing with gamblers such as yourself and will immediately think that you're just another jerk with a bankroll. As always, be polite and be sure to say thanks for anything special one might do for you. If you happen to pass by a flower shop, pick up a couple of roses and have them delivered by a bellman. She'll remember you the next time you call, and she might be able to bump you up to a suite with no extra charge against your comp account if, for example, most of the standard rooms are taken. Consideration never hurts. Especially if the person you're considerate to has the power to pop you into some deluxe digs.

But there's a good chance that he'll say "yes." Hosts field a hundred requests a day and some of them are quite extraordinary, so you'll never surprise or insult these guys. Just do it.

Know Your Floorman

Now that you know how to handle the guy who approves all of your comps, your next big step is to become intimately familiar with the world of floormen and pit bosses—a world full of dealers and supervisors, computers and clerks, front money and markers, counts and fills, rating slips and relief bosses, and endless paperwork. By the time you finish this book, all these terms and procedures will be second nature to you and you'll know your floormen almost as well as they know themselves.

Always remember that floormen are both your friends and your antagonists. They're the ones who assess your play and relay the information to the hosts and casino marketing. Based on the floorman's information, marketing makes a decision on your potential worth to the casino and how much in comps the casino is willing to give you to keep you on board. So your job as a comp wizard is to get into the good graces of your floormen on the one hand, and pull their strings on the other as if they were your personal marionettes.

Contrary to popular belief, most floormen earn less than hotel bartenders, cocktail waitresses, valet parking attendants, bell hops, *and* the dealers who work for them. On top of that, they have sizable wardrobe and dry-cleaning expenses and are paid by check, while most of the other people you meet working in the hotel take home a tip envelope every day.

The average floorman lives hand-to-mouth. He rarely gets to eat out at a nice restaurant or do much of anything else, especially if he's raising a family. Since most of these guys are struggling, the salient point for budding comp wizards to remember is that floormen can be bought cheap—if you know how to make the play.

A tie, a small gift certificate, a dozen golf balls, something your company sells, an off-premises comp, almost any little token

Complimentary Chain of Command

Casino Operations

VICE PRESIDENT CASINO OPERATIONS
Reports to Hotel President.
Defers comp decisions to subordinates.

CASINO MANAGER
Reports to VP Casino Operations.
Defers most comp decisions to subordinates. Can approve credit, airfare, walking money, and all other comps.
Interacts only with high-level gamblers.

SHIFT SUPERVISOR
Reports to Casino Manager.
Approves credit, airfare, walking money, and RFB.
Limited interaction with most gamblers.

PIT BOSS
Reports to Shift Supervisor.
No credit or airfare approval. Approves room and restaurant comps.
Extensive interaction with table players.

FLOORMAN
Reports to Pit Boss.
No room or gourmet restaurant approval. Approves buffet and coffee shop comps for two.
Extensive interaction with table players.

DEALER
Reports to Floorman.
Has no comp authority, but can influence floormen regarding comp decisions.
Extensive interaction with table players.

Marketing

VICE PRESIDENT MARKETING
Reports to Hotel President.
Defers comp decisions to subordinates.

CREDIT HOST
Reports to VP Marketing.
Makes numerous comp decisions. Approves credit, airfare, walking money, and all other comp requests.
Interacts with rated gamblers.

you can think of will be paid back in spades on your rating—as long as you find the right bosses. This isn't to say that you're trying to bribe them. You're simply befriending fellow struggling human beings who happen to make subjective ratings on your play. All right, all right, so you *are* trying to bribe them. What are they gonna do, shoot you for being nice?

Say you have a boss who especially appreciates you (after you've dished off a gift, of course). Which of your bets do you think he's going to remember when he's completing your rating slip? The little bets that'll force you to pay a $300 hotel bill when you check out or the big ones that'll ensure everything's comped and motivate you to come back as soon as possible?

Sometimes you'll observe a boss for a while and won't be able to get a handle on his or her personality. All you have to do is make an offhand comment to the dealer about the boss, such as, "Does she ever smile?" Within ten seconds you'll know all you need to about your floorman. Trust what a dealer says; they're usually pretty honest about the bosses working behind them.

In order to nurture at least a couple of bosses on every comp-counting trip, you'll need to recognize the different *types* that work the casinos. Some of them can be spotted in seconds. Some you won't be able to get a handle on until you check out, unless you prod them for your ratings while you're playing.

The Good Bosses

The good bosses are the guys you can use. It really doesn't matter if they're smart or dumb , hard working or lazy, stable or goofy. What matters to you is that you can trick or bribe them to get more stuff. Generally speaking, if they're congenial, busy with other affairs, or too damn self-absorbed to pay any attention to you except when they have to, you'll get more comps by playing in their sections.

Carey Casinova

He's the original casino love god. Married four times, his current wife is a dealer in the same joint, but he's still got all the moves. You can spot him in seconds. If he's not hitting on the cocktail waitresses, he's leaning over the tables, trying to get a gander of some sweet thing's layout while ignoring three $100 tables with rammin' jammin' action going on all around him.

Usually a handsome guy, he's a flashy dresser with perfectly coifed hair, and in constant need of attention. He'll flirt with every woman from 21-year-old racehorses to 90-year-old wheelchair-bound blind women. He's glib, knows all the casino jokes, and talks the talk with the best of them. A generous sort, he won't have a clue what you did on the game until it's time for you to leave.

He's easy to stroke. If you're male, all you have to do is brag about how slick he is to the ladies on your table when he's within earshot and he'll double your rating immediately. If you're female, he'll do whatever he can for you, as long as you laugh at his jokes. Don't ever let him think he has a chance with you, though, because if you turn him down, your rating will suffer accordingly. If you do go for his lines and wind up in an amorous relationship, you'll hit the grand slam of comps. Until he gets tired of you (usually about two days).

Gary Greedhead

He's got his hand out to everyone. Ostensibly to shake it, he's also trying to subtly shake you down. Often a real estate broker on the side, he wants to know where you're from, what you do, and how often you come to Las Vegas. A walking chamber of commerce billboard, he wants to talk business with you. The conversation invariably ends up with a discussion about how little floormen make and how nice the hotel's gift shop is.

He's best played with a three-way squeeze: buy him off with an inexpensive gift, bet small the 90% of the time he's hustling other customers, and tell him you're interested in investing in Las Vegas real estate, if he happens to hear of any good deals. He will.

Benny Buttkisser

He's so busy sucking up to the shift bosses, trying to make his fellow bosses look bad and generally stirring up shit, he has little time to actually watch the games. Although he appears to be very efficient at rating his players, he has no desire to socialize with them and if you leave him alone, he'll leave you alone.

If you can read his dealers' body language when he talks to them, you'll know right away that he's the kind of guy who'd rat out his own mother if he thought he'd get a promotion. He's especially susceptible to compliments you give his boss about him, if you make sure he overhears you.

If you can bring yourself to write a glowing letter to management about him, he'll automatically triple your ratings on your next trip.

Honey Happycheeks

Dressed like a $1,000 call girl, she's new to the trade (of working for a check, that is). Formerly one of top management's concubines, she's a little long in the tooth for them now (pushing 25) and they've insisted that the casino manager break her in as a dealer.

After extensive seasoning of, oh, about five weeks, and following a lengthy visit "upstairs" on one of her breaks, she miraculously gets the first promotion that comes along, bypassing the 34-year-old mother of three who's just finished her masters at UNLV in Casino Management. She's usually extra friendly, has great interpersonal skills and, if you're lucky, comes with all her vaccinations.

Known to date even 80-year-old trolls if they have enough chips, she's an easy pick-up if your bankroll can stand the bludgeoning. Although she still has trouble adding to 21, she knows the *exact* average bet and line of credit of every male in the casino with a credit line over $50,000.

Warning! She's to be avoided by male comp wizards betting more than $250 a hand (unless you're looking to get lucky), because she'll gun every bet you make and be on you like a chicken on a June bug. She'll ignore you if you keep your ACES play within the $25-$100 range.

The Gift That . . .

Although I've told you to lay something on the bosses if they're especially nice or you need a favor, you really shouldn't give them anything unless you're reasonably sure to get something in return. Once you find a boss or two willing to go in the tank, use these handy hints when forking over the graft.

• Never ever offer a boss cash. Virtually all casinos will terminate a boss for taking currency from a player and you could put someone in a bind if he thinks no one is watching.

• Give them something cheap. It's the thought, etc.

• Every male floorman in town has to wear a suit five days a week. They all need ties. Make it conservative, or the other bosses will hooray him when he wears it to work.

• Women like flowers. Too bad. They're too conspicuous.

• A $10 three-team parlay bet is a favorite among bosses. It makes them think of you for the whole weekend and it gives you both a common enemy—the house.

Strangely enough, if you're an average-looking female betting gobs of money, Miss Happycheeks will often give you a higher average bet than she should, because even though you may have an excellent education, great career, wonderful family, and more money in blue-chip investments than she can conceive, she feels sorry for you. But if you're a knockout, look out. She'll give you a rating all right, and it ain't gonna be a 10.

Mary Mary Kay

Very personable, she's a recovering drug addict trying to get out of the business by hustling all of her dealers to join her pyramid play while she pretends to watch her games. Often a born-again Christian, she never has a clue about what's going on in the pit. Although oblivious, she's a nice gal who's been splattered a few times herself and would never do anything to hurt you, hence your ratings stay high.

Danger! If she tries to bring you under her sales spell, under no circumstances should you ever suggest that what she's doing is a pyramid scheme, because it's really "network marketing." To

. . . Keeps On Giving

- Even big bosses get golf balls. No one seems to care if a player lays a dozen or two around the pit. Even if your favorite boss doesn't play the game, he'll probably give them to his boss, so no one gets hurt when you hand them out.
- Off-premises coffee shop or restaurant comps are a major motivator for bosses to nudge rating slips. If you can, get the comp with an open date so the boss can go on his day off. Warning. An off-premises comp will put the boss on notice that you're a comp wizard. Only offer them if you *know* he'll do something special for you in return.
- Be discreet. If only a couple of bosses are scoring all the loot, the other bosses get jealous.
- Never mail a boss a gift. His boss gets his mail first and hand-delivers it to him. If your buddy gets too much booty in the mail, he'll fry.

even hint that you believe otherwise will probably find your rating slip in the garbage. However, you can appear to be fascinated by her big-buck networking ploy. And you are—as long as it nets you big-buck comps.

Sammy Serious

A college-grad tweezer-butt with visions of being the CEO in twenty years, he wears Brooks Brothers suits, wing tips, power ties, needlepoint button-down-collar shirts, and a smug look at all times.

A guy who's read all the books, he counts down every blackjack player winning more than $500, but doesn't know a thing about how comps work (they didn't teach comps at Cornell). He's never made a laydown in his life and has about as much street sense as, well, a street.

These guys are great to comp-wizard on (now it's a verb), because they might as well be blind for all they can see through their tortoiseshell glasses.

Willie Wiseguy

He can be anywhere from 30 to 70, but he's seen it all, and done it all. Usually not too worried about his appearance, he's constantly on the lookout for crossroaders (casino thieves). A former casino bandit himself, he doesn't believe card counting works, let alone comp wizardry.

He's a guy who'll plant himself on the big game in his area and hawk it with a vengeance, making sure to keep the dealers and other players as uncomfortable as possible. He'll pick the cards up out of the discard rack and inspect the backs and sides any time someone makes a non-book play that wins, and he'll ignore your piddly $25-$100 play all night. As far as a comp wizard is concerned, he might as well not even be there except when you're making your first and last bets.

Mr. Whiskey

He's a hail fellow, well met, parties with the customers, and usually has a pretty good handle on what's going on around his area. The only thing is, he doesn't give a damn. Look for a big gut, nose blossoms, a big smile, and an ill-fitting suit.

He's especially vulnerable to golf balls, fight tickets, and food comps from somewhere else. If you're even close on the rating you need, tell him, and he'll do everything he can for you, *if* you make his shift fun. If you're a boozer coming with a buddy or two and want to raise some hell in the casino, this is your man.

The Bad Bosses

While it may take you a session or two to find the best bosses for your particular style of play, it won't take you long at all to discover the bosses dedicated to making your vacation a bummer. Bad bosses are creeps. They don't like you and they'll make you pay for trespassing into their territory. Sadly, you'll find them in every joint. As soon as you identify one, move to another pit.

Ms. Ima Movinup

An anal retentive, you can't crack her shell with a grenade. Dressed for success (at a "Fierce Feminists" convention) she volunteers for all the latrine details and loves to work the schedule, fill out employee termination reports, call dealers in on their days off, and make sure they work overtime if they need to leave early to pick up the kids.

Effervescent as a tree sloth, she never talks to customers unless spoken to and then only to talk down to them. She thinks all dealers are pond scum unworthy of her omnipotence and really believes she's next in line for a big move up the ladder of command. She doesn't realize that everyone in the joint, from the casino manager to the porter, hates her guts and she's got about as much chance of getting the next promotion as you do.

She's easy to spot, with bad hair and fully accessorized drab outfits to match, including eyeglasses that went out of vogue in the early '60s. She does everything by the book, except ratings, which she consistently under-values, because she thinks that the more she can chisel you out of, the better it looks on her record. You're better off not playing in Ima's pit at all than risking your bankroll trying to pry a comp loose from her clammy paws.

Bobby Burnout

An incurable cynic, he won't do anything for anyone and why should he? It's not like anybody's ever done anything for him.

Usually sporting a 10-year-old suit (which was out of fashion then), he can't understand why, after 15 years of playing slots, snorting coke, and dating 17-year-old high school dropouts, he's still busted and no one will give him a shot at moving up in the organization. A real pleasure to be around, he's the only floorman in Las Vegas who thought UNLV should have fired Tarkanian.

Hopelessly mired in the twilight of a mediocre career, he's miserable, hates casinos, hates dealers, and especially hates customers who make him work by asking for a comp or a rating. Usually chewing gum and leaning against a podium, he won't rate a $5,000 player unless he's asked. A dying breed (from cirrhosis and lung cancer, mostly) small pockets of them remain and you should avoid them at all costs (almost always your comps).

Lydia Lithium

You came here to party. She's come here to die. Poor Lydia has seen more therapists than Woody Allen, who've all convinced her that her clinical depression isn't her fault. If not hers, then whose? It must be yours. You're the one making her work this shitty job.

Have Your Rap . . .

Most people trying to trick the house lie to the bosses when asked where they're from or what they do and they often get caught if they haven't thought out their stories ahead of time.

A card-counter friend of a friend once sat down at a high-stakes table, trying to be invisible. A boss came over and introduced himself.

"So, where you from?" asked the boss.

"L.A.," said the gambler.

"You fly or drive in?" queried the boss, just being friendly.

The card counter, trying to look like a real sport, quickly fibbed, "I flew in. My own plane."

"Oh yeah?" the boss said. "What kind of plane you got?"

"Uh, uh, a Cessna," mumbled the counter.

"Me too!" beamed the boss. "What model?"

Now the counter was finished. All he could do was utter, "A two seater," while he got up from the game and skulked away, knowing he could never show his face in that boss' pit again.

Sometimes she's almost serene when the psychotropic drugs are kicking in, but even then, why should she help you? It doesn't matter anyway. Nothing does. She never smiles, dresses like she's auditioning for the lead in "Dark Periods," and doesn't really have the energy to write $100 on your rating slip when $25 is so much easier.

Even if you could somehow get her to boost your ratings 200%, it wouldn't be worth it, because you're coming to Las Vegas to have fun and a party-on-the-hoof she ain't.

Harry Hannibal

The serial floorman. He liked to drown puppies, pull the wings off butterflies, and start fires when he was a kid. Then he learned martial arts at 15 so he could stomp the crap out of the popular guys in school.

Now he's got the perfect job: watching people lose their life's savings. He doesn't have an interest in the house's money at all. It's *you* he cares about, perversely. He underrates everybody and

. . . Ready

The lesson? Don't make up a story about something you know nothing about. Here are some handy tips when creating a new personal profile for yourself.

- A lot of players like to talk on the games. The first question is invariably, "Where are you from?" Use a big city, but you'd better know something about the city you claim to hail from.
- If you're pretending to have a different occupation, make it an obscure one and have a working knowledge of it. It's kind of hard to claim you're a junk dealer if another scrap-metal guy happens to be on the table and starts asking you what they're paying for a ton of iron back home.
- To avoid casual conversation, the best thing you can claim to be is a salesman. Whether it's used cars, aluminum siding, or whole life insurance, no one in his right mind will want to know anything about your business, for fear that you might actually tell them.

will rip your head off if you ask for something.

He's hard to spot, but here are some clues. If you shake his hand and it feels like a newly opened tube of Pillsbury Buttermilk Biscuits, back off. If you ask him where he's from and he says "Why?" get up and leave. If he smiles and pats the dealer on the back every time she draws to a 21 and sweeps the board, pick up your chips and go.

Paula Paranoid

Nervous as a cop in prison, she knows she doesn't have the heart for this job and thinks that she's going to be discovered at any minute. Casinos being what they are, the bosses beat her up, the dealers beat her up, and the customers join the fray any time they get a chance.

Doing anything to avoid confrontations with her bosses, she always defers any decision, including comps, to her superiors and she'll underrate you if she's brave enough to rate you at all.

Usually assigned to the lowest-limit games in the house anyway, there's nothing you can do to convince her to take a chance with your ratings. To prove that she can't be bought, she'll cut your actual average bet in half if you do something nice for her. Usually wearing a dress with those pooched-out things on the shoulder and a doily collar, she should have been a school teacher, except the third graders probably would have beaten her up, too.

Jersey Jack

How can I put this delicately? How about, "He's a punk"? Yep, that works just fine. Reared in Camden and other Garden State garden spots, Jersey Jacks are famous the world over for exporting their rude behavior to sunnier climes. He hooked up with corporate in Atlantic City and got a transfer to Las Vegas, but he hates the town and isn't afraid to tell anyone within earshot how much nicer it was to live where it was cold and dirty and congested with other rude people.

A know-it-all's know-it-all, he's usually a head bobber with a sneer who's never really had his butt kicked (he wouldn't talk to people that way if he had). No matter how big or rich you are, he'll get in your face and bray his unwanted opinions on any subject, ranging from how overrated the Cowboys are to what a joke national health care is.

He has a double-digit IQ, but you just can't trick him with your ratings because, with him, everything's a contest. Fair play and social graces aren't included in the rules. If you're actually averaging $75 a hand and he sees you bet $25 once, that's your rating. You got a problem with that?

The Average Bosses

Finally, there are a lot of bosses who are neither good nor bad. They just are. They rate you according to what they see, they're reasonably pleasant, and they won't go out of their way to do anything for you or to you. That's okay. With just a little bit of effort, they can be brought right into the fold and you'll still get your free vacations with some refined ACES maneuvers.

Manipulating Bosses

I know, this is supposed to be a more sensitive decade, where we all hold hands, eat bowls of bird food, and think nice thoughts about everyone even if we hate their guts. Manipulating people probably doesn't fit the new-age consciousness so well, but look at it this way. The house makes the rules. And you have to play by the rules. Therefore, you're ultimately being manipulated by the house. Now, just think of it as if you're giving the house a little of its own medicine. Besides, you'll have to do it if you want to win.

You should cozy up to floormen and pit bosses whatever the size of your bankroll and level of comps you're after. But there are different styles for different stakes. For starters, the main idea to getting comped with a smaller bankroll is to get noticed, not rated. You get *rated* by going through procedures that we'll cover in the next chapter; in the rating game, your play is tracked by the floorman, then that data is sent upstairs to marketing, where your comps are determined. You get *noticed* to earn a comp from a floorman or a pit boss who can give you something on their own accord. In most places, floormen can give an untracked player a comp for two in a buffet or coffee shop and sometimes a casino room rate, and pit bosses can get you comps for rooms and the more expensive restaurants.

How do you get noticed? Simply buy in for a few hundred when you sit down. The dealer has to notify the floorman. When the boss looks over to OK the buy-in, ask him for a drink. This serves several functions. First, it puts the boss on notice that you're there. Second, it lets him know you're a sport, even if all you order is ginger ale. Make your largest bets early when the boss is watching; when he turns his back, settle in for the table minimum. Even three $25 bets initially will leave you another $125, with $50 in red chips to chum while you're earning your comp. When you've played an hour, lay down another large bet or two, call the boss over, and make your pitch for a meal ticket.

Another way to approach floormen for comps is to decide beforehand exactly what kind of comp you want. Say you'd like to treat your wife to a gourmet meal at Caesars. Call over a boss and ask him something like this, "How much do I have to bet and how long do I have to play to get a comp in the Bacchanal?" If the boss says, "You'd have to go four hours at a $250 minimum," you might decide that the Bacchanal is out of your league. Then you could say, "Well, how about the buffet?" Now you'll know exactly what's expected of you to qualify for the comp, whether it's high level or low. And the boss is put on notice that you plan to fulfill his requirements and will expect the comp in return.

A final bit of advice. Be nice. Don't lead off with something like, "Wattaya gotta doota get a comp around here?" Try something smoother like, "Have I played long enough to get a coffee shop comp for two?" Half the time the boss will say yes. The other half of the time he'll say no, but he'll follow up by telling you to play for another 30 or 40 or 60 minutes, however long it is until he'll feel justified in granting your comp—or until he goes on break. If it's the latter, he knows he won't be on the game when you ask again for your comp. That's okay. As soon as the boss' relief gets there and settles in, ask the replacement boss if you can get your comp. If he hesitates, tell him that the other boss said you only had to play till then to qualify. If he still says no, ask him to page the other boss. That'll clinch it, because it's a hell of a lot easier to write you a meal ticket than it is to run down some guy who's back in the help's hall, lying to a cocktail waitress.

Milking Floormen

Use the following tips to get everything you need from the floormen.

• Be nice. I can't overemphasize this. Believe it or not, bosses are human. In a casino, the nice guys go to the airport in limos.

Jerks fight for buffet tickets.

One of the most important aspects of ACES play is controlling yourself. It's easy to be an ass in a casino and you'll run into a lot of them when you play. The bosses and dealers put up with

What To Wear

A question often asked by first-time Las Vegas visitors is, "What should I wear?" The answer as far as comps are concerned is simple. "Money." As long as you've got some chips on you, you're "wearing" all you need to get the joint's respect. A fat cigar-smoking bailbondsman in a torn T-shirt with suspenders who bets $500 a hand looks a lot better to a floorman than an Armani-clad investment banker who just bought in for $60 and makes a big deal of firing three bucks a pop.

Men

If you've got money, Hollywood's okay. Conservative's okay. Poolwear's okay. Glamour's okay. Western's okay. Geek is *not* okay. Nine out of ten guys who get thrown out of casinos for counting cards fit the following profile: they have pasty skin, drink mineral water or juice, laugh through their nose (if at all), and wear clothing once fashionable in Iron Curtain countries. A dead giveaway is a short-sleeved velour shirt to go along with that casino tan. Where do they get these duds anyway? Is there a "Nerds-R-Us" out there somewhere? Anyway, you're better off looking like a pimp than someone with a degree from MIT. And nobody wants to look like a pimp.

Ladies

Wear whatever you find comfortable. Your comps might move a smidgeon upward on a high-limit table if you're dressy dressed, but most times it won't matter. Bosses know in their bones that the overwhelming majority of people who've tried to put one over on the casinos have been male. (I'm betting on you to even things out real soon.) You'll be noticed, and you might get ogled, but you'll rarely be suspected of anything. If you're dressed a little too flashy, though, you might attract some unwanted attention. The comp-counter look is casual.

a lot of crap. But the premium casinos have zero tolerance for players who abuse the staff or other customers, regardless of their level of play, and any untoward comments or gestures will either get you tossed out the door or rated with the "scumbags." That is, your rating slip will mysteriously find itself in the 21-pit garbage can.

• Always ask a boss for some inside Las Vegas information. Everybody likes to share a scoop. People enjoy feeling smart and they'll like it if you think they're smart. If you think they're smart, you must be pretty smart too, and a darn good guy.

• Take the boss up on a recommendation (restaurant, show, golf course, etc.) and thank him later for steering you to the right place, even if you hated where he sent you. People like having the chance to help and if you acknowledge that behavior, they will want to help even more.

• Brag to other players at the table about how nice the casino and its personnel are. Say something bad about The Mirage (unless you're at the Golden Nugget or Treasure Island). Say it's too big, too crowded, too expensive—it doesn't matter what. The folks working in the other clubs are jealous of Steve Wynn's flagship and they'll almost always agree with you.

• Try to give the impression that you're a big player at other premium clubs. This is easy to do. Just drop a few names about other shows, restaurants, etc. Always finish with a compliment about the casino you're playing in.

• Tell the boss how impressed you are that his joint doesn't worry about winners or losers. Every boss in Las Vegas likes to be thought of as a non-bleeder. This is real easy to do, too. You'll be hard pressed to make up a tale too outlandish about the jittery floormen at Bally's or the Barbary Coast.

• Every boss thinks he's sharp. As far as he's concerned, so do you. As far as you're concerned, he's not.

• A lot of bosses will look you up in the computer and tell you how far you can go on your comps if you make them your friends.

• Always say goodbye to the boss. Show her your chips. Tell her how much you bet and show how much you lost. Don't whine. An easy exit from the game goes something like this.

Tell the dealer you're quitting. Stand up. If the boss has her back to you, wait until she turns around. Count your chips in your hand, but hold your ground for a minute or two. Then give the chips to the dealer and ask for "color" (exchanging smaller chips for larger chips). She'll have to get the boss' attention. If the boss is busy with something else, she'll nod to the dealer and continue what she's doing. The dealer will color out your chips. Don't leave. The boss will eventually come over. When she does, hold out your chips or point to them on the table.

"You're too tough today," you tell her as you spread your chips so she can see exactly how much you've lost. "Maybe I'll get even tonight," you laugh. She'll pretend to feel the pain of your loss while secretly being relieved that she doesn't have to listen to you snivel. Now's the time for the clincher. Say something like, "I was lucky to get away with anything at all after losing both of those hundred-dollar (or double whatever your biggest bet was) double-downs." Important: if you're nudging your bets up verbally, make sure at least two dealers have been on the game before you get too outrageous or they'll bust you good.

You don't have to repeat this exchange verbatim. Just puff a little with your own style in a way that's comfortable for you. Whatever you say, as long as it includes something about losing and betting big, and comes without a whine, can't hurt you.

Where to Sit Down

You're finally ready for the last step in "Bracing for ACES" before you get to the actual playing of blackjack and practicing your comp counting. It's time to sit down at a table.

Table selection is an easy, yet vital, consideration in ACES play. The number-one criterion for selecting a game is to find a busy spot. The most important thing you can do to make a boss think that you're a bona fide high roller is bet big, but you only make your big bets when he's watching. And if it's busy, the boss will have a lot of other things on his mind, most of them more important than watching you and tracking your bets.

First, find a busy blackjack pit with lots of green-chip ($25) and black-chip ($100) play. Use your instincts and pick a boss you think you'll like. Watch the boss from the outside. He'll have three or four tables in his section. There's an invisible line between the floormen's sections and they never, ever, get involved with customer relations, disputes, or issuing markers in another boss' designated area. Most bosses will at least casually glance at all the games in their section every few minutes. Be patient. It'll seem like an eternity while you wait to determine the best seat, but it won't take long. Keep moving while you look. People who stand like a statue and stare at blackjack games for more than a few minutes raise the hackles on dealers, players, and bosses and immediately become suspect of contemplating various nefarious activities.

Walk around both sides of the pit to make sure you can evaluate every potential seat. If the boss is intently watching a particular game, sit diagonally across the pit, on a busy game in his four-table section, as far away from the big action as possible. That way, he'll only look in your direction when someone asks for something. When he comes over, bet it up. As long as he's there, keep betting big. You have to be willing to make protracted big bets while the boss is watching.

Sit in a position where you can see him at all times without having to "rubberneck." Caution: if you're sitting in the first or sixth playing spot and a boss stands beside or behind you, assume he's watching and bet accordingly.

Watch the Boss

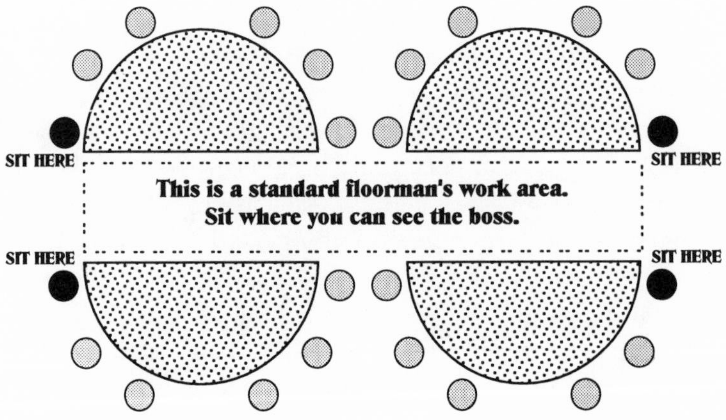

Hiding From The Floorman

Here are some other, more subtle ways to mask your play after you've become acclimated to the casino environment.

• Sit at the end of the pit on a corner table. This way the dealer blocks the boss' angle of vision, and the players sitting across from you on the other side of the table block his view as well. On top of that, you can always see his body, but he can't see your bet. Of course, he might come over and stand next to you, but if he does stand there and gander at your bets (and hardly any of them do), he'll soon wind up trying to support himself against the roped stanchions that keep the tourists from walking through the pits; it's not a real good spot for professional podium leaners.

• If the table has a tall (6-inch or more) placard designating the table limits next to the last betting spot and your back will face the boss when you play, sit next to it. Unless the boss has a perfect angle on the game, he'll have trouble seeing your bets and your peripheral vision will always let you know when he is there. (You can also use the pile of ashtrays that winds up at one corner of the table to block your bets.)

• Sit at the table so that your back is to the boss (end or first seat) and scoot your chair in toward the pit so that he can't see your bet at all unless he's directly in front of your game. Although you won't be able to see him as much as you'd like, he won't be

Block the Boss

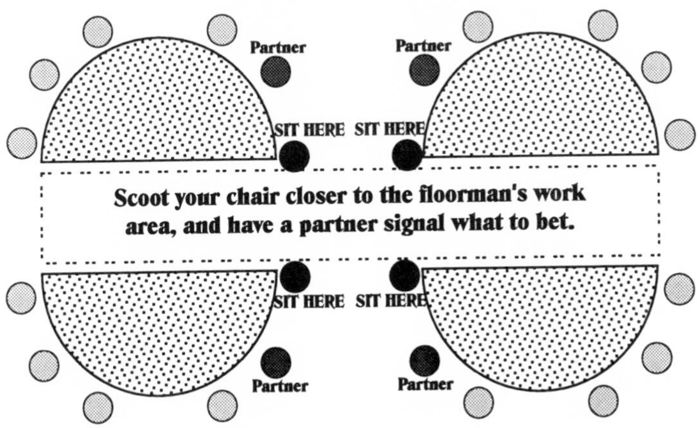

able to see you either. This works especially well if you have a friend on the table who can watch him all the time and signal you when to bet it up.

• Always make your big bets when the boss is looking. If he's still watching you, no matter what happens, your next bet should be big too. If the dealer shuffles, leave the bet out. As soon as the boss turns his back, I like to snatch the chips and make a small bet. After the shuffle, many professional players prefer to leave the bet out, particularly when they suspect the dealer is getting a little torqued. Sometimes you're worried about the dealer communicating information to the boss, sometimes you're not. If there's a question, make a bet for her. If she thinks you're up to something, you'll know right away.

• Try not to leave a table if you've played with the regular dealer for more than ten minutes; she'll have too good a bead on how much you've really been betting. It's always best to leave just after the relief dealer comes in, if possible.

• Make two or three big bets when you are about to leave.

• Make a bet for the dealer on your first bet. If the boss asks her about your average bet, she definitely will remember that you're a tipper and might say something good.

• Even if you don't buy into the theory of tipping dealers, you must make a bet for the dealer on your last hand. If the boss asks her how much you bet, she might give you credit for being a sport. While tipping at the end is a given, I've found that it's much easier tipping a little bit early on to get them on your side right away than it is trying to override an hour or two's worth of animosity with a measly bet at the end of your play.

4
The Mechanics of ACES

Boiled down to its basic elements, ACES involves playing a perfect game of blackjack, manipulating bosses, masking bets, and slowing down the game. By now you should have a good handle on the first two elements, blackjack and bosses, which were covered in the previous chapter. The fundamental concept of masking bets was also introduced in "Bracing for ACES"—make your big bets during the few moments when the boss is watching and revert to smaller bets when he's not. Additional techniques for masking bets—tricking relief dealers and bosses, playing with a partner, even tipping—are explained in this chapter. The final element, slowing down the game, could be the most critical of all, because sitting at a blackjack table getting credit for time played but *not* risking your money is nothing less than pure comp profit.

Play Slow

Speed kills. It's true about methedrine and it's true about gambling. As an ACES player, your objective is to minimize losses while maximizing comps. That means you have to reduce your exposure to the house edge (at blackjack) by playing fewer hands.

Here are the basic guidelines for choosing a blackjack table with an eye toward playing about 30% fewer hands than the house credits you for.

- More players are better than fewer players.
- Fewer decks are better than more decks.
- Cards dealt face down are better than cards dealt face up.
- A party atmosphere is better than a somber one.
- A shallow cut is better than a deep cut.

The best all-around blackjack game I can imagine is a single decker with six other players at the table having fun with a dealer who takes time to tell jokes and laugh with the players—especially during the shuffle. An okay game has four friendly people, four decks dealt face down, with the cut card placed smack dab in the middle. The worst game imaginable would be a face-up six-decker with a deep shuffle point where you're playing head-up against a fire-breathing speed demon. Get it? The more elements of "slow play" that you can combine, the better.

All right. Now that you've found a busy table and plopped yourself down in a wizardly position, you're ready to go. Here are some longcuts to a blackjack game that can significantly reduce your hands per hour.

• Avoid the quick-draw artists like the plague. The average dealer gets around a full layout about 60 times an hour. The ones wired on crank can spit out 90 rounds in the same 60 minutes—brutal for comp counters. Look for friendly, talkative dealers, as well as for older dealers, break-in dealers, or dealers on depressants (you'll find more of them downtown, rather than out on the Strip where drug testing is almost universal).

• If your dealer is younger than 30, ask him questions. A lot of the kids in Las Vegas really can't talk and deal cards at the same time. If you find one who's chatty and has to stop the game to underscore points in his conversation, make sure he knows that you're fascinated with his patter.

• Show your hand to other players. Ask how they'd play it.

• Take your time when you split and double. Scratch your head. Furrow your brow. Sigh once or twice. Talk to someone on the table about the merits of the play. You'll usually find at least one "expert" on every table who'll be glad to tell you how to play your hand. If one of your co-players is from New Jersey, he'll give you advice whether you ask for it or not.

• Sit out a hand or two at every opportunity. If the timing's right, or if your act is good, you might be able to miss a hand when the cocktail waitress takes your order or brings your drink. If you can make the dealer and floorman believe you have a strong superstition or two, it can take you a long way. For example, if you're on a double-deck game and someone new sits down, sit out until the dealer reshuffles, making sure to mumble something about the new player "changing the cards." Or if you're playing at a shoe game and a new player pops in for one hand and you lose, sit out a hand or two, again complaining about how the jerk "messed up the cards."

• If you're on a face-down game, anytime a player in front of you doubles down, stop the game and ask him what he got before you act on your hand. Almost everyone will peek at the card and show it to you. This eats up an enormous amount of time. If you can get everybody at the table extra cozy, you'll put a major hobble on the game.

• If you'd like to bet for the dealer, stop her just before she deals the cards. Ask her how you can make a bet for her. She'll be glad to stop the game and show you. Before she deals ask her if she gets to keep her own tips. When she says "No," ask her, "Why not?" The resulting diatribe, while often more long-winded, ill-informed, and opinionated than you'd normally care to suffer, is sure to eat up at least a minute of her time.

• If you're playing two hands and want to tip the dealer, stop her just before she delivers the cards and ask her which hand she wants her bet on. If she tells you to pick one, say "Eeny-meeny-miney-moe, catch a dealer by the toe. If she hollers..." Going through the whole verse before putting down the chip grinds out a lot of time, but you run the risk of being labeled a tweezer butt for life.

• Pocket your silver. Then, when the waitress brings your drink, ask the dealer for small change, which often stops the game in mid-hand while the waitress holds her meat hook over the table.

• If it's real busy, try to find a nonsmoking table. Then take a smoke break every 30 minutes or so, whether you smoke or not.

• If you've got the guts, spill a drink across the table while the cards are still on the layout. I know it sounds easy, but spilling a drink on purpose and making it look like an accident is hard to do. Still, it's worth plenty during a comp-wizarding career. Between toweling off the layout, drying off your chips, and bringing a new deck in, you've just picked up five minutes of free play. The best time to do this is when you're handing the dealer a tip. How can she get mad when you're giving her money? Only do this once per floorman per trip or you'll either get cut off or hammered on your rating. But one spill's okay. They see it every day.

• If you enjoy baiting the bull, instead of betting a green chip, bet $31.50, with one green chip, one red, one dollar, and a fifty-cent piece on top. Win or lose, this type of "barber-pole" bet requires two or three extra dealer motions on every hand. As an added bonus, you get to stop the game a lot to ask for change for your bets. Barber-pole betting can save you three to five hands an hour if done adroitly.

Please. While effective, you should only resort to barber-pole bets when you're stuck with a rude dealer. If you are, it's great sport to watch the blob get torqued out and slow the game to a crawl just to show you how miserable you're making her life. Heh, heh, little does she know she's making you money in the meantime. To guarantee sending her to the coronary unit before her time, ask for change for a dollar and make a big deal of betting 50¢ for her when you bet $106.50 for yourself. If you win, toss her the dollar with a flourish, making sure to say something cool like, "Who loves you, baby?" or "Could you deal a little faster, please? I'm on a roll!" You wanted slow? You got slow.

• Have a friend page you. This can save at least five minutes every hour.

• Have a friend play with you. You can really slow the game down discussing each other's hands (see "Playing with Partners").

• A great play is to get into a session when they're changing cards. In most houses that deal face-up, the six-deck shoes are changed every 24 hours, usually in the wee hours of the morning. If they play a face-down shoe game, the cards are changed about every four to six hours. Single-deck cards are changed every hour, double-deck every two hours. (These are general times that apply to all but the worst sweatshops, where the decks are replaced any time it looks like you might actually be winning.) Make sure to ask a dealer when the cards are changed. If you make it a point to be up at an early hour to catch the change of cards on the face-up shoes, scout out a big pit. If you see a boss changing cards a couple of tables away, sit down and hand the floorman your rating card. Bet big for the moment. Shortly, the boss will be messing with the cards on the pit stand so you can bet small. The new cards will get to you in a few minutes. When he brings the decks to your game, bet big again. The dealer will take five to fifteen minutes to inspect, wash, and shuffle all the cards. Sit there. Have some coffee. Ask her questions. Learn something.

When the cards are ready to go, bet small if the boss isn't watching. Usually at this time of morning, he's not. Play slow for a couple of hands and then, when you're sure you can get his attention, put a big bet out and call the boss over. Ask him what they do with the old decks. He might give you one, and it's a good time to show the boss one more big bet before you get up. If you're in a megaresort, go to another pit and work the same ploy. Artfully executed, you can get in 20-30 minutes of risk-free "play," but be forewarned, it is boring to watch someone shuffle cards all morning.

• Make a big deal out of it when you're asked to cut the cards. Then you can decide that you're not lucky and hand the cut card to someone else. On a double-deck game you can hold onto the cut card after you've put it in the deck. The dealer will pull the deck back and you'll still have the cut card in your hand! It's good for some grins on the game and it'll get you up to 30 seconds of non-risk ratings. There are lots of other cut-card plays. You can fumble with it and drop it. You can try to literally throw it into the middle of a multiple-deck stack. Or you can tilt the cut card and try to insert it sideways (for a laugh).

• If a couple of people get up, bet two hands. There are two advantages in doing this. You can keep the game moving as slow as molasses, and the bankroll swings will be smaller with two $25 bets rather than one $50 bet. There is a risk here, however, which you have to nip in the bud immediately. Some floormen, actually a lot of floormen, will look at someone betting two hands of $25 and give them an average bet of $25. Rating slips don't have a "number-of-spots-played" category and many bosses are too blockheaded to combine the two bets into one average bet. If you play two hands, call the boss over while the dealer's shuffling. Make two big bets. Ask him if you get rated for both hands. If he says "no," stack the two bets up on one spot. When he turns his back, pull some chips off (if you want to).

Shuffle Up

If the game conditions (rules, decks, busy, good boss, etc.) look about the same and you can't quite make up our mind where to play, "clock" the shuffles. Some dealers take as long as five minutes to shuffle a shoe. Compared to the buzz saws, who finish in a minute or two, you'll be able to save a minimum of three hands per shuffle while the dealer gives the pasteboards a full massage.

If you can find a chatty dealer, now is the time to talk it up. Many otherwise diligent workers see the shuffle-break as downtime and socialize with the customers during the shuffle. Since the cards aren't available for dealing, they reason that they are not doing the casino a disservice by engaging in extended conversation. They'll often come to a dead stop in the middle of mixing the cards to underscore a statement or wait for a punchline and inadvertently (or not) double the down-time in the process. With three or four slow shuffles an hour (you really can't expect more if the dealer is that sluggish) you'll save around a dozen hands an hour and cut your expected losses by at least a fifth and sometimes much more.

If the shuffle and game speeds are close, watch where the dealer puts the plastic card in the deck after the cut, because when it comes back out the dealer has to shuffle again. While card counters want deep penetration (that means they want the deck dealt as far down as possible before a shuffle), a comp counter wants just the opposite. The shuffle point doesn't affect the return per hand of a basic-strategy player, but it has everything to do with how often a shuffle is necessary. Bad penetration, where the dealer cuts a lot of cards out of play, means many more shuffles and fewer hands. It gets better.

MAX FACT: Sweatshop card-counter countermeasures can benefit comp counters.

Some sweatshops instruct their dealers to cut every shoe in half. They also make the dealers do things like break the cards into nine different piles and shuffle them twice as long if someone gets ahead $500 or so on the game. Sweatshops only get out about half as many hands as the premium joints, but they'll be damned if they're going to let somebody win without suffering for it. Thanks.

You can scout these sweatshops from the comfort of your home by subscribing to Stanford Wong's *Current Blackjack News*. Wong's newsletter identifies the casinos that deal blackjack with good and bad penetration. The places with bad penetration are listed in a category of "Bad Comments." As far as comp counters are concerned, the sweatshops with bad penetration are where we want to be.

The shuffle also comes into play in bet masking. The biggest bet you will ever make is the one you will never make. It involves timing the dealer's shuffle. You can tell when she's about to shuffle by watching for the plastic cut card; its appearance during play signals a shuffle at the conclusion of the round. When you see the card, it's time to strike. If you've busted or hit a blackjack and been paid, immediately put an extra big bet (up to 10 chips) in the betting circle. If you're in the hand till the end, wait until she picks up all the cards and then make a huge bet. In most clubs the dealer has to shout out "Shuffling" when she reaches the end of the shoe. The floorman will acknowledge her. If he comes to the table and watches the whole shuffle, including the cut, you've got to bail out. It looks pretty suspicious to pull your bet back, so if the boss is hawking the game, slowly pull the bet back behind the betting circle and say "Which way is the restroom?" Leave the chips there. Even while you're gone the boss will see your big bet, so not only will you get the benefit of not playing at all, you'll also look like you're betting big while you're away. Make sure the boss is not looking when you sit back down . If you bet big during the shuffles, you'll have big money on the layout up to 10% of the time with no risk at all. But as a last resort if the boss keeps watching, let your big bet play. It can't hurt your rating.

Pick Your Times

Have you ever wondered why you never see a clock in a casino? Or what the real purpose is for all those God-awful red and yellow lights blazing over the slot carousels that emit sounds like an egg timer gone bad? Or why the temperature in a casino always hovers around 68 degrees? Or why most breakfast specials start at the same time most folks are getting into bed? Or why unlimited drinks are free to players and why the women serving them aren't wearing any clothes? I'll tell you why. Because the casino wants to bombard you with so much sensory overload that you forget where you are, why you're there, and most importantly, that you're supposed to be in bed.

Time flies when you're having fun—ask the great-grannies who aren't even thinking about going to sleep at 3 am on a Monday night. And time stands still when you're not—witness the 25-year-old dealers who glance at their watches 15 times an hour to make sure they're not getting cheated out of 30 seconds of their breaks. Who knows this better than anyone? The big boys who run the casinos, some of the greatest time manipulators in the world. And you thought Salvador Dali could melt the hands on the dial!

Casino managers want to relieve you of your bankroll, and they rely heavily on timing to do it. You want to relieve them of their comps, and advanced ACES play takes into account all of the casino timing considerations.

Although the top joints in Las Vegas are busy most of the time now, weekends are definitely best for blending in. If you can only come a couple of times a year, come when it's really hopping. The craziest times are the traditional American three-day holidays, along with Super Bowl weekend, Cinco de Mayo, Mexican Independence Day, Chinese New Year, and anytime there's a big convention or boxing match. It's easy to get lost in these crowds, but sometimes risky during the ethnic holidays if you and the bosses are the only English-speaking people in the pit. This often causes a floorman to hang around you more than you'd want.

If you like to raise hell on New Year's Eve, Las Vegas is the nuts. The hotels invite their good players to big parties. Big-time celebrities come to these deals. You shake their hands. You meet the owners of the casinos. You dance to big bands, eat gourmet food, drink good champagne, and see hot shows—and none of it goes against your comp account. It's so busy your floorman won't have time to come up for air, and he'll be hard pressed to observe your play five minutes an hour.

When you refine your ACES play, you'll develop your own timing based on what you (and your partner) want to do when you're not playing blackjack. Do you want to party all night? Then play blackjack during the day. If you like to lounge by the pool, play golf or tennis, or shop all day, then play at night. It's always busy when the marquees ignite, so you'll have no problem disguising your limited play.

Graveyard shift, from 4 am to noon in most joints, is usually pretty quiet. If you scout around, though, you can find busy, high-action areas in the premium joints. In the smaller places it's best to party or sleep during graveyard shift and play when it's busy.

Play During the Count, Breaks, and Shift Changes

You'll need to do a little detective work in the joints to find out when the dealers and bosses change shifts and when they take the count (usually about the same time, but not always). You can use some simple investigative techniques to get the staff to spill their guts. You don't have to be Kojak to get the information you want, but you don't want to draw any unnecessary attention to yourself, either.

Walk up to any dealer. Try to find a dead game. If there aren't any, sit down on a low-limit game, order a beverage, and play a few hands. Then ask the dealer what time the shift changes. She'll tell you. Pretty cool, huh? Then ask her if the bosses come in at the same time. She'll tell you that too. You getting the chills yet? Now go for the coup de grace and ask when they take the count. She might get a little annoyed (unless you've been tipping her), but she'll tell you that, too.

A Typical 24-Hour Casino Day

2:30 am	Graveyard pit bosses and shift bosses on duty. Security guards lay drop boxes around pits.
2:45 am	Count begins.
3:00 am	Count completed. **Old rating slips closed out.** **New rating slips started.** Drop boxes pulled. Outgoing bosses tally the take.
3:30 am	Graveyard floormen relieve swing floormen. Floormen give rundown on all rated players.
4:00 am	Graveyard dealers relieve swing dealers.
10:30 am	Day pit bosses and shift bosses on duty. Security guards lay drop boxes around pits.
10:45 am	Count begins.
11:00 am	Count completed. **Old rating slips closed out.** **New rating slips started.** Drop boxes pulled. Outgoing bosses tally the take.
11:30 am	Day floormen relieve graveyard floormen. Floormen give rundown on all rated players.
12:00 noon	Day dealers relieve graveyard dealers.
6:30 pm	Swing pit bosses and shift bosses on duty. Security guards lay drop boxes around pits.
6:45 pm	Count begins.
7:00 pm	Count completed. **Old rating slips closed out.** **New rating slips started.** Drop boxes pulled. Outgoing bosses tally the take.
7:30 pm	Swing floormen relieve day floormen. Floormen give rundown on all rated players.
8:00 pm	Swing dealers relieve day dealers.

The rest is easy. All shifts last exactly eight hours. If it's 10 am and she tells you the current shift is over in two hours, it means that the graveyard shift starts at 4 am. The day shift will be coming in at noon and going home at 8:00 pm, when swing shift takes over. If swing shift starts at 8:00 pm they'll go home at 4:00 am, when the guys on graveyard slog in to start another happy day.

The Count

Your first major strike will come when they "take the count." Two pit bosses (not floormen) will come to the table and conduct a chip inventory, while the security guards scurry around, pulling the drop boxes that hold the money and putting new ones on the games. Pit clerks will run up and down the pit, trying to reconcile all the markers.

Sound hectic? It's nothing compared to what happens to your floorman. While you're sitting there, minding his business, he'll be up to his Fruit of the Looms in paperwork. He'll be furiously trying to write down everything the pit bosses are dictating about the chip inventory, while simultaneously trying to close out (complete) all of his shift's rating slips and start new ones for the new bosses coming in.

This is a great time to wizard on your floorman, because he has to fill out as many as 24 new rating slips and doesn't have a lot of time to do it. He'll only see one or two of your bets, at best, while he's trying to make a final determination on how much you gambled during his shift, as well as notate on the new rating slip what your average bet is for the guy relieving him. He also has to scan the chip racks at all four of his tables, order fills before the new floorman comes on, and complete a new chip inventory for the new guy. Whew! It's fast. It's furious. It's fat city. The magic twenty minutes before and after the count is when we strike. Our M.O.? Bet big and hide chips.

When the floorman comes to your table and closes out all the rating cards, he will try to note: how much you bought in for, how many chips you have, your win/loss (he'll base it on how much you've bought in for versus how many chips you have on the layout), your time on the game, and your average bet. You can tell when he's closing you out because he'll have all the rating slips in his hand and be scanning each player's chips and betting spots,

Coloring Up

Bosses in most places are required to keep a running log of $100 bills dropped on the game and any conversion of $100 or more in chips. This is done to keep track of table inventory and player win/loss, and to keep pilferage to a minimum. If you're on a busy game in a premium house with black-chip play, the boss won't pay a whole lot of attention when the green chips are converted into blacks (the dealer might not even notify him about it) and often won't notice who they're going to. On a $25-minimum table where nobody else is betting big, any time you convert green chips, make sure to make that a "big bet moment" in case the boss actually pays attention to the dealer. If you see someone else coloring up or coloring out with black chips, either make a big bet or sit a big bet behind the betting circle and take a break.

while frantically writing down all the data. For as long as it takes him to close your table out, bet big (from your miserly little pile). You'll know when he's finished, because he'll put all the rating slips from your table on the pit podium and move on to another game. Whoopee! Now you've got a new rating slip that says you're betting three or four times your actual average bet. And when the new boss relieves him and does his rundown on your table, of course you'll be betting big again and getting your unjust rewards.

Whether you want to keep playing or not is up to you. If you're ready to leave, go ahead. If not, you're in a great position to rack up some big bet ratings for at least an hour or so while the new floorman drinks his coffee, greets the customers, ducks his boss, hits on the cocktail waitress, and talks with the other floormen about last night's ball games.

Hint. If you hear a lot of racket and see security guards dropping empty metal cans throughout the pit, it means the count is imminent (within 30 minutes). Don't get up. Stay and play through the count, even if you were planning to leave, because you always want to get a second rating slip started. Why? It's not unusual for an unrated person to immediately take your spot when you get up. The incoming boss may not remember the face that went with your rating slip, and if you get up and leave without signalling the boss to close you out, you could easily earn comp credits on somebody else's play while you're out at the pool or taking a nap. What happens to you if a guy sits down and plays an hour or two and only bets $25 a hand when you're rated as a $100 bettor? Only good things.

MAX FACT: There's no such thing as a bad rating. If you're a $500 bettor, give the boss your VIP card even if you're goofing around and betting $20 a hand. It's impossible to make a bet that hurts your rating. Why? Because every single bet adds something to your equivalency.

Breaks

Bosses work a standard eight-hour shift with two "short breaks" lasting 20-30 minutes, and a "lunch" running 45 minutes to an hour. These are good times to pad your rating.

For example, if you know when a boss is going on his 45-minute lunch break, you can get there 10 minutes earlier and bet big. Then bet the table minimum while his relief is on the floor and bet it up again after the regular boss returns. You'll get in about an hour's play doing this, but the hour that you play could have an actual average of about $25 and a posted average of up to $150 if you do it perfectly. It's not easy the first few times, but it can be done after you've cased the joint during a trip or two. If

A Break for a Break

If your regular boss takes a short break, take one for yourself. Ask him (or the dealer) when he'll be back. Don't get up until he disappears from the pit. Put your chips behind your betting circle, toss the dealer a dollar, and tell her you need to make a pit stop. No one will say a word if you're gone less than 20 minutes. And you'll miss 10 or 15 hands while you're away. Remember this: rating slips have no provision for breaks.

you pull this off once on each shift, your comps will cover anything you want to do, within reason, with greatly diminished risk.

You can easily maneuver around the floormen's early breaks on day shift if you watch when they open games in the high-limit pits. Scope them out on Saturdays. Bosses in most joints normally have the same schedule on Sunday. If you get a boss you like, learn his schedule and stick with him (especially when he's away).

As a courtesy to the bosses relieving them for their breaks, floormen normally make a notation of your average bet on your rating slip and then give the relief boss a rundown on the rated players in his area. While the floorman is pointing out the rated players on your game, bet big. When he goes on his break, start betting small or take a break. Don't quit playing until the floorman on break comes back. Then bet big a few times and call it a day. Or, if you want, you can take a break while the regular floorman is gone.

Taking Breaks

Top-notch ACES players understand the dollar value of taking breaks. The example below assumes that you're betting $100 a hand on a .5% game. (For $10 bettors divide the savings by ten.)

Type of Break	Time	Savings
Waiting for a drink	1 minute	$ .50
Watching change of cards—1 deck	2 minutes	$ 1.00
Waiting for a shuffle	3 minutes	$ 1.50
Going to the bathroom	5 minutes	$ 2.50
Answering a page	5 minutes	$ 2.50
Watching change of cards—6 decks	10 minutes	$ 5.00
Breaking with a boss (coffee)	10 minutes	$ 5.00
Breaking with a boss (lunch)	30 minutes	$15.00

Each hand takes approximately one minute to complete.
Every hand you sit out will save you 50¢ in expected loss!

Warning. You shouldn't take more than a 20-minute break when the relief floorman is watching your game, especially when it's busy. If someone is clamoring for your chair and you're not there, the floorman may pick up your chips and make you forfeit your seat.

Grandfathering In

At selected times, you'll get the opportunity not only to play the floorman, but to play the traffic flow as well. Here's one method that's especially juicy.

Scout out a premium casino pit about noon on Saturday to find out where they put the high-limit games. Come back Sunday morning when it's slow, usually before 10 am. Scope out the same tables, and find one with a $25-minimum sign that has a couple of black-chip players banging away. Mosey right in, making sure to buy in for at least $1,000. Make your first bet $100, wait for the boss to turn away, then settle in betting one green chip at a time.

Within an hour, the casino will start filling up and the boss will put a "$100 minimum" sign on the table, but he'll tell all the green-chip players that the raised stakes are for new players only, and that they're "grandfathered in" (they may continue betting $25). Now it gets good.

Make a spectacle of betting at least $100 as soon as the sign is posted, $200 if your bankroll can stand the swings. Why? Two reasons. The first is obvious. The boss is watching you. The second deals with human nature. Most bosses, heartless though they may seem, don't like to embarrass customers. They get a slight twinge of guilt about demeaning green-chip players by putting up the $100 sign. If you smile and bet twice the minimum, the boss will think you're pretty swell, and he'll remember that big bet when he summarizes your action with his relief, who's due to push him off duty within the next half hour if you've timed your play right.

Then, while the boss is busy getting ready for the changing of the guard, go back to betting a quarter. But when his relief comes in, bet it up again. Now you've gotten in about two hours of play at an actual average of a little more than $25, but someone in marketing's going to think that you're a certified high roller.

When the new boss is settled in and the dealers have changed, it'll be time for you to call it a day. Stand up, shake the new boss' hand, and tell him you're going to lunch, but you'll be back later. Say something nice about him, the joint, or the dealer and politely ask, "What was my average?" If he says anything less than $100, point to the minimum sign and ask him how you could possibly bet less than $100 on a $100 game. Nine times out of ten, he'll agree. If he does, mumble something about playing two hands most of the time, too. You'll get your $100 average and sometimes a lot more.

Now, I've already told you that the boss on duty usually notates your average bet only once (unless it's time for the count). Why, then, is it important for him to think you're okay? Because when he gives his relief a rundown on all of the players in his area, it's important for the incoming boss to think that you're okay, too.

Changing of the Guard

In a busy joint, the changing-of-the-guard process (new boss coming on shift) is almost always the same, but don't expect to see the emotionless troopers you encounter at Buckingham Palace. It's hectic. Paper's flying everywhere. The boss going off duty is often cranky. The boss coming on is usually a little logy (and maybe a taste hungover, to boot). And they both have different agendas. Here's a sample scenario of two experienced floormen going through a change of shift while you're working on your ACES.

The boss going off duty (we'll call him Bucky) wants to go home. Now! The boss coming in (Rico) is still in a fog. Rico wants as much information as he can get from Bucky so he's not left high and dry.

Bucky's tapping his foot and holding up his left arm, glaring at his watch. Rico's at the end of the pit talking to a dealer about blowing a bet on the Dodgers. Rico finally sees Bucky grandstanding and hustles up. "Jesus, I'm glad to get out of here today," Bucky grumbles.

"Tough shift?" Rico asks.

"Those turds have been bugging me for eight hours," Bucky snarls as he points to a table full of obnoxious drunks betting blacks every hand. Bucky hands Rico their rating slips. Rico arches his eyebrows as he sees "$25" listed for their average bets. "Screw

Surprise Ratings

Most often the floorman will watch your play immediately after you hand him your VIP card, but sometimes it'll be during the course of the session. If it is, it's easy to spot if you keep your eyes peeled.

If you see the floorman pick up all the rating slips from the pit podium and write something on them, it generally means one of three things: he has nothing else to do, a bigger boss is hawking him, or he's evaluating everyone in his area. Whichever the case, bet big. Some bosses keep the rating slips in "tubs" (clear plastic containers attached to the blackjack tables). If he uses the tub, you'll see him pull all the slips out, so bet big.

If he happens to choose your table first and sneaks up on you when you're betting small, say something like, "I think the guy who wrote these money-management books makes all his money selling books." Not only will you be 100% right, you'll also put the boss on notice that you move your money when you're winning. Try to engage him in enough small talk to keep him around until you win one more hand and stack your biggest bet while he's watching. If the conversation continues for another hand and you win, bet big again. If you lose, drop back to a smaller bet (though not real small).

Most times the last few big bets you make will influence your final rating. As soon as you're *sure* he's not watching you anymore, bet small and don't bet big again until the next time he's watching you.

'em," Bucky grins. "I see 'em betting quarters, and I told the cocktail waitress to cut 'em off."

"I got you," Rico laughs.

Bucky points to your table as he goes around the layout, handing each slip to Rico. "This broad bought in for two hundred dollars and *all* she's got left is four thou. Numb nuts here's in five thousand and his credit's all up." Now he points to you. "Take care of this guy, he's all right. He's in a thousand, betting a hundred, maybe two. The guy on his right is Mr. K. Who the hell knows what he's doing? He's been busting my chops all night.

Took out nine markers at a thousand a pop and bets five hundred a hand. He's blown about two thousand in blacks since we took the count."

"Ball buster, huh?" Rico throws Mr. K's rating slip in the trash. (Trust me on this one. I've done it myself.) "We'll see whose balls get busted when he checks out." (The hosts might not be too thrilled, either.)

They run down the other two tables. Bucky hands Rico the table inventory sheets. "You wanna see if the racks are right?" Bucky asks.

Rico knows he came in a couple of minutes late. He gives Bucky a little break. "What if they're not? We'll probably be open tomorrow anyway. Get out of here while you can still beat the traffic." Bucky bolts out of the pit and Rico's on his own.

He spots a cocktail waitress, orders coffee and juice, and walks around the tables, checking the table inventories. When he gets to the first table, the drunks unload on him. "That other boss is a real asshole," they moan. Rico knows he's in for a long haul and retreats.

Now you get to make Rico's day. Tell him that you've got this comp down the street for dinner tonight that you can't use and wonder if he knows anyone who might want it. He'll snatch it from you before you can finish the question.

This is the perfect time to tell him you've got to leave, but you'd like to know what your average bet is. If he looks down and you're betting $200, it's almost a lock that he'll smile and say, "How's two hundred sound?" Look him in the eye and say, "That's fair," and you'll have just played two hours at about $50-$75 a hand and have two hours of $200 action logged in the computer with your name on it.

Look Like a Loser

All the world loves a winner? Not in Las Vegas they don't. You'll be a lot more popular around the casino if they think you're a sucker. Why? Casino bosses don't have to explain losers, but they do have to tell the big cheeses what's going on if someone wins.

I've been in and around the business for 25 years and I've never once seen a casino manager dress down a boss after the house won. I have seen more than a few underlings get fired when they couldn't explain how the shift just got frapped while they weren't looking.

Bosses like losers. From the worst sweatshops to the softest spots, every boss wants to win. It's human nature. They've been told since they were three years old that winning is everything, and here you are trying to beat them. Do they feel sorry for you when you lose? Some do. And a lot of them give losers better ratings.

Another plus in looking like a loser is that you won't be scrutinized as a potential cheater. If, for example, you're up a couple of thousand in a mid-size hotel, your floorman has to identify you to a bigger boss, as well as the eye-in-the-sky, before your winnings get out of hand and he's left holding the bag without an explanation. Everybody passes the buck until it stops with the casino shift boss, who'll come over and watch the game a few minutes or go "upstairs" with surveillance and observe you without you knowing it. This is especially counterproductive if you're comp wizarding, because the same boss might also review players' comps with marketing and when your name comes up he might find it noteworthy that the floorman gave you a $75 average bet when he saw, with his own two video cameras, that your actual average bet was less than $25. If he suspects that a boss is giving you an inflated rating, all hell'll break loose downstairs and you'll be about as welcome as a boil the next time you show up in your boss' area.

The bottom line is, be aware of what's going on around you. If another player on your game is winning like a pig, it often means everybody else is too, particularly if the dealer is busting a lot. As soon as you see "heat" on the game (two or more bosses watching intently), make a big bet and get up and take a break, no matter how much you're up or down (or how "cold" you think the dealer is). Go powder your nose or get a drink, then ease back in when the heat has died down and the bosses are once again tending to other matters.

It's not easy to do if you're the biggest player on the game (so try not to be), but it's important to learn how to hide chips. The reason for squirreling those chips away are many, but if a floorman compares your stash on the table to your rating slip, and it looks like you've lost $500 or $1,000 in an hour or two, he'll be hard pressed to believe that you only averaged $25 a hand and he'll probably give you a $75 or $100 rating if your last bets were made cognito.

If you *are* a loser, you won't have any trouble looking like one. In this case, try to limit your losses during any given playing session. If you do go on tilt and start betting too much, you're liable to be taking the early flight home and paying for your room. Double trouble. Don't do it.

Note. It's a good idea to carry some chips into the game, and then "swallow" (or hide) them after you've taken a marker. Now you can tell the boss you lost even if you wind up paying off the marker by saying something like, "Ain't this swell, I get to use the leftover chips from last night's fiasco to buy back today's marker too." Since you should be playing on a crowded table, the floorman won't be able to trace a few hundred in chips and you'll be the big winner, er, loser. Loser-winner. Aw, you know what I mean.

Hide Chips

As you've just seen, hiding chips is a key element of comp wizardry that you'll need to master. Unless you catch an outstanding winning streak (which will happen every now and then), once you've become proficient at salting away chips on the sly, the floormen will think you're a loser every time. It's imperative that you hide the fact that you're hiding chips, so you'll have to learn a few moves.

There are several methods that work, and unlike picking a game or schmoozing a floorman, you can practice these at home. First of all, you'll need some chips. If you don't have any, go buy some. You can get a hundred plastic poker chips for a couple of bucks at Wal-Mart.

Professionals use a number of time-tested techniques for snaking chips off a game. Here are a few of the simple ones.

The Palm

My personal favorite, and one of the easiest to master, is to cup your hand over the top of a stack of chips and squeeze until two or three chips are wedged in your palm. Lift your hand from the stack and continue squeezing, with your palm pointed downward. Look at your knuckles. Can you see any chips? Neither can anyone else. Now, keeping your hand pointed down, reach into your jacket for a mint. (Tic Tacs are best. They don't fill you up.) Release the pressure on the chips and they'll fall into the pocket. Pull out the mints and *voila*, you just "lost" $50-$75 and you get to offer the dealer some candy. With just a little practice at keeping your palm down, neither the dealer, the bosses, nor the other players will ever see you stashing chips.

The Smoker's Palm

If you smoke, you can snag two chips every time you reach for your cigarettes using the palm move. To do it right, keep your smokes in one pocket, your matches in another, and fill both pockets with chips.

The Sloppy Pile

Another favorite, particularly of the card-counting gentry, is to keep your chips in a disorganized pile in front of you until you cash out or change color when you leave. The dealers and bosses never know when chips are missing from your hill of reds, greens, and blacks because they never know what the value of the hill of chips is in the first place. This works best with a loose, open jacket or a jogging suit with an inside pocket. All you have to do is pick up a few when the dealer is having a discussion with the players on the other end of the table and drop them in. Nobody'll ever know.

Chip Under Glass

This move takes a little practice, but if you're pounding drinks, it's a beauty. Just hold a couple of chips under your glass or cup. Pick up the glass from the bottom and hand it back to the cocktail waitress when she brings your new order and palm the chips. Be sure to block the dealer's view with your body. Be careful. Cocktail waitresses don't like to make change (some don't know how).

If the chips slip out of your hand and land on her tray, she'll invoke her union rights and have every reason to believe that those $100 chips were her reward for fetching you 70¢ worth of whiskey. Your fingers are fair game if you try to snatch the chips back. Drink girls' bites have been known to kill.

Load the Purse

Women get all the breaks. Hiding chips is a snap if you carry a purse. Most clubs won't let you put your purse directly on the table, but you can hold it on your lap. Just leave it open a little and every few minutes, while the dealer is watching the other end of the table, drop a couple of chips in.

Break Time

The last great way to hide chips? When you take a break, leave just a few chips behind your betting spot and take the rest with you. When you return, put about three-quarters of your chips back on the layout and fire it up again. If you run out of chips, take another marker and no one should be the wiser. Important. Don't take any less than half of your stack out of your pocket when you return or the dealer will get suspicious.

Getting Busted

Now that you've learned how to hide chips, you have to be prepared in case you get busted for hoarding them. The worst thing you can do is make a boss think you're up to no good. If you suspect a boss is wondering who hid the chips—if you detect a boss giving you the evil eye or if she asks loudly, "What happened to all the greens?"—come clean quickly and innocently. Start pulling them out of your pocket and show her where the chips are. Have an excuse ready for hoarding the chips. Lines such as, "This is how I keep track of what I'm winning (or losing)" are heard every day. The boss might think you're goofy and a pain in the butt, but she won't think you're doing anything out of the ordinary.

It's not a bad idea to pocket chips in the exact amount of your buy-in or marker. A lot of players, especially when they get ahead, stash "their" money, while leaving the "house's" money on the table to play with. Of course, this is pure money-management mythology, because if you win it, it's your money. But the boss won't question it for a second if you pull out the buy-in and say something about the house's money—especially if some lint, paper scraps, and God knows what else accompany the chips.

Now that you've come clean, ask the boss if she'd rather you keep them on the table or change them for bigger chips. Her primary concern isn't that you're winning or losing, but whether she has to make a needless fill. If you can gloss over the situation with a smile and some cooperation, she probably won't dock your rating and the worst that'll happen is that your rating will be accurate.

Some Pointers For Hiding Chips

• If you keep your money in neat stacks (most people do), don't ever try to hide a big pile at once. The dealer will notice that your chips are gone and it will make her suspicious.

• If there's a lot of green-chip action on the game, it's better to remove greens from view than blacks, which bosses track more closely. If there's not a lot of green-chip action, you can swing with the black chips, but only when the bosses are busy elsewhere.

• To prevent the bosses from having to make needless fills, never take more than two stacks (40 chips) off a game.

• If you're a $25 bettor and you change up a stack of greens for blacks, don't put the blacks in your pocket. Put only the denomination of chips you're actually betting in your pocket, unless the action turns into a monster and you find yourself caught up in the fever, betting black chips along with everybody else. If the game becomes a magilla, you'll probably want to leave anyway, because too many eyes will be on the layout.

• Get as many chips off the table as you can before calling the boss over and making your last bet.

• If you've just swung with a pocketful of chips before going to lunch or dinner, make sure to unload and count them in front of the waiter just before ordering. You might get wet when the waiter and busboy start slobbering all over you thinking they're going to score a big chip tip, but the extra attention and service they lard on you will be well worth it.

Quick Quiz

Q. You're a champion chip-hider and you look like a big loser. You've just made a big bet and "lost" the last of your chip stash. The boss asks, "Anything I can do for you?" What do you say?

A. No thanks, my host is taking care of everything.
B. No thanks, I'm staying across the street.
C. No thanks, I just ate.
D. Yes.

A. It's D. So what if your host is a sport and you're staying across the street and you just ate? If someone offers you something, take it. It doesn't matter if it's a line pass to see the free *Salute to Singers who Died of Drug Overdoses* afternoon revue or the ptomaine special 99¢ 24-hour eat-till-it's-gone breakfast buffet. You can barter it for something else, offer it to a floorman in another joint, or toss it to a tourist who isn't as wily as you.

Be Nice

People who are used to gambling in Atlantic City might have trouble grasping this concept, but instead of being rude, try being nice. You'll get more stuff. If you've never been to the Land of the Grim, perhaps you need a little primer on how they act out there on the East Coast. First, in Atlantic City it's imperative for everyone on the table to tell everyone else how to play their cards. Even—no, particularly—if they don't know how to play their own. Secondly, everyone, including the dealers, cocktail waitresses, bosses, and fellow players, is considered an enemy. Third (to the major detriment of comp counters), everyone is in a hurry to lose. Players don't talk to each other, unless to complain. They never talk to the dealers, except to argue. Dealers don't talk to the players. And anyone who tries to strike up a conversation with the dealers, bosses, or other players gets a serious hairy eyeball.

Call me a dreamer if you will, but even though I've become somewhat cynical after hanging around casinos most of my days (and even more of my nights), I still believe that a positive attitude

Dealer Mistakes

If the dealer makes a mistake, say something like, "That's why they make erasers," and tell him how amazed you are that he doesn't make more, considering how many hands he has to deal every day.

If a dealer makes a mistake and overpays you, overlook it.

If the dealer makes a mistake that's going to cost you money, *stop the hand.* If the dealer forgets to give a person a card, or doesn't give herself a hole card, or forgets to give you your double down, take your time before deciding what to do. If you have a clear advantage, continue the hand. If it looks like you're going to get whipped, try to bail out.

Say you've doubled down on ten, the dealer's got a five up. She forgets to give you a card. She turns over a ten in the hole. Let her hit out. If she busts, demand to be paid for the double. If she makes a hand, it'll probably be called dead.

What if she forgets to give you a card and turns over a five in the hole? Let her draw out. If she draws your face card, demand to be paid. If she busts, demand to be paid. If she draws out a multi-card hand, let them call "No hand."

After she's made a hand, never let them go back and give you a card. You're better off pulling your money back.

If they give you the option of continuing or tossing in your cards before the dealer draws, make the decision in your favor. If she's got a big card up and you don't have squat, fold. If she's got a little card up and you've got a total of 10 or 11, double. When in doubt, bail out.

gets you more in life than a negative one. And I know it sounds silly, especially coming from someone who makes a living teaching others how to exploit favorable situations, mathematical and otherwise, but I think that people with a good attitude lose less money than the grumpheads.

While a positive attitude doesn't carry a lot of scientific weight, psychologically it makes all the sense in the world and the reason is simple: if you're nice, people will like you, and if they like you, they'll give you more stuff. And free stuff, need I remind y'all, is what it's all about.

In order to make sure that you don't act like a donkey on a blackjack game, I've included a few pointers for those who are graduates of the Eastern Seaboard School of Charm.

• Let the floorman be the expert. You're supposed to be a sitting duck. Be humble and let him know you respect what he has to say.

• Don't ever lie when asking for something. If you're ever caught lying, you'll lose your credibility forever. Bullshitting's okay. People like to be bullshitted as long as everyone knows that it's bullshit. Most good bosses and all good hosts are professional bullshit artists.

• Don't ever challenge a dealer. If a question arises, be a gentleman. If another player is a chronic jerk, be extra nice to the dealer. When the beef starts (and it will), always take the dealer's side in the dispute. Do the same with the floormen. If you're on their side, they're on yours. If it gets really ugly (and you think you can take him), get in the jerk's face and back him off the game. You'll be a hero forever. If you're not the type who goes for cheap physical violence, you might want to needle him to the point that he gets aggressive, then let security finish it for you. You don't want the misery to last too long, however, or too many eyes will be on your game and your ACES maneuvers will lose their effectiveness.

• If you lose a dispute, lose it with a smile. The floorman will respect your ability to take defeat graciously and he'll thank you for it on your rating slip.

• Never make a promise you can't keep. Don't tell a floorman you'll do something for him if you can't do it. If you make a promise and do perform (such as giving him an off-premises comp), he'll welcome you like a long lost friend. If he expects you to do something for him and you embarrass him, you'll be lucky to get eye contact, let alone a decent rating, the next time you play in his area.

Tipping

It might be a prerequisite for becoming a managing general partner in a major accounting firm, but being a stiff in Las Vegas is a big-time no-no. Virtually everyone who works in the gambling business once worked for tips. If you can't let loose of a nickel chip now and again, you'll get absolutely no respect from the staff, no matter what you're wearing, what movie you just starred in, or how much you're betting. If, on the other hand you're "George"—a great tipper—you'll get the benefit of the doubt every time an iffy situation pops up, and believe me, on blackjack games, iffy situations pop up a lot.

The key to ACES tipping is to stay within your budget and try to get at least double value for your tips, especially when you're gambling.

On the Tables

The reason you're currently mastering ACES is to earn free vacations. Vacations are supposed to be fun. All it takes is a few bucks ($5-$10) every session to get the dealers on your side. When it comes down to crunch time, and a busy floorman has to ask a dealer what your average bet was, you'll definitely get the best of it. Here's how it works best for me.

On my first or second hand, preferably while the boss is watching, I put a five-dollar chip on top of my bet and tell the dealer it's for him. When I win, I give him five and bet the other five for him again. (When the bet made for the dealer remains in the betting circle, the player controls the chips; when the bet is placed outside of the circle, the dealer controls the chips.) I know it's going to cost me five dollars going in, but it may make the dealer a lot more than the $10 if you hit a streak. If the dealer complains when I don't give him the whole amount, I *leave*. Again, a free vacation should be fun, and it is astoundingly uncomfortable to sit at a table where a dealer rags you for *giving him a tip!* Go to another table in the same boss' section and try again. I've found that about 10%-15% of dealers get mad when you don't give them the full amount; I've also found that they're the same dealers who can work an entire eight-hour shift and never smile. Why

King George

Among the famous, guess who was the greatest, the King of all King tippers? No surprises here: Elvis. He reportedly gave away over a dozen Cadillacs to Las Vegas Hilton employees.

Frank Sinatra wasn't quite on his level, but when he'd attend any party, wedding, or special presentation, he'd hand out $100 bills to everybody working there. He did this from the late '50s well into the '80s. You can say what you want about the guy, but he's a sport.

Other great celebrity "Georges" include Tony Curtis, Dean Martin, Sammy Davis Jr., and Richard Pryor.

Not all celebrities are classy. I once had a summer job driving a taxi on the Strip. Milton Berle (who was only making about $25,000 a week) got into my cab at the Dunes. I took him to the Stardust. The fare was $1.30. He gave me a one-dollar Dunes chip and three dimes.

Some of Las Vegas' other legendary stiffs include Pete Rose, Bruce Willis, Jerry Tarkanian, Bill Cosby, and George Blanda.

subject yourself to such a grim scene? Though you don't want to table-hop, when confronted with a rude dealer, you should move.

When I make my last bet, I always make sure to put something up for the dealer. If I've booked a nice winner, but they don't know it, I go ahead and bet $5 or $10 "for the boys" (only when the boss is watching). It may not seem like much to you, but it adds up for them.

A lot of times players try to tip the floorman. So do I, but only under certain circumstances. I ask the dealer if the floorman can take a tip. If she says "No," I wait until she goes on a break, then call the floorman over and make a big bet for him. When he tells me he can't take it, I say, "Too bad, you're a really nice guy," and pull it back. If the dealer tells me the floorman can take a tip, I shut up. Either way, if he gives me a super rating, I try to scrounge up an off-premises comp or cheap gift for him somewhere and give it to him with a flourish just before I finish my last play.

Most casino hosts aren't allowed to accept gifts, but they all do. They make pretty serious money by Las Vegas standards and a measly $25 or $50 token won't move them nearly as quickly as it will a floorman or a pit boss. If you've massaged your boss well enough, your computer standings will ensure that you get what you want anyway. If not, you may have to rely on the old tie routine again for the host.

Note. If you like to go to flea markets, sometimes you'll find a stand hawking silk ties and scarves that cost less than $6 each. If you know you're on your way to Las Vegas, pick up half a dozen. They'll pay for themselves tenfold.

Cocktails

Bosses and dealers sometimes watch how you handle yourself with a cocktail waitress. You're gonna have to give her something. If two of you are together, one of you should give the waitress a dollar. If you're by yourself, give her the smallest denomination you have available (50¢ is okay). It is never necessary to tip more than a dollar for a drink. Drinks do not go against your comp balance. Order something expensive. If you order tobacco with the drink, the same dollar covers both.

Now that you know how to sorta look like a "George" on the table, you still need to set your budget for the rest of the trip. Unlike on-table tips, which affect your ratings, other tips are entirely up to your conscience. Here's what I do.

Restaurants

For poor inattentive service, I often leave no more than five percent. For rude service, I leave a penny and a stinging note (although some waiters I've known take it much more personally if you stiff them). For outstanding service, I'll often leave up to 20% of the food bill. It isn't necessary or expected to tip 15% of the total bill if you've had several bottles of comped wine that are marked up 300% to begin with. Also, you can subtract the taxes when you figure your toke.

Oftentimes, a busboy or busgirl will pay a lot more attention to you than your waiter, especially the savvy ones who know how to perform for a tip. In these cases I always slip the busboy a couple of bucks, and watch his eyes light up. Then I decide if the waiter is worth the full 15%.

Similarly, especially in gourmet restaurants, if you've really done well and are feeling like a sport, you can drop a couple of extra chips around the room; they'll remember you the next time you come in. The danger here is that the next time you eat there you might be stuck big and then you'll feel like a heel when you tip according to the rules of Max.

Housekeeping

Maids are the most underappreciated members of the hotel's service crew. While custom dictates leaving $1-3 a night (on the dresser or table top) depending on the room and service, very few people do. I suspect the reason is that it's hard to walk away from your money when you can't see who you're giving it to. It's a lot more comforting to find your maid and give her the tip personally. You'll feel better when she thanks you profusely, even if you can't understand what she's saying.

Others

Limo Driver: You're supposed to be a high roller. Give him $10.
Bellhop: A dollar a bag is standard.
Skycap: A dollar a bag is standard.
Front Desk: Not necessary, unless they've lost your reservation and they're sold out. Then a double sawbuck ($20 bill) often works wonders when they're searching the data base for your name.

Who Pays the Tip?

It's the custom in Las Vegas, and a fine custom at that, for the guest(s) of a comped player to pick up the tip (what with him taking all the risks). Handle it any way you want, but if you're playing with partners there are a few fun ways to determine who picks up the toke.

Guess The Check

Everyone at the table tries to guess the final bill before it comes. Whoever's guess is farthest off the mark loses. Basic strategy: Get in the middle if you can. If only two of you are playing (there is no middle), try to guess second. You can usually judge if the other person is way off high or low, then make your guess one penny more or less. In a three-person game, it depends on whether you are playing with beginners or veterans (of the game). With beginners, try to guess third, and put yourself between the first two guessers if they've left a gap. You'll have a lock. With veterans, go first or second. Second is better because you can bet a penny more or less in the direction you think is closer and hope that the third guesser chooses the side that puts you in the middle. If you go third, the first two will probably be a penny apart (take the middle if they're not), and you'll have to choose a side. If you don't have a strong opinion as to which side will put you closer, choose the side that puts the guy you like better in the middle. In a multi-player game, try to pick your spot, volunteering to guess next as soon as someone leaves a gap. Make a guess that lands in the gap and you have a lock. And if you know going in that you'll be playing the game, pay attention to the prices of what people are ordering.

Guess the Fortune

If you're having Oriental food, here's an easy one. Every person chooses a fortune cookie. Then you guess how many words are in your fortune. The one farthest away loses. Basic strategy: Always guess eight or nine. Fortune cookies rarely contain less than five or more than twelve words.

Guess the Number

This one's a bit more complicated and it takes a couple of minutes to play, but it's a lot more fun, especially if there's a big group at your table and the loser has to pick up a monster toke. Here's how it works. Have your waiter write down a number from 1 to 1,000. He can't show it to anyone. Then everybody takes turns guessing a number, in round-robin fashion, until someone gets it right. If a person guesses a number that's more than what the waiter's written, the waiter says, "My number's lower." The next person then has a narrowed range of numbers. After the next guess, the waiter says, "Higher" or "Lower" and the range of possibilities gets smaller. The loser is the person who finally guesses the correct number. The game is chock-full of excitement, especially when it gets down to a few choices.

Basic strategy. Always split the difference (as closely as you can calculate when you're under the gun). For example, if the range has been reduced to more than 260 and less than 462, choose 360. Say the last two numbers called were 300 and 320 (in a six-person game); if you pick 310, there's a good chance that someone will get "trapped" before it gets back to you. If it gets down to where there's only a four-number range with four players guessing in front of you, you get to watch them squirm while you sip on a $1.25 cup of coffee and contemplate ordering a post-dinner brandy.

Warning. Don't pick 666. Fundamentalist bleatings notwithstanding, Las Vegas waiters are notorious for picking the "mark of the beast." (Don't ask me why—I just write what I see). Avoid it like the devil. If it gets down to the last three or four numbers, always choose an even number. Why? When asked to choose random numbers from one to ten, more than 50% of the American public chooses 3 or 7. Don't be odd. Sixty-nine is another popular number among Las Vegas food servers.

Play With a Partner

Why should you play with a partner when you've already figured ACES out for yourself? A lot of reasons.

First, almost all comp criteria for RFB are designed to accommodate two people. The heartbreak of wasting unused comps notwithstanding, partying in a deluxe suite is tough if you're by yourself. It's ten times more fun seeing how far you can run up a tab in a gourmet room if you're with a friend (until it's time to leave the toke). If your partner's of the opposite sex you have the added bonus of knowing that, as long as you don't go completely off the deep end, you'll probably get lucky. That'd be a start of a good weekend even if you were staying home.

Secondly, you can combine two bankrolls and deposit more front money under one name to get better accommodations. At most hotels, if you put up $5,000 each and play right, you'll get anything you want. You can even ask for one card with two names on it. It depends on the hotel's policy. Some casinos let players share ratings and some don't. Make sure to ask before you make your play. If combining ratings is not allowed, put all the money in one account. Then, both of you can play and the floorman will credit both bets on one rating slip. Also, there are favorable bankroll implications for betting an equal amount spread between two hands instead of all on one (the fluctuations will be smoothed).

By playing with a partner, you both get to share the dream of the free vacation before you come to town and you get to partake in a wonderful weekend conspiracy against the house. Trust me here, folks, anything that smacks of subterfuge is infinitely more fun when pulled off with an accomplice. Winning is also more fun if two of you share in the joy and, believe it or not, losing's a lot easier if you share in the despair.

Several plays that we've already covered are more easily accomplished with a partner, i.e., slowing down the game and hiding chips. You can also play games to see who pops for the toke at restaurants and shows (see "Who Pays the Tip?").

An important consideration when playing with a partner is that floormen instinctively believe that you're betting more if your stack of chips gets a lot bigger *or* a lot smaller. If you play with a partner, both of you should take markers (unless you've combined your bankrolls into one account). The designated "loser" should keep slipping chips to the designated "winner" until the loser is out of chips, at which point the loser should call the boss over for another marker. He'll see that the loser's stack is history and the winner's stack will be doubled. The boss will figure that both of you bet more than you actually did if the stacks have significantly changed size. Pumping up the winner's stack might sound contrary to getting chips off the layout, but remember, this is partner play.

Always bet big when the boss brings the new marker. The loser can sit out each time a new marker is signed. The winner should make a big bet when the boss is completing the loser's marker at the table.

Try to sit next to each other. It's hard to maneuver chips underneath the table when someone's sitting between the two of you (unless you get real friendly real fast). When the dealer is focusing on a player on the opposite side of the table, casually slip

The Danger of Playing With a Partner

As much fun as it is to skin the casinos with an amigo, there's a bunch of reasons why some people shouldn't play with a partner when chiseling comps.

• Las Vegas is the divorce capital of the world. You'll know why if you play for an hour or two with a spouse who's a bad loser.

• If you make a mistake while your partner's watching, you'll hear about it for the next ten years.

• If your partner makes a mistake while you're watching, she'll hear about it for the next ten years.

• One of you may want to gamble while the other works on his tan. If you come back a loser, someone will be depressed.

• If you like to gamble lots of hours, you'd better bring someone who likes it too, or she'll get mad when you don't want to go shopping, see the dam, see a show, eat dinner, go dancing, take a break, or sleep.

• If you play for hours and insist that your non-playing partner sits there and watches you play, you are a jerk of the lowest order.

a couple of chips underneath the table to your comrade. If you think the dealer suspects you, hand your partner five or more chips in clear view. Then he can say, "It's about time you paid me off, chump," or something of the sort to diffuse the situation.

This works really well with green chips. A $500 stack is more than three inches tall. If the loser manages to move, say, $1,500 over an hour or more, the winner's stack will be huge and the loser can say things to the boss like, "Every time I bet $25, I won and every time I bet $100, I lost." Your actual average bet will probably be around $25-$30 with judicious ACES play, but this will encourage the boss to give you at least a $50 rating.

Danger. If the two of you are playing together but not sharing a bankroll, the designated loser must determine beforehand a fixed amount that he'll give the designated winner. I've seen a lot of friendships strained over honest miscues made in the heat of battle.

There are a hundred ways to protect yourself. The easiest for me goes like this. The loser decides to give the winner $1,000. For every $100 passed, each puts a dollar chip in a special pile. When each has five chips, change the dollars for a red chip. Both can confirm the accounting at this point. When both have $10, the entire $1,000 has been passed.

If you notice that the dealer is seeing your hands going underneath the table, another way to exchange chips is to place your own chips in your partners betting circle. How? Just reach over and put some chips on the other guy's stack before the dealer pitches the cards. Then, after a winning hand, the winner only gives the loser back a portion of the loser's winning wager. This takes a little practice beforehand.

If the dealer is wiping out the whole table, both you and your partner should palm a chip or two off the table every few minutes. Make it look like carnage to the boss. She won't know where all the chips went, but she'll be happy anyway.

If you're both playing on the same account, don't take two markers. It'll piss off the boss.

Getting Together

Here's a prime play if you need an extra seat at your chosen blackjack table. The fact that everybody, down to the rankest amateur, knows that you never split tens is good news for you. Say there's only one seat on a table and you want to play with a partner. How do you get her a seat? A surefire way to open up another spot is to make a small bet and split face cards against a dealer's small card the first chance you get, making sure to announce your play with something brilliant like, "Well, I came here to gamble." Over the long run, it won't cost you much because splitting tens against a dealer's 4, 5 or 6 is not nearly as bad a play as standing with a 12 against a dealer's 7, yet people do that all the time and nobody lets out a peep.

When you break up your 20, you'll be sure to get some dirty looks and maybe some downright rude commentary about your cognitive abilities. When the other players start popping off, smile and tell them you love to split tens, you do it every time, and it works just fine for you. When they tell you it affects the other player's hands, shrug and say, "So?" If they continue their harangue, tell them you'll play your money and they can play theirs.

About this time the dealer will be hitting your first split face card. If it's another face card, split it again. Incredibly, Hebrews, Buddhists, Moslems, Hindus, and atheists alike will suddenly be spiritually bound as you hear them bellowing, "Jesus Christ!"

Now it gets fun. If you get another face card, split it again. By this time your tablemates will be snorting mucus all over the layout while they're questioning your heritage and contemplating moving to another game or punching you out. Here's a sure-fire way to move them along. If the dealer busts out, look around the table with a cocky, self-congratulatory smile and say, "See?" If you lose, flash your teeth and say, "It's a good thing I'm rich." If the dealer has a big card in the hole and would have busted if you hadn't split tens, but now draws out to a 20 or 21, duck.

Play to Your Bankroll

I was cold and lonely. It was my sophomore year at Nevada Southern University (soon to be dubbed UNLV). Everybody had gone home for the holidays but me. The heating system was on the fritz, the maintenance man was out of town, and my high school sweetheart was waiting for me in Texas. Talk about the makings of a country tune!

The year was 1967 and UNLV wasn't even NCAA then. There was only one dorm on campus and virtually everyone living there was on an athletic scholarship of some kind. All of us jocks had menial jobs around the campus that paid more than we were worth, but I had found a few joints that would let me gamble at 19. I'd managed to put most of my money down the maw of the blackjack tables all semester long and had $7 to my name. Hardly enough to get back to my sweetie. I was desperate.

I drove through a patented Vegas ice-cold windstorm in my roomie's car and parked at the Aladdin. I forcefully strode up to a blackjack table and told myself to let $1 ride six times, pick up $64, and buy a one-way ticket to Amarillo. The first buck lasted one hand. My luck held steady as I lost the next six hands in a row. Now I was, cold, lonely, and broke, too. Two weeks of eating leftover dorm food by myself was staring me in the gut. I almost hurled as I vacantly stared around the casino.

The waitress brought me a double whiskey sour. I chugged it and walked back outside. The wind was blowing about 50 mph now and I couldn't really tell if the tears streaming down my face were from frustration or the bitter wind blowing toward Texas. I got back in my buddy's car. Then it hit me. I remembered that my good old roommate Ron Carter had a habit of keeping small change in the glove box for parking meters. I pushed the button on the glove compartment and looked in. Smiling up at me was an old Indian-head nickel. I caught my breath as the adrenaline rush jolted me. I was still in the game.

I squeezed the nickel and wondered what I should do with it. Go downtown and play the penny slots at the Pioneer? Nope. I was getting back up on the horse that throwed me. So I stomped right back into the Aladdin to teach 'em a lesson! I started stalking the slot machines, looking for an unwary single nickel slot that was waiting to be hit. Never anyone's fool at 19, I knew that if I watched an old lady play a machine until she was out of nickels, then that machine would be due to hit. I tried to calm myself as I semi-casually walked between a row of slots.

Like a messenger from God I heard an angel's voice beckon, "This machine's janky!" I turned and stared. A 300-pound woman wearing a house dress and hair rollers was pummeling a nickel machine with her fists! Paydirt.

I gulped deep breaths, hoping she'd step away from my machine after administering the pounding. She stepped back and dug into her purse. I seized the moment. Swooping in, I elbowed her out of the way. As I dropped my last nickel on earth in the slot she roared, "Hey, that's my machine!" and yanked on my letter jacket. I ignored her and quickly pulled the handle as I stared at the $50 jackpot sign blazing from the top of the machine. I dared to look down as the reels spun.

Bar. Yes!

Bar. Yes!

The last reel seemed to spin forever. Please God, yes. One time, one time for me! Sally, I'm coming home!

Bang!

Lemon.

I lost.

While listening to the woman hackle me mercilessly, I waited for the cocktail waitress. It seemed like hours before she brought me a drink. I hammered down another free whiskey sour and drove back to the dorm and sat in my room, staring out at the lights on the Strip. Unable to stand it any longer, I packed my suitcase and drove out to the Showboat on Boulder Highway and parked the car. Braving the elements, I trudged down the highway with my thumb out and bag in tow and hitchhiked through 1,000 miles of high-desert winter without a penny in my jeans. That's a hard ride home.

And wouldn't you know it? When I got back to Texas, I couldn't even buy my girlfriend a Christmas present and she dumped me for some chicken-necked guy in the theater arts department at the local junior college whose dad ran an Amarillo car dealership.

What can you learn from this tragic story? The same thing that 19-year-old kid did. If you're betting more than you can afford to lose—that is, if it's going to change your lifestyle if you blow it—you're betting too much. As poor as I was in those days, I shouldn't have put a quarter in a Coke machine, let alone go up against one of the joints with everything I had.

To you, it might mean that you'll never know the pleasure of staying in a deluxe suite and flying first class, but you can still get good meals and other freebies if you play within your means.

The Means And The Ends

What are your means? That depends on how you look at things. There are two ways you can size up the bankroll you have at your disposal for comp hunting.

- You can assume that every dollar you have is part of your comp-hustling arsenal.
- You can set aside only as much money as you can reasonably afford to lose if your luck turns sour.

MAX FACT: Anyone who loses his life savings trying to get a comp is serially stupid. (I urge you to choose the second option.)

Possible Results

I hate to do it, but I'm now going to tell you about some really geeky stuff like standard deviations, elements of risk, probability, chances of ruin, risk tolerance, and bankroll parameters, and use a bunch of other words that you might have to look up. Some of what you're about to read here might scare you, some of it might go a little over your head, and some of it might put you to sleep. I didn't even want to include it in the book, but the publisher made me put on some nerdly duds and do the dirty deed. If you're a stout-hearted math maven, you'll love this stuff. But even if you're not, try to slug your way through it, so you'll know a little something about the risks you face financially when you gamble for comps.

Up to this point, I've talked mostly about expected results (usually expected losses, because losses are inevitable when you play negative-expectation gambling games). The expected result is the measure you need to evaluate the trade-off between your monetary losses and the comps you receive. But when considering how high you can comfortably gamble, another measure is equally important: *possible* results.

What if you were offered this proposition:

Bet $100 on ten separate flips of an honest coin. On each flip, if the coin comes up heads, you win $100. If it comes up tails, you lose $100. Regardless of whether you are ahead or behind after the tenth toss, you get dinner for two at The Bistro at The Mirage (worth about $100).

Realizing that a coin flip is a fair game, you might analyze the gamble like this:

Probability says there should be five heads and five tails. So I should break even and get the dinner free.

Your analysis would be correct; the deal is good in terms of the expected result. But have you considered that the coins might not land exactly five heads and five tails? What if things go badly, and heads comes up only four times while tails comes up six? In that case, you'd lose $200 in pursuit of your $100 meal. Can you live with that outcome? If you can't, you'd better not play the game. If you can, then consider that it could be worse. It's possible that the coins could fall as follows:

Heads	Tails	Result
3	7	-$400
2	8	-$600
1	9	-$800
0	10	-$1,000

(There's an equal chance that the coins will fall unevenly in your favor, but since no one I know takes winning as hard as losing, we'll concentrate on the downside.)

As you can see, dire things can happen. The worst result, 0 wins and 10 losses, will occur on average once every 1,024 series of 10 coin flips. It's relatively unlikely, but if it happened to you, you'd probably blame me, so I'm letting you know right now in order to get myself off the hook.

What if the proposition stipulated that the coin be flipped 100 times, 1,000 times, or 10,000 times? Should you be concerned about the possibility of losing every coin flip in those propositions? No, you shouldn't; the odds against losing 10,000 (or even 100) times in a row are unfathomable (about the same as meeting an honest politician). But there's still a significant amount of risk associated with the gamble, and it's important to have a handle on how much.

To determine the realistic boundaries of possible losses (and wins), statisticians use a measure called standard deviation. Calculating the standard deviation (from the expected result) for gambling propositions tells us how bad things can get, and allows us to set our gambling levels accordingly. Check out the chart on the next page.

This analysis covers a play of 60 hands of $10 blackjack (representative of what it takes to earn a buffet comp for two). The information needed to assess risk is contained in the data under "Possible Results." About two out of three people who play 60 hands of blackjack at $10 per hand will finish with a result that is within one standard deviation (1SD) of the expected result (a $3 loss). That is, 68% of players will fall somewhere between a loss of $90 and a win of $80. Approximately 95% of all results will fall

Buffet Comp for Two

Hands	Bet Size	Casino Advantage (basic strategy blackjack)
60	$10	0.5%
Expected Result	-$3	

Possible Results	Minus	Plus
1SD	[$ 90]	$ 80
2SD	[$ 175]	$ 165
3SD	[$ 260]	$ 255

between -$175 and +$165, an area within two standard deviations (2SD) of what's expected. And three standard deviations (3SD) will encompass about 99.7% of all outcomes, which means that it would be highly unlikely to win or lose more than about $260 after 60 hands of play. For practical purposes, you can assume that minus three standard deviations is as bad as things could get. Consequently, you should be mentally and financially prepared to lose up to $260 to chase the $15 buffet comp.

As you play longer and bet more in pursuit of the bigger comps, the possible losses become greater.

Full RFB Weekend #1

Hands	Bet Size	Casino Advantage (basic strategy blackjack)
500	$150	0.5%
Expected Result	-$375	

Possible Results	Minus	Plus
1SD	[$ 4,100]	$ 3,300
2SD	[$ 7,800]	$ 7,000
3SD	[$11,400]	$ 10,700

The numbers in these examples look brutal, but remember, three standard deviations is the outer boundary. Few losing sessions will be this bad, and it's equally probable (or improbable, depending on how you look at it) that you will experience a favorable departure from the expected result and win $255 with your buffet, or $10,700 during your RFB weekend. Remember too, the risk is no different from what you face whenever you gamble anyway. What *is* different is that now you're getting something back, the comp, which improves your gambling result no matter what happens. At worst, the comps act as a hedge against bad luck. Let's take a look at three trip scenarios.

Scenario One. You're stuck like a hog, can't win a single big bet, and wind up losing $4,500, so your net loss is almost three times what a vacation would have cost you retail. On the other hand, you've been in the race and you've had the best of it all weekend. This is when you get to ask your host if he'll qualify you for full RFB next trip (see "The Next Trip's Free"). If he says yes, you get another vacation for nothing, so now you're only marginally down, and you've still had a good time, and you may even have graduated from novice to intermediate comp-wizard status.

Scenario Two. You've put in plenty of hours and your losses are what you expected them to be, about $200. But you've had ten times that in fun, frolic, and freebies, and your entertainment expenses have just been pared by 90%.

Scenario Three. You win like a pig *and* you get the free stuff.

Be careful. Scenario Three may be the most dangerous of all, because now you think you can't lose. The next time you play, you'll feel lucky and bet more than you should. If you do step it up and catch a losing streak, you'll blow your whole bankroll and the only vacation you'll have coming is if you stay somewhere with some cousins you don't like, or spend two weeks listening to your kids pummel each other while you cuss me and cook weenies with this book, burning it page by page.

Getting back to what's reasonable, everyone's risk tolerance is different. I like to consider the range covered by two standard deviations to make my bankroll decisions. Approximately 19 out of 20 times, my result will fall within the range covered by 2SD, and I'm comfortable with that. I never bet so much that a terrible run (like the -3SD result in the RFB Weekend chart) would take me completely out of the game because the comps that my gambling earns make me a big winner, and allowing myself to be stopped-out because I bet too much would be foolish.

Bankroll Parameters

After a while, you'll learn to make good decisions regarding what you can afford to bet based on your experiences. As a beginner, however, you might need a little general advice to get your bearings. The bankroll recommendations that I make here, and throughout this book, are based on the type of analysis I've just shown you. Most of the time, I'll lean to the conservative side, with the stated bankroll requirement being large enough to withstand a negative fluctuation of three standard deviations. If you are comfortable with more risk, you can go with a smaller bankroll.

I'll start with the obvious. If your bankroll is less than $500, you really shouldn't be betting more than $10 per hand; if you do, those pesky swings can eat you up in just one two-hour session. Even at $10, over the course of a weekend the swings could gut you completely. So comp counting for things like rooms and gourmet meals is out of the question. But that doesn't mean you can't play judiciously to your $100-$500 bankroll and earn comp classics and low-level comps.

If you're packing $500 to $1,000, you can raise it up to bet, or represent (see "Apparent Average Bets," below), a $20 average for a couple hours at a time. This will get you buffets, coffee shops, some casino rates on rooms, and even some low-end gourmet.

Serious comp counting starts at about $2,500. Now you can bet $25 for four hours or $50 for two and score some middle-range gourmet and low-end rooms, as well as everything else already listed above.

RFB begins at $5,000. At this level, you can afford to make the two-day plays required for RFB at a few non-premium casinos. They'll expect a $50 minimum for at least eight hours. A $5,000 bankroll can handle it, especially when you start rigging the game with a few ACES moves, i.e., slow-play.

As you move up from $5,000, you'll qualify for RFB in better and better joints. If you have $10,000 in the bank, spend $2,000-$3,000 annually on vacations, and have a good job or retirement benefits that ensure that you'll never want for the necessities in life, a big loss won't impact you as much, and you'll be able to bet up to $200 when the time is right and $25-$50 when no one's paying attention. If you follow ACES strategy to a tee, you'll be in for a lot of fun for a long, long time. Your swings at this level and betting scheme will vary from an $8,500 loser to an $8,000 winner during any eight hours of play, but that's at the extreme. Two thirds of the time, your results will fall within a range of plus or minus $3,000.

What you'll win or lose is ultimately up to the gods of gambling. What you'll get back in comps is entirely up to you. Use these guidelines and your good sense and you shouldn't get into trouble.

The House Edge

Reducing the house advantage by improving your blackjack skills or playing games with better rules will save a significant amount of money over time, but it will barely affect the short-term swings. Here's the RFB Weekend chart again, only this time, the casino advantage is 0.2% compared with 0.5% in the example on page 113.

Full RFB Weekend #2

Hands	Bet Size	Casino Advantage (basic strategy blackjack)
500	$150	0.2%
Expected Result	-$150	
Possible Results	Minus	Plus
1SD	[$ 3,800]	$ 3,500
2SD	[$ 7,500]	$ 7,200
3SD	[$11,200]	$ 10,900

Notice that while the expected loss is reduced significantly ($150 down from $375), the possibility of dramatic swings in either direction still remains. There's no getting away from risk.

Apparent Average Bets

An important part of ACES play is making it appear that your average bet is larger than it really is. To accomplish this, ACES players make lots of small bets, and a few big bets. In most cases, this approach will benefit you in two ways. First, you'll reduce the total amount gambled and, thus, lower your expected loss. Second, you'll soften the bankroll swings. Here's an example.

Let's assume you want to portray the $150 average bet necessary for the RFB Weekend. The bet-mix that follows, when executed properly (boss sees all the high wagers and misses most of the low), accomplishes this.

10	hands	at	$300
30	hands	at	$200
50	hands	at	$175
410	hands	at	$100

Five-hundred flat bets of $150 amounts to $75,000 in total action. The mix above reduces the amount wagered by more than 20%, down to $58,750. Look what happens.

Full RFB Weekend #3

Hands	Bet Size	Casino Advantage (basic strategy blackjack)
500	$117.50	0.2%

Apparent Bet Size: -$150

Expected Result: -$117.50

Possible Results	Minus	Plus
1SD	[$ 3,200]	$ 3,000
2SD	[$ 6,200]	$ 6,100
3SD	[$ 9,300]	$ 9,100

The expected loss drops to $117.50 from $150, and risk (the potential swings) is also reduced. These benefits occur naturally when you apply the basic bet-masking techniques described throughout this book. Be aware, however, that these effects will be less pronounced during plays of short duration, or plays in which your biggest bets are either much larger (in proportion to your other bets), or more frequent than shown here.

Expected Loss and Refueling

Look back at the charts in this chapter. You'll notice that the "expected result" number in each is preceded by a minus sign. This means you're losing money. It's a bizarre quirk. Even though you are winning overall (after factoring in the comps), if you play long enough, you will lose your entire bankroll. But don't despair; the gourmet meals, free booze, late hours, and adrenaline rush of playing thousands of hours of blackjack will probably have killed you before then anyway.

If you want to take full advantage of what the joints are so greedily serving up to the masses, you'll have to replenish your bankroll from time to time. But I don't want to hear any sniveling about having to reach into your pocket. If you go to New York City and take in a couple of Broadway shows and stay at the Plaza and eat at Four Seasons, you go home a thousand or two poorer, easy. Would you replenish that vacation money? Of course you would. Is it money down the drain. Yep. Do you ever have a chance of getting it back? Nope. What's my point? When you come to Comp City, it's almost 50/50 you'll be going home with more money than you brought, while somebody else pays the bills.

Don't be misled. ACES isn't for everyone. If you don't have a ready source of income and you don't have the ability to augment a bankroll when negative fluctuations strike you down, perhaps you should immediately refer to "Free Whiskey," retire to one of Las Vegas' many free saloons, and contemplate how you're going to get steady work so you can take advantage of the pearls of wisdom in this book.

Quick Q & A

Q. Is there a way to reduce risk when playing for comps?

A. Yes, there are two things you can do to smooth the swings. The first is to bet less for longer periods of time. A host may tell you that you have to bet $75 for four hours, but that's just a benchmark. You can bet as little as $25 a hand if you play 12 hours a day, and you'll be worth just as much to the casino as someone betting $75 a hand for four hours because the total action is $18,000 either way. Casinos use a method called a "four-hour conversion" to provide this betting flexibility. Betting less, longer, will produce less severe bankroll swings. Of course, you'll have to give up more time to play. (See "Four-Hour Conversion" in the "Appendix.")

The second thing you can do is combine playing results with a fellow comp wizard. Whether you travel together or separately, sharing wins and losses over the course of a few trips will result in gentler swings. This only works if your partner is someone you trust. A lot.

Q. Should I set myself a stop-loss for each trip.

A. Unless you have a bankroll that far exceeds the minimal requirements, you probably should. Not because it's mathematically correct, but because it'll rip you apart emotionally and you won't have fun on the trip if you go home feeling like a sucker for taking such a bashing. On the upside of a loss (huh?), the house will give you the benefit of the doubt and usually nudge up your comps if they know that you're a big loser, particularly if your losses look quite a bit larger than they actually are (see "Look Like a Loser"). If you do have a big bankroll, you should continue playing, because all you can do is continue to earn. If you're on a strict budget though, stop your losses at some point and enjoy your comps.

Q. What if I lose 40% of my $10,000 bankroll on a single trip. Does this mean I can still make the same big bets as when I had the $10,000?

A. No. You now have a bankroll of $6,000 and your big bets will have to be reduced accordingly until you've replenished the bankroll (either via a favorable swing or with new cash). Conversely, if you win $4,000 on your trip, your betting level can (not must or should, but *can*) be increased, and you can bet more to get better comps the next time. You'd be much better off, though, to set the winnings aside to use to replenish your bankroll after a bad trip.

Cash or Credit?

Bankroll	How to Show It	How to Play It
\$20-\$1,000	Cash	Don't get rated. Don't deposit money. Don't use markers.
\$1,000-\$2,500	Cash	Same as above. Churn money.
\$2,500-\$5,000	Cash or credit line/ front money (smaller clubs)	If cash: same as above. If credit/front: use markers, get rated.
\$5,000-\$10,000	Credit line/ front money	Take markers. Get rated.
\$10,000 and up	Credit line/ front money	Take markers. Get rated. Play for airfare.

Use Markers

A proper understanding and utilization of markers is a must for the advanced "society-chip" (\$25-and-up) comp counter. Markers are a mystery to most low- to mid-level table-game players, but using them is not that complicated.

When you arrive at the table, you hand the dealer your VIP card and the dealer calls the floorman over. You ask the boss for a marker in a specified dollar amount, at least 10% of your credit line or front-money deposit (but never less than \$500). The boss starts filling in a rating slip in your name and there's a brief wait while the pit clerk verifies your account and signals the boss to proceed.

The floorman tosses a "lammer" (a small plastic button denoting the amount you're getting) onto the table and tells the dealer to give you the money. The dealer then cuts out the chips and passes them to you. Now you're in action! A few minutes later, the floorman brings you a document (two pages separated by a carbon) that looks like a large bank draft. This is the marker. He hands you the marker to sign. Before you sign, politely make it clear that he's distracting you from the high-stakes action, and make a big show of making a large bet while he's watching. Now you get to wait until the hand is over to inscribe your John Hancock on the marker, smile, and hand it back. Be sure to autograph it with the exact signature you used on your credit/deposit forms or he'll be coming back to your game to make you re-sign it and you'll have to make an extra big bet or two.

By now you should realize why it's beneficial to take markers at every opportunity. All that paperwork not only slows down the game, but also requires the floorman to watch your first few bets, which you inflate to enhance your rating.

Choke Points

Choke points are the average bets and minimum player wins that a floorman has to report to a pit boss. Also, if anyone is betting more than the average or winning more than the minimum, the game will attract at least two sets of eyes.

	Premium	**Other Strip**	**Sweat-shops**	**Down-town**
Average Bet	$500	$200	$100	$100
Gross Win	$5,000	$2,000	$500	$1,000

Premium—Mirage, Caesars, MGM, Treasure Island, Golden Nugget, Desert Inn, Horseshoe.
Other Strip—Everything from Hacienda down to Vegas World, excluding premium and sweatshops.
Sweatshops—Excalibur, Circus Circus, Slots A Fun, Gold Coast, Barbary Coast, Luxor.
Downtown—All downtown hotels, except Golden Nugget and Horseshoe.

When you're ready to quit, make sure to bid farewell to the floorman, while you bet a full slab of chips, of course. Also make sure that he sees the size of your bet. When you're confident that he has duly noted your high-roller posture, it's time to leave. Now you have the choice of buying back your marker right there at the table or simply leaving with the chips you have in front of you.

If there are more chips on the table than you owe on your marker, then it's okay to redeem it—in other words, buy it back. Tell the dealer that you'd like to pick up the marker and hand over enough chips to pay it off (if you've taken several markers but only have enough to pay off one, that's okay, too). The floorman gets the marker from the pit clerk and hands it to you. You can either take it with you to discard later, or rip it up right there and hand the boss the pieces.

Many high rollers make a triumphant show of this ripping-up ritual—it signifies victory. However, from a comp wizard's point of view, it's more advantageous to your rating to look like a loser and skulk away than it is to redeem your markers at the table. Also, by redeeming your markers with the floorman, you may have to make a number of large bets while the paper transactions are completed, as opposed to just a few before you walk.

Whether you redeem or walk, the boss then completes your rating slip, which the pit clerk posts for marketing's scrutiny. The markers are sent to the cage at the end of the day (usually between 2 and 3 am). If you want to pay off your markers later, just go to the cage and pay them off with cash, a personal check, or travelers checks.

Special Tips for ACES Players

• Floormen hate "marker churners" (players who take a marker, pay it off, take a marker, pay it off, ad nauseam). If you insist on keeping a boss frazzled by burying him with needless busy work, he'll burn you on your rating slip. Don't do it. When you take a marker, make it big enough to cover at least 10 average bets. If you're a few hundred short of redeeming it when you leave, don't pick it up with added cash. Tell the boss you're going to try another pit and walk with the chips. The simple gesture of not making him go through the hassle of redeeming your marker will work in your favor when he fills in the most important space on your rating slip—the one marked "average bet."

• If you're not going to take a marker for at least $500, don't put the money in the cage. Any marker smaller than that labels you as a cheapo and nuisance. Most bosses won't write it up, especially on the Strip, where they're not allowed to. You'll get a lot more respect from the bosses by buying in for a couple of hundred dollars cash. And you'll get noticed when you buy in, so you can make a couple of large bets in pursuit of buffet, coffee shop, or room comps.

• Unless you plan to bet at least $25 a hand, don't put money in the cage or establish a credit account. Taking a marker for $500 and betting $10 a hand is bad form. The boss will note how much you're betting and think that you're a wimp or a moocher trying to pull something over on him, because you're taking way more money than you need. Buy in for cash if you're a smaller player.

• If you cash out large amounts of chips at one time, you'll draw attention to yourself, because the cashiers have to ask if you have any outstanding markers. Make sure to cash out in small amounts to maintain the look of a big loser.

• You don't have to worry about losing your VIP card in a casino. The only signature verification the casinos use is in the pit clerk's computer terminal. There's nothing on the card to show a stranger what your signature looks like, and all marker signatures are verified within minutes. Some scuz buckets have tried to rip off other people's accounts in the past, but they're picked off 99% of the time, and sent to jail 100% of the time when they are.

Regulation 6-A

Many players in Las Vegas don't want anyone, including but not limited to the IRS, their bankers, and even the casino, to know their business. Unfortunately, the casino economic system is set up in such a way that the casino, your banker, the IRS, even your letter carrier get to put their noses right into the middle of it. If you move a lot of money around the tables, it's important for you to understand how the casino reports transactions to the federal government.

Please understand that I'm not advocating evading taxes, laundering money, or doing anything contrary to a single one of this country's laws, but you need to understand what you're up against so you don't create unnecessary problems for yourself.

Aldous Huxley wrote in *Brave New World* that the laws are designed so that "Everyone has to break at least a few in order to survive." He was right. You don't believe it? Just examine the innumerable statutes in your state regarding sex between consenting heterosexual adults. If you're a Catholic priest, *maybe* you haven't fractured any of those laws, but the rest of us, we're offenders.

Did you realize that there are more than three hundred million laws in the U.S.? (No? Well, that's because I made it up, but come tax time every year, it sure seems like it to me.) Forget rolling through stop signs, breaking the speed limit, and tearing the tags off mattresses. All of us, at one time or another, have committed a crime, some of us for the thrill, some of us for the money, some of us because we thought the law was wrong, and most of us out of blind ignorance. Now, at least, you won't have ignorance as an excuse.

Regulation 6-A is a relatively simple cash-reporting procedure ostensibly designed to thwart money laundering and identify people who carry around large amounts of cash. On its face, the regulation is simple. Any cash transaction over $10,000 must be reported to the IRS. The IRS office in your region is notified of the transaction and acts accordingly. (I don't know what that technically means, but I get this little tick going in my left eye just thinking about it).

A word of warning. Don't test them. The U.S. government is one of the most inefficient behemoths ever conceived by man, with three notable exceptions: our high-tech Army kills people better than anyone around; our deep-pockets Justice Department is unparalleled at putting people in jail; and the beloved IRS has no peer at making your life miserable. Trust me on this one, folks. Don't try to trick 'em. You'll lose.

Now that you know you shouldn't try to trick 'em, here's how to do it. The key provision in the regulation is that any *single* transaction over $10,000 is reportable. Transactions are broken down into at least four categories: drop, money plays, deposit/redemptions, and chip purchases. Here's what each category means:

Drop. The money the house takes in when you buy chips on a game. This means (theoretically) that if you drop $1,000 ten times, you are at the limit.

Money Plays. Money wagered directly in the betting spot. If you win, the casino pays you in chips. If you lose, they take your money. If they take over $10,000, you'll be reported. So it's only losing money-plays bets that matter.

Deposit/Redemptions. Front money you put into the cage, and money you use to pay off casino credit.

Chip Purchases. Money you use to purchase chips at the cage. Not one player in a thousand buys chips at the cage. The only reason you'd do it is if you're up to something sneaky and the cage people know it. It raises red flags throughout the casino and is to be avoided by solid citizens such as ourselves.

Here's how it all works. The meter starts running after your first "loggable transaction." This occurs when any of the above transactions exceeds $2,499. The pit boss will hand a new rating slip to a pit clerk and ask if the casino has your identification on file (photo ID, current address, Social Security Number, etc.). If they do, the boss won't say anything to you; he'll simply complete a report.

If your ID is not on file, the boss will put you on his "No ID" (aka "NOID") list for the day. The pit clerk will also notify all the

Winnings Are Not Reportable

Regulation 6-A is not designed to catch gamblers who win, but to ferret out guys lugging around ill-gotten gains. Even the government understands that if you cash out $12,000 on Friday night, that's no guarantee that you'll get home with any money come Monday morning. You can cash in $10,000, $20,000, even $50,000 and up in chips with no Reg 6-A report necessary.

other floormen on that shift that you're a "NOID." Your cash transactions will then be closely monitored for the rest of the day until the clock turns over (explained below).

In most casinos, once you hit, say, $5,000, your floorman will approach you and ask if you know about Regulation 6-A. If you say yes, he'll tell you exactly where you stand for the day. If you tell him no, he'll tell you about the regulation, explain that if you exceed $10,000, you will have to show ID or you won't be able to play in his casino any more. ("Any more" in this instance means forever, until they have your photo ID.) This also means that if you're barred in the Las Vegas Hilton, you can't play in the Reno, Laughlin, or Flamingo Hiltons either. If you've got good comp karma going in these places, don't risk losing it over something silly.

In the classier joints, they'll also hand you a summary of the regulation, but they won't give you any clues on how to circumvent it. Don't ever, under any circumstances, put the boss in a position to compromise himself by asking him how to get around the regulations with questions such as, "What time does your 24-hour clock start?" "Can I go to another pit?" Or, "Can I buy chips from another player?" Soliciting this type of information understandably makes bosses very uncomfortable, as they can lose their work cards and go to jail for giving you tips on defrauding the government. On top of that, the house can be fined up to $50,000 the first time a boss gets caught helping you sneak around the regulation.

In the smaller joints, if you're getting into the $2,500 range on a single play, you're probably the focus of too many eyes to make any ACES maneuvers in the first place.

If you're in a bigger club and you're concerned about your cash transactions being logged, you can buy in for $2,499 and money plays for $2,499 and then change tables. Now, if you buy in for another $2,000 on a different game, you're still okay, because your transaction has to be over $2,500 on a *single game* to start the meter running. The floormen will probably be aware of your status, but they're not obligated to start logging you, and they won't—unless they don't like you, that is, in which case they'll take delight in hassling you by strictly adhering to cash-reporting regulations. Once it's going, every cash transaction of the same

ID Or Not ID

If you're on the sneak and don't want the casino to know your real name or address, you'll need to know a couple of things.

• Using an alias when you gamble is not against the law, and it's done every day in Las Vegas. As long as you're not trying to defraud anyone, you can give the casino any name you want and sign that name to a comp slip.

• Generally speaking, cash players are the only ones who won't be asked for an ID.

• Most hotels require at least a credit card with a name on it when you check in at the front desk. The hotels that don't—you can call first and ask—will require a cash deposit (usually $100 or less) for incidentals. If they don't want to see ID when you check in, you can get your room comped under an assumed name. If they do require ID, and you don't show one, you'll be limited to food, show, and special-event comps only. When checking out, if you're due a refund on your incidentals deposit, you'll be asked for ID.

You Have to Show ID	**You Do Not Need ID**
Checking in (most joints)	Applying/receiving a VIP card
Depositing money	Getting rated
Applying for credit	Obtaining a comp
Cashing a check	Using a comp
Exceeding $10,000 cash	Checking out
Hitting a big jackpot	
Redeeming incidental cash deposits	

• If you're hiding, be careful what games you play. The joints must obtain ID and issue an IRS W-2G form before they can pay you off on any of the following big hits: keno ticket for $1,500 or more; bingo game for $1,500 or more; slot/video jackpot for $1,200 or more; race book or sports book winnings of $600 or more if it exceeds at least 300 times the original wager.

• Don't even think about trying to circumvent the cash reporting laws by using fake ID. This will put you in the company of money launderers, racketeers, and tax evaders.

type, no matter how small, is credited toward the magic $10,001 figure.

In the casino megamalls, each *pit* has its own reporting requirements, because it's impossible for a single floorman, or even a single pit boss, to watch a player who may bounce in and out of a hundred different table games. This means you can hop from pit to pit when you're approaching your limit with little risk of being discovered. However, it's hard for me to envision any competent comp wizard ever needing to blow more than $10,000 in a day to get everything he wants anyway.

Each hotel determines the starting time of its 24-hour clock. Some start at midnight, some start at 2 am, and some start as late (or early) as 6 am.

Rumor (from, shall we say, well-placed sources) has it that any transaction over $25,000 is also forwarded post haste to the Treasury and Justice departments in your locale. Not good. Not good at all.

I understand that this will only apply to about ten percent of the readers, but if you are a high-rolling comp wizard, there are some problems that need to be addressed before you do something stupid.

• If you're pocketing $100 chips, you'll have to cash the chips slowly and discreetly at the cage. At the premium casinos such as The Mirage, Hilton, Caesars, Horseshoe, and MGM, you can cash up to $4,000 at a time on a busy night without the cage calling the bosses and telling them the amount of the cash-out. At the smaller clubs, $1,000 at a time seems to be the choke point. The reason a comp wizard doesn't want the boss to be aware of the cash-out falls under the "look like a loser" category.

• Don't, under any circumstances, excessively churn your money and make so many re-buys that you go over the $10,000 top. I've seen more than a few players come to Las Vegas with less than $5,000, buy in with the whole thing, cash out $6,000 or more at the cage, come back to buy in again, and then be told that they can't play any more unless they produce valid ID. This sits well with neither the casinos nor the players, as the casinos often lose a good customer and the players put undeserved heat on themselves out of sheer ignorance.

• If you're making money-plays bets, don't ever bet so much

that you're liable to go over the $10,000 if you have to split or double down. For example, if you're betting $300 a hand and you're already at $9,000 and get four aces, you could wind up putting $10,200 down the chute.

If you find yourself in this trap, there are two ways to weasel out of it if you're crafty. One, buy chips for the splits. Two, if you're already pushing the envelope on your buy-ins, you can buy chips from another player at the table. (It's a little left of kosher, but there are no reporting requirements for purchasing chips from another player.) It's not in the casino's best interest to report you—if only from the extra-paperwork point of view.

• If you deposit anything less than $100 bills at the cage, the casino will put your small bills in a safe and give you the same bills back when you cash out, so if you are a money changer, depositing front money won't do you any good at all.

How Regulation 6-A Changed History

Before the IRS, Treasury Department, Nevada Gaming Commission, and casino owners developed this system of controlling cash transactions, it was a common occurrence for a young man, usually wearing an expensive jogging suit, to approach a dice or blackjack game carrying (literally) paper bags full of small bills. When asked what he did for a living, he was invariably in "investments." Strangely enough, a lot of them seemed to have sinus problems, too.

These post-adolescents carrying huge wads of cash would plop $50,000-$250,000 on the table and fire it up. Once all of the $10s, $20s, and $50s had gone down the chute, they'd head to the cage and convert their chips to $100 bills.

The government stepped in. They wanted to make the casinos report everyone who bought in for $2,500 or more in a single day. The casinos, recoiling in horror, countered with $20,000 a day. The Nevada Gaming Commission offered a compromise. They suggested establishing a system of controls to which every licensed casino had to adhere. The system, based on the Bank Secrecy Act, established the reportable cash figure at $10,000 a day, the same as the nation's banks and S&Ls.

But the government balked, because casinos weren't under their control. What was to stop them from violating the process?

The Gaming Commission provided several assurances, including civil and criminal penalties to any gambling licensee who aided and abetted money launderers up to and including the loss of the establishment's license. The government reluctantly agreed.

But now there was a gnashing of teeth up and down the Strip. "We'll lose all our big play!" they cried at Caesars. "How can we compete with the islands, where their hands aren't tied?" they moaned at the Hilton. Share prices of the stocks in publicly traded casino companies quaked as antsy stockholders waited for the worst. What happened? The casinos stopped catering to street criminals and targeted, instead, the much broader-based market of urban professionals.

About this time, Atlantic City was blossoming on the eastern seaboard and many people were getting their first taste of gambling. Granted, the service stunk, as anyone who's ever been to Atlantic City will attest, but a lot of people who had never been to Las Vegas decided to give it a shot.

Steve Wynn, never one to sit idly by while his half-billion-dollar debt service loomed, attacked the market with a vengeance. He zeroed in on the readers of *Forbes* and *Fortune*. Many came. They, too, discovered that Las Vegas was the nuts. Incredibly, they were not only getting value, but also the ultimate hedonistic escape. The industry exploded as major corporations and stock brokerages throughout the country touted the viability of the casino business as never before.

What happened to the criminals? Nothing. They figured out how to launder their money elsewhere and kept coming along with all of the square Johns after all. Caught up in the new family atmosphere, Vegas' newly elected sheriff, John Moran, swept all the hookers off the Strip and respectable guys actually started bringing their wives with them!

And something else happened. The wives saw that Sin City wasn't such a bad place and started letting their husbands come to Las Vegas by themselves to conventions and on business trips. Try that in New Orleans.

Bottom line? It might sound like a wild theory and you'll never read this anywhere else, but it's my firm belief that Regulation 6-A was one of the final catalysts that forced Las Vegas casinos to become "respectable," and the city has prospered because of it.

Getting Money

Personal Checks

Cashing out-of-state personal checks at the casino cashier is easy, so long as you have a major credit card and a driver's license or another valid form of photo ID. Most joints have a cash limit of up to $200; Caesars will give you up to $1,000. You don't have to be a guest at the hotel where you want to cash a check. For locals, some casinos require a local check-cashing bank card; others accept a driver's license instead.

Travelers Checks

Exchange travelers checks for cash at the casino cage. You cannot buy chips at a table with travelers checks.

Cashier's Checks

Casinos will honor cashier's checks under the proper conditions. If you want money as soon as you arrive, first buy the cashiers check back home and call the casino with the check number and amount. The casino will call your bank during business hours to confirm that it's good. If you bring a check with you without preverification, it won't be worth a dime unless the bank it's drawn on is open for business, and even then it might take a day to clear.

When a cashier's check is approved, most joints will credit your front-money account for the entire balance. They won't just fork over a slug of hundreds that you might blow somewhere else.

No money orders.

Local Payroll Checks

Casino cages keep a file of approved employers. If you work for any established company in town and have photo ID, there's never a problem. In fact, it's usually worthwhile to cash your paycheck at a casino, to take advantage of promotions that reward you with comps.

Government Checks

All government checks are greedily, er, greatly appreciated by the joints. Just show some ID and you'll get your cash fast.

Cash Machines (Credit Cards At The Cage)

These are not ATM machines. They don't spit out cash, they don't set a limit, and they don't require a PIN number. You'll find them near the cage in every casino in town. All you have to do is drop your VISA, MasterCard or, yes, American Express in the slot and punch in how much money you want. If the transaction is approved, a check is printed in the cage. Then you just go over to a cashier, show some ID, sign the check, and you're back in action. Sound easy? It is. That's why you should know a thing or two about this easy money before you destroy your credit.

• Cash machines charge up to 11%, up front, for the money you get. The casinos and the machine company split the proceeds. You're already an 11% underdog (some of the worst odds in the house) and you haven't made a bet yet.

• Cash machines keep a running log, complete with addresses and amount taken, of every chump who uses them. The machine company adds that information to its data base. That's some pretty private information. You probably don't want your name on a mailing list labeled "Degenerate Gamblers Who Can't Control Themselves and Make Really Stupid Decisions About Money."

• After you pay the fee to the casino and the guys who put the machine in the joint, you get to pay your normal interest rate on the revolving charge card: 15-18% a year on the principal, which includes the 11%. Oy!

No-Interest Casino Loans

Once you're established, the casinos will give you up to thirty days to pay off your gambling debts. That's a pretty good float if you work it right with interest-bearing accounts or short-term investments. I've heard of isolated promotions where a casino has allowed players to buy chips from the cage with a credit card, then submitted the charges as a purchase, not a cash advance. This would also give you a float for a month, but I don't know of any casinos that are doing it now.

The Last Resort

If you're really stuck, look in the Yellow Pages under pawn shops—but read the pawn-shop section in "Superstitions and Admonitions" first. And if *all* else fails, you'll have to call someone for an emergency infusion. This is where you find out if there's anybody left in the world who cares about you. If you can find someone who does, you can get a wire transfer through a bank. Or have them forward it through Western Union on Fremont Street downtown or at the Barbary Coast or Gold Coast. The charges are steep for cash-to-cash transfers: from $15 for a $100 transfer, to $50 for $1,000. It goes up from there on credit-card-to-cash transfers.

Living With the Losses

Now that you're a professional gambler (playing for comps, of course), you have to understand the ebb and flow of the business. There will be good times. There will bad times. During the bad times your character will be tested. You won't believe it possible to lose so many hands in a row, but it is. Viscerally, you won't understand the negative fluctuations, and you'll think that you're being cheated. You're not. If you know an engineer, ask him for a print-out from a random number generator. The numbers will appear to be anything but random—you can find evidence of any pattern you want to, if you look hard enough. The ups and downs are inevitable and you'll simply have to learn to live with them.

So what if you lose? As the sage Ernest P. Worrel is fond of saying, "Them's the grits." It happens. Live with it. Don't despair. The longer you play, the more likely you are to profit. A casino owner worth his salt never "sweats" the money as long as he knows he's got the best of it. If he books a loser, he knows he'll be a winner the next time, or the next time, or the next time. It's not easy, but it's the only way he survives. Emotionally, the same principles apply for an ACES player.

Now that you're this far into the system, you're actually thinking about trying to live like a high roller, but you're still afraid of losing money. Why? Because like most of us in the "reasonable" world, you've been led to think that you can't win. After all, you never really won anything significant, right? Pardon me, but that happens to be crap! You're already such a big winner it almost defies belief. How? I'll tell you.

The average man expends about four hundred million sperm with each act of love. Let's assume your parents married at 25. Let's also give them the benefit of the doubt and assume they had sex 50 times a year for 20 years. That gives us 20 years times 50 acts of love times four hundred million sperm each time. That comes to four hundred billion little spermies and yours won! That's four hundred billion to one! Now that I've put to rest that you are a winner, let's talk about how to handle yourself when the inevitable losses happen.

You just lost money. A lot of money. You feel like an idiot, a jerk, a loser. Now you're without a dime and you've got another whole day to stew. What do you do? Get stewed for free to drown your misery (see "Free Whiskey")? Maybe. But no matter how miserable you are for having lost so much money, you can still hold your head high, because you had the best of it going in, and you've got the best of it now.

If you have access to more discretionary dollars, go get them and get back on the merry-go-round. It's the only way you'll learn how to ride the rough terrain. If you're out of jack because you bet way more than you should have, you'd better go home and reassess what you're doing. You may not have the discipline to be an ACES player, or you may be playing for more sinister reasons than getting a free vacation. If you are, you're on your own, in more ways than one.

Everyone can be a hero when he's on top. An honest measure of someone's character is what he does when he's down. Do you really think it does you any good to curse the dealers and snarl at the bosses? Hell no, it doesn't. On top of that, if you behave like a lady or gentleman, you still get one hell of a vacation for the money you blew and you might be invited back next time RFB and won't even have to gamble, so you'll have the best of it by far even if you've lost your stash.

I'm sorry if this sounds like sermonizing, since I'm about as far away from fire and brimstone as a man can be. On the other hand, I'm not bragging when I say that behaving with grace under pressure is one of the few admirable traits I managed to develop in my formative comp-hustling years, and it has served me well.

In the casino business, as well as in life, nobody likes a sniveler and nobody likes a snitch. If you show some class, they'll give you a pass. If you whine, you won't get a dime more in comps, and you might get a lot less. If you point fingers at other people and blame them for your losses, you'll definitely get a lot less and you might not get invited back at all, let alone for a full-comp RFB no-risk romp the next time you get the urge to come back to town.

Living With the Wins

Strangely enough, you see much more erratic behavior in Las Vegas from the winners than you do from the losers. Sure, the losers get goofy and bang their heads on tables and abuse the staff, but the winners? They go completely off the deep end. Why? Lots of reasons. First of all, guys who have always thought of themselves as losers are suddenly self-anointed heroes and their egos aren't even remotely prepared to handle it. Secondly, a lot of guys who've just won a thousand or two for the first time have never in their lives had a thousand or two to blow on something frivolous. So what do they do? They run to the casino men's clothing shop and buy a $500 jogging suit (retail value $79). They order two bottles of $150 champagne up to the room. They might even call up a couple of $300 hookers. Then they go downstairs and regale anyone who will listen with tales of gluttony (as if they've invented debauchery that very evening).

The third and underlying reason that most folks lose control when they have newfound wealth is that they simply aren't wired to handle instant, albeit unearned, success. It happens in all walks of life to those who suddenly achieve fame and fortune. How many times have you seen a struggling businessman, actor, or athlete suddenly get wealthy overnight and then immediately start to believe his clippings? It happens every day in Sin City.

What does this have to do with me, you ask? A lot. First of all, remember, you're supposed to look like a loser. Giving the old "Yeehaw," along with tossing $25 chips to cocktail waitresses, doesn't do a lot to enhance that image, amigo. Nor does suddenly betting $500 a hand as soon as you're up a thousand or two. It looks good for your average bet, but it puts a whole lot of unwanted attention on your game.

So much for image. What should you do if you stumble onto a monster win? Put the money in a safe place (that you can't reach if the adrenaline and booze start taking control) and continue to play as if you were on the same budget you started with. Why? Because the next time you come you could lose an equal amount and then you won't have enough to continue your comp-wizard career in the fashion you've now become accustomed to.

Here's what happens to most gamblers. They come to town and lose, say, $1,000. On their next trip they win about $1,500, but they spend the hell out of it. The third time they blow around $500, and then maybe lose another $300 the fourth time out. Now they've made four trips and their bankroll's down $1,800 when it should stand at about a mere $300 loser. Do you see what's happening here? If you don't salt away the winnings, over time you won't have anything to play with. Take it home and put it in the bank. It's the only way you'll survive the swings.

Warning. If you win real, real big your first time in town, don't let it go to your head. When I was a pit boss on the Strip in the late '70s, I watched a Texan who owned a chain of lumberyards win over $100,000 on a $1,000-limit dice game on his first trip to Las Vegas. He was back the next week and lost $40,000. No problem, he had a system. He came back two weeks later. Before long he was a fixture at the tables, not only losing about $10,000 a day, but neglecting his business. He took his eye off the ball and failed to see the oil glut that was destroying his state and it took him about six months to lose everything he had, because he "knew" he could make up his business losses by shooting dice. In less than eight months from the moment his plane touched down at McCarran for the first time, he was a break-in blackjack dealer at Binion's Horseshoe. I haven't heard what happened to him since then, but I'd be willing to wager a bundle that whatever he's doing, it's not quite as good as owning a chain of lumberyards in Dallas.

The moral of the story is, it doesn't mean a thing if you win today—the joints always have the edge. Unless you're playing for comps, that is.

The First Time

Nothing's easy the first time. That doesn't mean it can't be fun (think back, folks). You've done all the preliminary work. You've scouted out a good joint, played blackjack for a couple of hours, gotten along well with a nice, busy floorman, made a couple of smooth ACES moves, tipped the dealer just right, and all in all settled pretty smoothly into your new role as a relaxed comp wizard. Now you're ready to ask for your first comp. Gulp.

The heart races. You know that not everybody gets a comp the first time they ask. Sweat soaks your palms, your mouth's dry, and your voice cracks as you look at the boss and croak, "Can I get a comp?"

You hold your breath while he looks at your rating slip. He's the judge and jury. You secretly think, "What kind of person am I?" He lets you know when he smiles and says, "Sure, where you wanna go?"

You exhale and confidently say, "Where's the best place to have lunch?" He offers the buffet or the coffee shop. You wisely nod and say "Coffee shop," knowing full well that coffee shop is a misnomer in Las Vegas, a place where everything from prime rib breakfasts to king crab dinners is served. He starts to write out the comp. By now you're almost frothing. He hands it to you and you try to control yourself as you grab your partner and sprint to the head of the invited guest line to wolf down your first free meal.

The waitress hands you the menu. You feel guilty and giddy as you scan it, looking for the most expensive things you can find. Yippee! They've got a $14.95 T-bone, $7.95 shrimp cocktails, and glasses of designer wine at $4.50 a pop. You order four glasses. That dinner salad doesn't look too bad, either, and you're going to put a serious dent in the dessert tray you spied on the way in. Two pieces of $4 cheesecake? Go ahead. You've earned it. Besides, it might be another eight hours until you get your second-ever comp, so bulk up.

You spend a leisurely hour and a half running up the biggest bill you can, leave a nice tip, pat your expanded waistline, and sip coffee while you contemplate who you're going to tag for tonight's free dinner.

You're a comp wizard. There are 40 or 50 places out there for the taking, and now they're all *yours*. Welcome to the club.

5
Other Games

Up till now, all the discussion has been about blackjack. That's because none of the other casino table games are particularly well suited to comp wizardry. The house edge for most of these games is both fixed (non-reducible) and known, which means that except in cases where you find extraordinary conditions (casino mistakes, short-term promotions, exceptionally slow action, and the like), you won't be able to fool the bosses or the trick the system sufficiently to overcome the house's built-in advantage. For example, it's impossible to play baccarat at less than a 1.17% disadvantage, yet it's precisely this number which the comp-reimbursement system is based on. So the comps you earn simply can't make up for the money you lose getting them.

The fundamental moves of comp wizardry (playing slow, masking bets, etc.) will help narrow the spread between your losses and the comp gains, but will rarely, if ever, net you the big gains you'll find in blackjack. Of course, gamblers play baccarat, craps, roulette, and other casino games every day, anyway. If you do, you should get comped for your action. At the very least, the comps function as a partial hedge against losses.

This isn't to say that no other game in the casino is worth playing for comps. At one game, video poker, you can even eke out a small profit with perfect play, and be a big favorite by taking advantage of the perks available when you belong to slot clubs. Even playing slot machines can pay off if you're a slot-club member. So we'll deal first with slot and video poker machines.

Slots and Slot Clubs

Slots. Hmph. In the olden days the sharpies had a saying about slot machines. "The only way to beat 'em is to cheat 'em." And cheat 'em they did (but that's another book). I don't want to even suggest that you cheat anybody, not when you can get the best of them playing ACES on a blackjack table, so I suppose we should stop right here because slots truly are one-armed *bandits* and you'll never have the edge going up against them. Right?

Wrong. C'mon. Give me some credit here. Twice as many people play slots and video devices as play all of the other games combined. These machines account for roughly 65% of the tax revenue the state takes in from gambling. Did you think old Maxwell was going to let you down on your favorite game? Nope, you can beat 'em and beat 'em bad. How? Two ways: first, by joining slot clubs and second, by learning optimal strategy for beatable video poker machines.

Most of the major joints have slot clubs. All you have to do is show up at the casino Welcome Center and join (which is as easy as filling out a grade-school raffle ticket). You'll be issued a VIP card that you insert into a card reader on the machines when you play. The reader tracks your action, and you are awarded points in accordance with the number of coins you play. The points can be redeemed for free rooms, shows, meals, gifts, and sometimes cash.

A major benefit of slot-club membership is getting on a casino's mailing list. With all the new casinos coming on line, competition is frantic, and the joints now constantly mail out free offers to their cherished slot customers. The favorite giveaway is free rooms, especially at times when occupancy levels are running low. Take the time to join the slot club in every casino you patronize, if only to get your name into the casino databases. If you work the system hard and play your cards, er, slots, right (one master wizard I know managed to accumulate 49 free room nights on a 50-day stay), you'll never have to pay for a room again. It takes a little more legwork than ACES play, but if you're on a tighter budget, and if you like playing slots and video poker, it's the only way to go.

Beating Them Over Time

You can hardly expect the casinos to comp you more than they expect to win, so it figures that once you start to drop coins down the gullets of the greedy little slot machines you'll have the worst of it. And mostly, it's true. No matter how good the slot club, you'll be a long-term loser if you insist on feeding the bandits. The slots are set to beat you, and you can't outwit or outplay them. If you join a club, play a little every time you come to town, and take advantage of a free-room offer now and then, you'll be doing alright. But, if you want to beat them consistently, you'll have to learn a new skill—optimal video poker play. Video poker is similar to blackjack in that the casino advantage can be lessened, and even overcome, by a skillful player. The most important skill is learning to distinguish the good machines from the bad in terms of payback percentage. This can be done by analyzing the pay schedules that are posted on every machine. Many machines are beatable (or near beatable); the best pay schedules (that you have a reasonable shot at finding) for "Jacks or Better," "Joker Poker," and "Deuces Wild" machines are printed on the following page.

The best treatment of video poker for the beginner is contained in *Bargain City: Booking, Betting, and Beating the New Las Vegas* by Anthony Curtis. Another great tool is *Stanford Wong Video Poker* software, which you play as a game while you learn the optimal strategy. Then, once you have the basics down, *Winning Strategies for Video Poker* by Lenny Frome provides the proper playing strategies for machines with 50 different pay schedules. There are other good books; they're listed in "Resources."

Cashing In

In *Bargain City*, Anthony Curtis writes, "Slot-club comp disbursement is still an inexact science, which means there are loopholes just waiting to be exploited." I agree. When you learn the ins and outs of a few clubs, you'll figure out all sorts of ways to beat 'em. At some places, slot hosts will even comp the big players to food and drinks on top of what they give them in rooms and shows for

Jacks or Better (25¢)
Payoffs Per Coin Played

9/6 (99.5%)		**8/5 progressive (100%+)**	
Royal flush	250 *	Royal flush	250 **
Straight flush	50	Straight flush	50
4 of a kind	25	4 of a kind	25
Full house	9	Full house	8
Flush	6	Flush	5
Straight	4	Straight	4
3 of a kind	3	3 of a kind	3
2 pair	2	2 pair	2
Pair of jacks or better	1	Pair of jacks or better	1

* *Royal flush payoff with five coins played, $1,000.*

** *Royal flush payoff with five coins played, $2,200 or above.*

Wild Card (25¢)
Payoffs Per Coin Played

Joker Poker(101%)		**Deuces Wild (101.1%)**	
Royal no joker	400 *	Royal no deuces	250 **
5 of a kind	200	4 Deuces	200
Royal with joker	100	Royal with deuces	25
Straight flush	50	5 of a kind	15
4 of a kind	20	Straight flush	9
Full house	7	4 of a kind	5
Flush	5	Full house	3
Straight	3	Flush	2
3 of a kind	2	Straight	2
2 pair	1	3 of a kind	1
Kings or better	1		

* *Royal flush payoff with five coins played, $1,175.*

** *Royal flush payoff with five coins played, $1,000.*

their slot-point redemption. If you learn how to play perfect video poker strategy and can determine where the best games are, you'll get the best of the comp system. Here are a few more ideas.

After you've signed up and joined the club, buy in and get plenty of coins. Make sure you get *two* slot VIP cards (tell the hostess that you play two machines or get a second one in your spouse's name with the same account number). Find a busy area where two machines are vacant. Put your slot cards into both machines. Dump all of your coins out into the tray of the machine in front of you but play the other one occasionally. Always play coins in that machine, not credit. Then, when another person wants to play that machine, say it's okay, but you'd like to leave your card in for the credits. Most people don't have cards and won't give a hoot if you get the credits or not. Now you can earn double for your play, or just sit and watch your new "friend" play while he racks up slot-club points for you.

If you don't worry about raising suspicions, here's a surefire killer comp earner. A lot of progressive video poker machines around town eventually accrue a jackpot which gives knowledgeable players a positive expected return. Any jackpot above $2,200 on an 8/5 quarter progressive yields an advantage. It also brings semi-pro and pseudo-knowledgeable video poker junkies out of the woodwork because they've either heard (or just deduced) that a jackpot that high is worth playing. A lot of these underground misfits don't have slot club cards. What you want to do is sit at a bar where they have bar-top machines and order a drink, but don't play. As it gets busier and the jackpot continues to climb, you'll see the semi-pros slithering around the bar, trying to lock up a spot. If a guy wants your spot, you'll know. Offer it to him, but tell him you want to leave your rating card in the machine. He'll go for it and you'll be getting maximum coin advantage from a guy who can play about seven or eight hands a minute. If he hits, he might even toss you a little something for giving up your seat and if he doesn't, you're still going to get a free meal or a toaster, even, for being so darned kind.

If the progressive meter is linked to a stand-up machine, you can work the same ploy, but you'll have to play some hands before you snare a pro stalking the elusive jackpot. If you see someone in desperate need of playing, offer him the machine but insist that your card stays in. If he says no, so what? You can play it yourself. If the jackpot is over the breakeven number, you've still got the best of it and you'll be building up valuable comp points, too.

The Lazy Slot Club

Gearing up and maintaining a new slot club is an expensive proposition for casinos. To begin with, all the machines have to be fitted with card-reading devices. Then they need expensive software to track gambler activity, new employees to man the slot-club booths, printed matter explaining and promoting the club, a new branch of marketing to handle all the new data that the tracking system generates, and so on. Consequently, some of the casinos don't have sophisticated clubs that utilize all the new technology. But they still have slot clubs, because they know if they don't reward their good players with freebies, they'll play somewhere else. How do the lazy slot clubs rate you? By reviewing your buy-in receipts and occasionally observing your play. These situations are tailor made for comp wizardry. The key is to buy in often, and don't forget to get the receipts validated.

Las Vegas Advisor

If you want to stay up to date with video poker and slot-club wizardry, you ought to take a look at the *Las Vegas Advisor* monthly newsletter (see "Resources"). The *LVA* staff covers the Las Vegas slot scene like bulldogs, and your humble author also shows up nearly every month to keep you current on the latest comp opportunities.

Why Craps is Dying

Shooting dice was fun until the early '80s. Then, in an astounding display of ignorance of human nature, one of the new breed of crafty casino managers with an accounting background (but little else) came up with the brilliant idea of making dice dealers split their tips with 21 and roulette dealers 24 hours a day.

Before their emasculation, the four dealers who made up an eight-hour "crew" would split their tips four ways. This created a constant air of excitement, because everyone around the tables, gamblers and workers alike, was rooting for the dice to get hot. The dealer's nasal singsong would filter through the casino and the whole room would feel a buzz when the dice were hopping. And something else happened. Something magic.

Every time the shooter made his number, the whole table—no, the whole pit—was in on the profits. How? The gamblers betting on the shooter were knocking down a major score. The dealers were "partnered up" with the gamblers, who were making bets for them on nearly every roll. The boxman (who let the dealers hustle the gamblers) got a succulent layoff from the dealers and the floormen behind them were treated to a share of the spoils for discreetly losing their hearing every time a dealer hustled a player for a tip.

If it sounds like agony for players to have a crew of four dealers banging into them for tips, it was anything but. The minute you showed up at a dice table it went something like this.

You bought in for $500. The dealer looked up and smiled. The rest of the dealers sized you up. You might be a live one.

"Hello Mr. R. Nice to see you," the dealer said as you stuck out your hand. The dealer wasn't supposed to shake hands with players, but he elbowed the boxman who gave him the wink. The shake (and shakedown) was on.

"Hard sixes been coming in all day, Mr. R.," the dealer whispered as he leaned over to hand you your chips.

All right—this dealer's pulling for me, you thought as you handed him a red chip to put on the hard way (which paid $40 if it hit). "Hard six," you told him.

"Is that a two way, Mr. R.?" he smiled.

"Only if it hits!" you laughed, knowing you were being hustled, but not really caring.

Sometimes it hit, most times it didn't. But the whole time you were being stroked by masters every bit as crafty as the $300 stealth hookers who still mysteriously appear at your side as soon as you've got $5,000 in the rack.

On top of that, up to a dozen other folks at the table were also being pumped up by the croupiers. When it was your turn to toss the galloping dominoes, total strangers were in your corner, rooting their brains out for you. Talk about hero time. And the great part was that you, a lowly amateur, could roll those bones just as well as Nick the Greek.

Don't get me wrong. Shooting dice can still raise the old blood pressure 50 points in 50 seconds, but it ain't what it used to be. Players are still serviced a bit, but they never get to be part of the team anymore. In the old crew-for-crew days, dealers were willing to risk their jobs by hustling the big shooters (some dice dealers at top joints averaged $300-$500 a day in tips back then). The players knew it and reveled in the dealers' moxie. But the new breed of big bosses just couldn't stand it that a bunch of proles pushing chips around a dice table were making more money than they were, when, after all, they had business degrees and everything. Also, on a more practical note, money locked up by the dealers was no longer fair game for the house.

One of these days, and likely pretty soon when the old guard in the mid-level casinos start crumbling under the weight of the megaresorts, the owners will look at their percentages and realize that they made more money at the crap tables when crews split up the spoils table for table, even though the dealers took home better pay than their comptrollers. It wasn't just because the game was more fun and more people played, either. Dealers touted the players on high-house-percentage proposition bets, and when a player popped a $10 yo'leven at 15-1, he didn't mind putting a little something up for the dealer, even if the hustle was a mite less than subtle.

For now, the house's percentages have fallen, crap tables have been removed and replaced with blackjack games that even first-time players can get the best of (especially comp counters), and the thrill is gone. The only hope the casinos have of reviving dice pits and creating that old-style atmosphere with crap shooters is to train the dealers in professional customer-handling techniques (to tone down the hustle) and rely on the largesse of the diceheads for tokes. In Las Vegas. In a dice pit. Uh huh.

That said, what can you do to get the best of a dice game if you're a comp counter looking for a free vacation? Not much. Unlike blackjack (or roulette), each crap table is assigned its own floorman. Even when he's bombarded with paperwork, you can't hide your betting patterns, because a boxman (and sometimes two) sits on every game as well. The box knows what you're betting and in most cases he relays that information to the floorman when it's busy. On top of that, even the best bet on a dice table has a house edge at least triple what you face on an average blackjack game. In fact, some of the proposition bets (any craps, snake eyes, boxcars, etc.), are up to 40 times as bad.

If you still want to get the feel of what it's like to toss the dice and get the best of it, go downtown and bet $1 on the pass line. The expected loss on your bet will be about a penny and a half. Now if you order a couple of drinks and play an hour and get in, say, 20-40 line bets, you'll still be ahead; you might even be able to knock off a low-level meal chit. Bet anything more than that and you'll move back into the ranks of suckerhood.

Note. Some clubs give comp credit on line bets only. Others also give credit for odds, but the problem is that they reduce your comp-earned ratio accordingly. Although rumors abound, I've yet to find a high-stakes dice game that you can get the best of.

Roulette

It takes special circumstances to get the edge on a roulette game, but comp counting can work. It's all a matter of waiting for a perfect spot to play.

First, you need to know how to bet. The best bet? There aren't any on a roulette wheel. You'll get much larger swings betting single numbers, but the house advantage is precisely the same for every bet (except one, which is a little worse) on the wheel. You can't make a really bad bet. You can't make a really good one either. So you've got to be sure to land on the right game if you want to grind out some major comp value. Here's how.

Find a busy game. I mean a really rammin' jammin' table where hundreds of chips are piled on the layout every spin and the dealer is buried up to her neck. Wedge yourself into the game. Ready? Not yet.

Let's back up a minute so you can understand how a floorman watches a roulette game and what he's looking for. His priority is to make sure that the payoffs on winning numbers are correct. His secondary objective is to keep the game honest by preventing 1) players from "past posting" (putting chips down on winners after the ball has dropped) and 2) dealers from handing off chips to accomplices. Does that leave him much time to watch and rate players? Not very often. Why? Ninety-nine percent of what he's responsible for occurs after the ball has dropped. Bosses never watch the ball spinning or the dealers "mucking" (cleaning up) the chips because they're too busy watching the chips go out. And they have to watch two or more games in most joints. That's good news, but only if you know a trick or two.

The first trick is spelled S.L.O.W. How do you play slow on a roulette wheel? It's easy. Only put your money at risk every three or four spins. This doesn't mean don't bet, it means don't leave your money on the layout. Confused yet?

All right, I'm going to digress again. Most roulette players like to buy stacks of wheel chips (each with its own color) so they can cover all sorts of numbers on the layout. Each player has a different color wheel chip (that's how dealers keep track of who bets what). Roulette players, unlike other gamblers, constantly move their chips all over the layout until the dealer stops all betting when the ball's got a few rotations left on the track. This creates a lot of motion and confusion. If everyone on your table is betting only "colors" (wheel chips), that's probably not a game for you. Why not? Because dealers and bosses know who gets each particular color of chip when the winners are paid.

But if one or two other players are putting green and black chips on the layout, especially on the "outside" bets (red/black, odd/even, first 12, etc.), they really don't know who's getting paid, especially if you take your time picking up your chips when you win. That's your game.

Remember, in roulette as in blackjack, you're working on the art of deception and misperception, trying to look like a big bettor and a big loser. To do this, come to the game with, say, $2,000 in black chips. Give the boss your VIP card. Don't make a bet until you've seen him start to write up your rating slip. Now bet five chips on red or black. As soon as he looks away, snatch back four chips. If he looks back, pile 'em on somewhere else. If he looks away, get 'em back. Don't worry, he won't be paying a whole lot of attention to you after he's filled out the rating slip; he'll be too busy verifying the multi-chip payouts. Besides, he sees this all the time from gamblers playing hunches, constantly changing their minds, and moving chips all around before the ball drops.

Now you can discreetly drop a couple of chips in your pockets every few minutes. Within an hour or two, after you've stashed the chips and taken a marker or two, it will appear that you've really taken a beating even if you were only nicked a little. Remember, you need a very busy game to take this to the hilt, and you'll have to make big bets at a game with a 5.26% edge, so this move isn't

Roulette Comp Wizarding

Most joints expect around 50 spins an hour on a roulette table. There's no skill involved and they know that no matter how you bet, over time you will lose 5.26% of your bets.

If you bet $200 a spin and the house assumes 50 spins an hour, your total betting handle is $10,000. At 5.26%, this amounts to an expected house win of $526. The house will then comp 40%, or $210.

On a big-time game a dealer is lucky to get a spin every three minutes. If you slam down $200 on a color or section when the boss is watching and snatch $100 back before the ball drops and "forget" to wager a spin or two, it's possible to make it look like you're averaging $200 every spin while you're really averaging only $100 playing about 15 spins an hour.

Expected House Win
50 spins x $200 x 5.26% = $526 expected win

Expected Player Loss
15 spins x $100 x 5.26% = $79 expected loss

Comps earned	$526 x 40%	$210
Player expected loss		$ 79
Net player comp gain		$131 *

**This still doesn't compare to blackjack comps, and it's tougher to pull off.*

for everyone. Always leave the game before all the other green- and black- chip players take off or the boss will be able to scan the chip rack and determine that you really haven't lost or won any money.

Another move, though it won't make you look like a loser (but will change your M.O. if you're playing in the same pit a few days in a row), is to fill your pockets with green and black chips you've bought and stashed away at other games. Get a marker. Now, to make it look like you've really been firing it up, add a couple of black chips to your stack every few minutes and you'll walk away a couple thousand "winner" after you pay off your marker. The idea is to create the impression that your bets are big enough to warrant a higher rating.

However you play, as always, tip the dealer, because the boss might ask him how much you bet and if you're a stiff, you'll get clobbered. Make a bet for the dealer just before you leave and try to leave after a new dealer has been on the game for only a spin or two.

As in blackjack, you can always take a break. Give the dealer a couple of dollars and ask her to hold your spot. Leave your chips there. Even though you're gone, the comp meter will keep running.

This roulette scenario works best during holiday and big-event weekends when it's especially busy. The prime times are during any Julio Caesar Chavez fight at the host hotel and Cinco de Mayo at any top resort. There are many legendary Mexican roulette players who bet huge amounts all over the layout.

A word about betting systems. A gambling system known as the "Martingale" is particularly favored by roulette players. In this system, gamblers double their bets after a loss. It only stands to reason that if the ball has landed on red 11 straight times that black should come up next, right? Wrong. The past 11 spins have nothing to do with what happens on the next spin. Don't use betting progressions. You'll eventually lose the ranch if you do.

Still not convinced? Read on. One Strip resort has installed six electronic signs above its roulette tables which display the last 16 winning numbers on each game. Gamblers (and some of these are smart people, for God's sake) will watch the displays and wait until, say, black has hit five or six times in a row and then they'll start chunking pretty good stacks of money on the red and doubling up every time until a red number hits. Any idea what the house's net result has been since it installed these devices two years ago? Here's a clue. The displays cost the house about $7,000 each. The house makes about a nickel for every dollar bet. Each board paid for itself (above and beyond the normal take) in less than six weeks. That's more than $40,000. At 5.26%, they took in $740,000 above their normal drop, much of it in progression sucker bets, in a month and a half! Yowser.

Quick Q & A

Q. *What if the eye in the sky sees me pulling chips off my bet and sitting out every other roll or so? Won't they alert the boss?*

A. No. Don't worry about the eye in the sky. Their job is to catch cheaters, not comp wizards.

Q. *Is there a best place to sit?*

A. Yes. Be sure to sit nearest the even-money proposition bets that you are making. If the only available seat is on the end of the table, make your bets in the 19-36 section, or on "odd." The closer you are to your chips, the easier they are to manipulate. You want to discreetly snatch your chips back. Leaning across the table every time makes discretion damn near impossible.

Q. *Should I try to befriend the roulette boss?*

A. No. If you're on the right game, he'll be too busy to make idle chit-chat.

Baccarat

Most Las Vegas visitors are afraid to cross the invisible barrier that separates the baccarat pit from the masses. Maybe it's all those arrogant bosses who look like the cast of a daytime soap or the tuxedo-clad dealers who glare at you standing there in your Levis and are every bit as welcoming as a French maitre d'.

Besides the snoot level, baccarat's a bad game. Yet it's the table game that virtually all players (mostly foreigners) with million-dollar lines of credit play. Its allure is the aura of glamour and exclusivity. You don't have to sit next to the Al Bundys of the world while you gamble, and you get to treat the American staff like the serfs and coolies back home.

Every joint on the Strip covets the monster international baccarat players, but only a few (Mirage, Hilton, Caesars, MGM, and Desert Inn) can snare the nabob suckers. Why? One guess! Comps, of course! No matter how much money they have, no establishment on the planet ever treats them better than the Las Vegas casinos who suck millions and millions out of them every year. Always trying to outcomp each other, Las Vegas casinos are the only resorts in the world that can afford to cover the walls of suites in monkey hide, spend thirty-five million on private golf courses, fly in chefs from Seoul to feed an entourage of four, and on and on.

How about you? Can you beat baccarat with comps? Not really. The limits in the main pits are too high to overcome with a cocktail, and the house percentage is too high to overcome with rooms, shows, and even food.

There is one great baccarat-based play for wizards of any level. You're broke. And starving. You can drink for nothing (see "Free Whiskey"), but you've also got to eat. Are you limited to the tub o' popcorn at Slots A Fun? No way. If you're well dressed, go into the baccarat pit at The Mirage, where a gorgeous little buffet is set up for the high-limit players. You'll find lamb chops, curry shrimp, tempura-style meats, and exotic Oriental delicacies that you add to slimy rice. Dish yourself up a couple of scoops on those teeny plates that rich people eat from, stand there and chow down, and nobody'll say a word to you.

If you want to feel real hoity toity, have the server, hovering there in the tux with a towel draped over his arm, prepare your plate for you. Then sit down in one of the $1,000 chairs while you regally inspect the surroundings and pretend that you're worthy of hanging out with the baccarat ilk. When a cocktail waitress comes by, order a double of her best cognac. Still broke? When she brings your drink, haughtily sniff and dismiss her with a wave of your hand like the peasant she is. Rude? Of course. Unique behavior? Not in a baccarat pit. It's a given among baccarat pit personnel that the more money you have, the cheaper you are and the worse you get to treat the staff. Be a real ass and everybody will think you're a genuine tycoon.

Race And Sports Books

Even the heavy bettors don't get taken care of very well here. Sports books' win margins are low (especially against the sharpies who bet big bucks) and their operating expenses are high. Consequently, most sports bettors can't even get a comp for two bucks at the ever-present snack bar. The best move here is to get a drink ticket (or tickets) when you make minimum bets ($11, sometimes $5.50). If you're a monster bettor, you'll get a buffet now and then, but coffee shop ducats are hard to come by, because the house thinks that anyone who frequents the books is a glutton. Good guess.

Poker

Poker players are considered a notch above sports bettors (and a rung below amoebas) by casino staffs. Why? Imagine working in a room with hundreds of people intent on fooling each other, every one of them trying to come up with a bad idea. The bosses grow weary of the scammers and squawkers and conclude that they're all a big nuisance. No matter their level of play, poker players rarely get high-level comps, but they can usually worm meal tickets for buffets, snack bars, and limited coffee shop comps. The best house for these is the Horseshoe, where almost any poker player can get a $6 meal ticket after a couple hours at the table. Considering the Horseshoe's good food, that's not a bad comp. Ask the poker shift boss for the chit.

If you're from out of town, try this move. Call one of the bigger poker rooms, talk to the manager, tell him you're coming in to play, and ask for casino rate on a room. A lot of times you'll get it. Depending on the hotel's normal rate, you'll save $30-$100 just for making a call.

One no-risk comp move the poker gang came up with is brilliantly sleazy. It works like this. The hotels all have toll-free 800 numbers. The poker chiselers know which ones go directly to the PBX operators. They have their buddies or family back east call the hotel, ask for the poker room at a pre-set time, and have them paged. Then the guy quits playing poker, gets on the phone and talks for 20 minutes or so and saves his mom or pals about $15, while the hotel foots the bill. Slimy? You bet. Surprising? Not a bit.

Pai Gow Poker

According to *Optimal Strategy for Pai Gow Poker* by Stanford Wong, you can achieve a breakeven game if you can engineer a situation in which you bank six to 14 times the amount of money that you bet when you aren't banking. That would be fine for your comps if you were getting credit for something like $100 in non-banking situations and $600-$1,400 when you bank. Unfortunately, most casinos will only credit you with the $100 average. The house figures about 25 decisions per hour at an edge of something less than 2.5%, so you can only accrue about $25 per hour in comps. This isn't always the case, though. I know of situations where a boss has factored a player's big banking hands into the calculation of the average bet. A $600 or $700 average in this situation is worth $150+ per hour in equivalency. But because of the enormous risk, it's not really worth considering.

Pai gow poker is a good alternative to playing 21 for a friend or partner who doesn't go for the blackjack grind. At a busy, high-action table, the pace is sometimes slowed to 15 decisions per hour or less. Now the expected loss of about $40 per hour is offset—though again, not overcome—by the $25 in comps.

If you could slow the game down to less than 10 decisions per hour (barely achievable), you'd have a comp wash.

Other Other Games

You can amuse yourself at keno, Caribbean stud, red dog, big six (wheel of fortune), sic bo, and other trumped-up casino table games while you wait for a drink, but they are all bad news for anything except whiskey and tobacco. Even then, they still don't compare to the more common table games. These are not the games for the comp conscious.

What It Costs To Play

Based on moderately crowded tables, one hour of play, and $100 average bet.

Game	Decisions	House Edge	Net Loss	Comps
Blackjack-Good Rules	60	0.2%	$ 12	$ 48
Blackjack-Bad Rules	60	0.6%	$ 36	$ 48
Craps-Pass Line	30	1.4%	$ 42	$ 17
Roulette	50	5.3%	$ 265	$106
Pai Gow Poker	24	2.3%	$ 55	$ 22
Caribbean Stud	22	5.3%	$ 116	$ 46
Red Dog	90	2.5%	$ 225	$ 90
Baccarat	100	1.3%	$ 130	$ 52

On games other than blackjack, net losses will be greater than the value of the resulting comps.

6

Everything You Always Wanted To Know About Comps (But They Were Afraid To Tell You)

Gimme an "R." Gimme an "F." Gimme a "B." What's that spell? PARTY! When you're in the grips of RFB, you'll find yourself shoveling eats and swilling booze like you've never done before. Is there a sound reason for going on a 10,000-calorie-a-day weekend? Of course there is. That it's free doesn't hurt, but you'll have an even stronger motivation for pigging out when it's on the casino's nickel. After a day or two of gambling, you'll find yourself developing a combat mentality. You'll want to hurt them. It'll be you against the house and it will be war. How do they attack? With their house advantage on the games. How do you counterattack? With your stomach. How do you win? By ordering it up.

Ordering from the bottom of the menu works if you're a full RFB customer or if you have an off-premises food comp. But if it's your first stay at a particular hotel, you'll have to take it easy to gain their trust before you're set up for the full hog-o-rama the next time out. Also, RFB comps oftentimes aren't issued as a complete package; there's a wide range of comp gradations. So, before we go any farther, maybe we should look at just what all the R, F, and B in RFB really mean.

"R"

"R" stands for room. After coffee shop meals, room comps are the easiest to get, especially if a free room—and not food or beverage—is what your sights are set on. Any pit boss can give a rated player a room comp (ask the floorman; he'll get it approved by the pit boss), and rooms are given away like candy to slot-club members. Whether your hotel room is comped or billed at the casino rate, it's a pretty straightforward deal. A bellhop schlepps your bags, shows you the bed, sticks out his mitt, and leaves. A couple days later you check out. Other than watching movies in the room, there's not much you can do there to run up your comps and they charge you for the movies anyway. Ho hum.

"F"

"F" stands for food. When you're F'd, you and a guest get to eat whatever you want. Now the house is starting to take a little risk, because two champion garbage-guts visiting a specialty restaurant for lunch and a gourmet room for dinner can stuff in about $150 worth of grease a day if they really let out the waistbands. Chomp.

MAX FACT: People with food comps go to the front of the line.

"B"

"B" stands for beverage. Next to airfare, B is the hardest comp to get. And rightly so. One bottle of vintage French wine in a gourmet room can hurt them more than all the R and F put together. That's why they demand such a high average bet before they dub you B'd.

Even when you're B'd, some joints have a choke point on the vintage wines. For example, it might be $50 for a party of two. If you're RFB and order something more expensive than that, the restaurant will call a host to ask if it's okay. If you're on your ACES, you'll probably be close. What to do? Order something less than $50 and then tattoo 'em with designer brandies after dinner. How can you tell what the choke point is? Ask the waiter. He knows. Chug.

"RFL"

That stands for room, food, and limited. It means you're still RF'd, (and you get a limo ride to and from the airport), but you're not allowed any room-service beverages, expensive wines with dinner, or more than two drinks at a show. If you want beverages, they'll let you charge it to your room and then they'll hit you with a bill when you check out. If you're L'd, order a modest wine with dinner. If you want drinks in your room, buy your own hootch at any of the Strip liquor stores. Some RFL weekends include shows, some don't.

Sample Weekend–RFL

Say you've played 10 hours at $50 a hand. The house assumes about 60 hands an hour, or 600 hands at $50. That comes to a total betting handle of $30,000. Of that, they expect to win about 2%, or $600. With a 40% equivalency, you'll have earned about $240 in comps. Now let's look at a typical weekend bill.

Room	Two Nights @ $75	$150
Dinners	Four @ $35	$140
Breakfasts	Four @ $15	$ 60
Lunches	Four @ $15	$ 60
	Total	$410
	Less Equivalency	-$240
	Difference	$170

Examine the chart above. The R and F total is $170 over your comp allotment. So, now you owe them $170 bucks. Right? Nope. They'll usually pick up the "difference," especially if you show a big loss for the trip. As long as it's within reason, and the comps are all for in-house meals and rooms, you should be okay. But at $50 a hand, you can see that your comp account couldn't handle the B.

"What," you ask, "if I only run up a $200 bill? Will they give me something back?" Yes, they will. A nice firm handshake and a hearty invitation to visit again. Casinos never give back unused equivalency. Kind of makes it hard to feel guilty about taking advantage of them, doesn't it? Go ahead, beat them up on the F; see what they'll let you get away with.

This example graphically illustrates the value of off-premises comps. Instead of running up $30 every morning in the coffee shop where you're staying, go next door and give them a play. In the premium casinos, you'll have to average $25 bets for an hour or so, which has an expected loss of about $5. But, you can run up a $50 tab without trying in any coffee shop worth its salt and save your host-hotel RFL account for a gourmet meal. Oink.

"RFT"

That's room, food, and teetotaler. If you don't drink alcohol, it makes zero sense to get B'd. In this case you want to maximize your R and F, or minimize it and get hard cash for your airfare. Some places don't make a distinction, and maintain the same criteria for drinkers and non-drinkers. If you run into that situation, you can still take advantage of it, particularly if you're getting room-service liquor. All you have to do is take home a few bottles for your friends. And what friends they'll be.

If you know you've got a hundred or so extra built up on your comp account, and you're room only, you can ask a pit boss to give you a comp to a gourmet restaurant and put "no alcohol" on the ticket. It's the booze that sends gourmet tickets through the roof; you'll be hard pressed to top the century mark without imbibing. Let them know ahead of time that you don't want the booze and it'll improve your chances significantly.

"RFB"

Once the casino observes your play and dubs you RFB, you'll be among the chosen few who can have everything in the restaurants, shows, room service, or bars that they want. That's *everything*. If you're not planning to make any hinky moves with airfare, you can rip and tear for three days and go home packing an extra ten pounds without breaking a sweat (until you try to button your collar come Tuesday morning). To get into the magical realm of full RFB, you'll have to show them an average bet that's about 40% more than you need to qualify for RFL. You'll be able to make up the difference in expected losses with a couple nice bottles of wine in the gourmet room or a single room-service lard-out.

Comp Classics

If you're new to Las Vegas and want to get your feet wet before making the plunge, scores of automatic comps are yours for the asking. If you're not new, but aren't quite ready to risk a lot of money, you can go a long way on these old-time freebies. You don't even have to play to get some of them. Most comp wizards use the classics as a matter of course, without even thinking of them as comps. I'll start with the most common, then lead you to some of the more obscure.

Drinks

Even if you've never been to Las Vegas, you've probably heard that juice, soft drinks, beer, wine, and cocktails are free to anyone who gambles, whether they're at the penny slots or in a private baccarat pit. A free drink gives you an enormous value advantage virtually every time you order one. Let's look at the math for earning drinks on a table game. I'll assume you're ordering a call-brand cocktail or imported beer that would cost you about $2.50 at any non-biker bar, and that you're betting $5 a hand. The chart below shows how long you can play the different table games before your expected loss catches up to the price of the drink.

Game ($5 bet)	Decisions per hour	House Edge	Decisions to lose $2.50	Time to earn $2.50
Blackjack	60	0.5%	100	1 hr.-23 min.
Craps-Pass Line	30	1.4%	36	1 hr.-12 min.
Roulette	50	5.3%	9	11 min.
Pai Gow Poker	24	2.3%	22	55 min.
Caribbean Stud	22	5.3%	9	25 min.
Red Dog	90	2.5%	20	13 min.

Remember, this is if you bet $5 per hand. All of these games except Caribbean stud and pai gow poker can be played at $1 to $3 limits. It takes more than eight hours of $1 blackjack play to accrue an expected loss of $2.50, the amount you'd have spent at the bar. You can even subtract a generous dollar toke for each drink and still come out way ahead. Order a drink every time the cocktail waitress comes by. Booze'll make you look like a sport and, if your act is good enough, a drunk and a loser. Coke, juice, even water will keep the fluids circulating and force you to take a break or two every hour, which will further increase the value of the drink!

So much for table games. In keno, the cheapest tickets cost about a dollar, and the house keeps about 30¢ of that on every game. Even here, you're getting drinks for about 10% of retail. If your ticket hits, ask for a drink chit when you cash it in. Sometimes they'll even give you two. Your edge? A bunch.

Go to any sports book and bet $11 on a game. Make it a game you're interested in. When you place your bet (worth about 50¢ to the joint), ask for a couple of drink tickets good at the bar. Now you get some great entertainment rooting for your favorite team, while you suck down your favorite beverage courtesy of the house. That's a hard one to top.

Anyone who buys a roll of quarters at a video poker bar gets a free drink. How free? Go ahead and bet five quarters on the

Recouping Cost Of One Drink

Number of pulls/plays (with maximum coins bet) necessary to equal expected loss of $2.50.

Coin Denomination	Slots 3-coins	Video Poker 5-coins
1¢	2,083	
5¢	556	263
25¢	134 *	400 *
$1	56 *	100 *

* *At these levels you should also be accruing comps via a slot club membership (see "Other Games").*

first hand. The house advantage on most bartop poker machines averages a percent or two, depending on the pay schedule. Are you willing to part with 3¢ for a Chivas on the rocks?

All slot players drink free. If you're just angling for the comp, play the nickel machines. The best move is to lurk around and spot a slot drink lady with an empty tray. That means she's taking orders. Cut her off at the pass while you drop your coins down the hole.

Local Phone Calls

Want to save a quarter? Good for you. A few nice joints out there will still let you pick up a house phone and have an operator place a free local call (ask if you can get "a local outside line"). You might have to search a little to find a casino where this still works. Almost all casinos used to give away local calls, but the free phone call is going the way of free cigars and cigarettes on the tables.

Tacky Gifts

If you're like the rest of humanity, every time you come to Las Vegas every cheap relative you've got tells you to "bring me a souvenir." If you want to look like a sport, you can go into any of a dozen grind joints and pick up ball caps, mugs, fanny packs, decks of cards, or really spiffy key chains that you wouldn't consider keeping for yourself, but will appease the souvenir hounds.

Funbooks

Funbooks are, well, fun. Why? Most of them give you free whiskey, free trinkets, and free money. Some even give you free food, free slot pulls, free rooms, and discounts on shows and rental cars, and they don't cost a penny. Although not as prevalent or valuable as they were in the early '80s when professional coupon hustlers took to counterfeiting them, funbooks are still offered by many casinos and are easy to get. Generally all you need is an out-of-state ID; sometimes a coupon from one of the freebie magazines is required.

Even when you have no interest in the other things funbooks offer, every single one of them contains coupons that have real cash value. They're called lucky bucks. Lucky bucks pay two-to-one, three-to-two, or seven-to-five on even-money bets. Without getting into the math too deeply, two-to-ones and three-to-twos are worth about 46¢ apiece and seven-to-fives are worth about 92¢.

Would you toss two quarters away if someone just handed them to you? No kidding. Just playing a couple lucky bucks a day can pay for a tip or two, and is as easy as picking money up off the street. If you want to raise lucky-buck gambling to an art, you can scoop up dozens of them every day and have a genuine fail-safe you-heard-it-here-first-that-it's-true *expectation of winning money every day while you're in Las Vegas.* Take a look.

Condition	**Player Expected Win (Loss)**
Bet 5 7-5 Lucky Bucks	$4.60
Bet 10 3-2 Lucky Bucks	$4.60
Bet 180 $25 Blackjack hands @ 0.2% House Advantage	($9.00)
Net Player Expected Win	$ .20

I hope you understand what you're looking at here. What it means is if you play just 15 lucky bucks, you will overcome your expected loss for three hours of $25 blackjack play, which can easily net you three coffee shop comps for two. Kind of makes you wonder about the poor slobs who are throwing their money away, doesn't it?

If a joint sees you abusing lucky bucks, which normally have a limit of a couple per day per person, they may tell you to stop using them. Big deal. Go play the lucky bucks given away next door.

Parking

Parking in downtown Las Vegas usually costs something. If you use a valet service, the zuke's about two bucks a car. If you park in a garage, it's pretty cheap by big-city standards, but still sets you back about 50¢ an hour. You can save the fees in most clubs' garages by getting your parking validated at the cashiers' cage.

Most validations have a time limit: if you go over four hours, you'll be charged the hourly rate until you pick up your car. How do you beat it? By "playing for parking."

You play for parking by making a token bet at a blackjack table and having a floorman or pit boss initial the back of the ticket. This tells the parking attendant at the booth that the casino is willing to pick up the whole charge. What's playing for parking worth? Whatever you owe, no matter how long you're over on the meter. If you have to bet $5 for two or three hands, even in a joint with bad rules, there's no way the expected loss can even come close to what you'll be saving. And, if you've left your car upstairs for a day or two, you'll save some real bucks. Call the boss over as soon as you make your first bet. He'll sign your ticket immediately.

Paycheck Cashing

This is a no-risk no-brainer that anyone who lives in Las Vegas is crazy not to take advantage of. A dozen or so casinos cash paychecks and let you spin a wheel, pull a handle, or scratch a ticket to give you some kind of chance at winning up to double your pay. The worst you can do is get a free drink. A lot of people get comped meals, cash, and other juicy prizes. Every once in a while, someone pops for the whole deal and walks out a thousand or two richer. Cash your paycheck at a bank and they're afraid you'll take the pen.

Low-Level Comps

Someone who comes to town with a $500 bankroll and wants to play as little as $5 a hand can still get comped. The key to getting stuff when you bet $5 (and up to $25) a hand is to get noticed, not rated. You get noticed to earn a comp from a floorman who can give you something on his own accord. In most places, floormen can give an untracked player a comp for two in a buffet or coffee shop. Simply buy in for a few hundred when you sit down. The dealer has to notify the boss. When the boss looks over to OK the buy-in, tell him you'd like a drink. This serves several functions.

First, it puts the boss on notice that you're there. Second, it lets him know you're a sport, even if all you order is a ginger ale. Make your largest bets early when the boss is watching and ask him how long you need to play for a buffet or coffee shop comp. Then settle in, making nickel bets. After you've played an hour or so, make your pitch for the meal.

Where should you play your $5-$10 game? Head straight to downtown Las Vegas. In fact, I recommend downtown to anyone coming to town with less than a couple of thousand. You'll be treated nicely and noticed readily if you're a $5-$25 bettor. The downtown joints give away more and are more relaxed than the clubs on the Strip, and the people you play with are more colorful. You'll meet degenerate gamblers, grannies from Iowa, fighter pilots from Nellis Air Force Base, cowboys, wiseguys, maybe even some people like yourself.

Downtown is more reliable for low-level comps than the Strip, thanks, in no small measure, to Binion's Horseshoe. It's the quint-

Some More Words . . .

Simply knowing the magic of getting the best of the casinos—playing basic strategy, applying comp wizardry, even trying out some advanced ACES moves—isn't enough. You also have to summon the gumption to go for the freebies. You might feel a little anxious or nervous about this crucial part of the game. Just take a deep breath, look the floorman in the eye, and go for it. The rewards are immediate, and you'll soon be awash in the warm, fuzzy feeling of getting your first comp. You'll savor your first taste of being treated like a high roller. And, you'll experience the sustained adrenaline rush that comes with getting the best of the big boys at their own game. Whether it's a measly buffet for two or a full RFB weekend, it doesn't matter. The key is to get out there and pull it off.

The first time or two you might be clumsy, but no one will know it. Even if someone does suspect it's your first play, so what? It's one of the most commonplace transactions in a casino. If you're really antsy, here's a tip. Go into a casino that

essential old-time gambling hall. Their blackjack game has excellent rules. The rooms are plain, there's no entertainment, not even a buffet. Just gambling, drinking, and meat and potatoes (and a little Mexican food). And they do it all with a turnover rate that would make the human-resources department at any other hotel in town run for cover. The dealers and bosses aren't well paid, but they're workin'. Binion's has served as a way station for down-and-out gamblers and scufflers since 1951. If you look at a lineup of dealers, you might see a guy who used to have his own joint in the Dominican Republic, one who just got out of the real joint, a kid working her way through UNLV, and an ex-casino thief. Play $2 a hand for an hour to get comped to a huge ham-and-eggs breakfast or a great late-night steak.

For lunch, go to the Four Queens across the street. Play Multiple Action Blackjack for a couple of hours at $5 a hand. There are three betting spots, so you'll have $15 on the layout every time they deal, but that's okay. It's a good game with good rules

. . . About Asking

you don't care about and practice your new trade for a few hours. Be bold. Say things you never would have said before. Try your lines on floormen you'll never see again. A friend of mine owns one of the country's most successful telemarketing firms. His salespeople practice their pitches on "customers" who would never use the product, even if they got it for nothing. Why do they call on these certain non-buyers? Because they're not selling, they're rehearsing. So what if they make a mistake? It only costs the price of a phone call. It might cost you a little more than that, but if you find a low-limit game, you'll still be ahead by ordering a cocktail or two every hour. By the time you finish your first session, you'll be a seasoned veteran. And hey, you might get lucky and get a free meal out of it, too.

While you're making your practice plays, you'll learn how to steel your nerves, acquire some flexibility, and develop the proper attitude for asking for the comps you so justly deserve.

and it's fun. A coffee shop comp for two can be worth as much as $40.

It's dinner time, you say? Buy in for a couple of hundred at the El Cortez and play a while. Then ask the floorman for a comp to Roberta's. The atmosphere is distinctly downtown, but the food is great. Try the venerable king crab legs or big Porterhouse.

The Lady Luck has the best all-around deal going for low-end play. Any $10 bettor who plays for three hours a day can get a casino room rate (as low as $10 weeknights and $40 on holidays). If you bet $15, you only have to play for two hours. They have great rules on their double-deck blackjack, the rooms are nice, and they treat their low-limit players like VIPs. In fact, their low-limit players *are* VIPs. Make sure you register with the floorman for the Burgundy VIP Club when you buy in.

If you want to deposit $1,000 in the cage at the Lady Luck (the only place in town where you should deposit less than $2,500), they'll give you a deluxe suite, gourmet meals for two, and put a limo at your disposal. You have to bet $50 a hand for two days. If you only want to play $25 a hand for four hours, you can still get a great gourmet meal for two worth at least $75. Not bad for an amateur comp wizard.

Off-Strip casinos are another possibility. Try the Gold Coast (play for an hour and go for the huge T-bone in the coffee shop), Palace Station, and Sam's Town. My favorite off-Strip casino, the Maxim, has an old-time policy of comping virtually everyone. It's within easy walking distance of anyplace you want to go on the Strip and it's staffed with some of the nicest casino people you're likely to meet. They have good lounge and comedy shows, a nice gourmet room, a decent little coffee shop, and damn good double-deck blackjack. Any $10 player can get a coffee shop comp anytime; the prices are so low that you'll have to strain to run up a $30 bill, but it can be done if you're a real swine. Any $25 player can weasel a comp in DaVinci's, the gourmet room, and casino rate on a room is easy to get. All you have to do is ask.

That's all there is to becoming a low-level comp wizard. A couple-hundred-dollar buy-in, a polite inquiry to the floorman, and you can score at least a meal on the house.

Soft Vs. Hard Comps

Soft comps include cocktails, food, rooms, and most in-house shows. Hard comps include airfare, tickets to fights and special events, and off-premises food, shows, and golf. Soft comps have the hotel's departmental profit margins built in to their prices, because they're purchased wholesale and billed to your comp account at retail. Hard comps, on the other hand, cost the casino real dollars every time you use them. Soft comps are easier to get than hard comps.

The distinction between soft and hard is critical to what a casino is willing to offer you. For example, it's easy to go to any show in a hotel you're staying in gratis, if you're RFB (or betting $125 a hand for four hours). To get your host hotel to pick up the tickets for Liza next door, which cost $60 a pop, you'll have to average a whopping $400 to $500 a hand.

Advice? If you really want to see Liza, stay where she's headlining or pay the $120 for the tickets. The same deal goes for golf. If your host casino doesn't have a golf course (or an ages-old agreement with one), you'll have to bet a lot of money to get to tour the links on the joint's dime.

Room Comps

I once asked a seasoned casino manager why a local player, who didn't require a room and only wanted an unlimited food and beverage comp, had to bet the same $125 a hand for four hours as the RFB guest who got food, beverage, *and* a room. He replied, "Rooms don't cost us anything." Of course, the rooms do cost something (maid service, linens and laundry, toiletries, etc.), but their (soft) cost is trivial compared to the (hard) cash some casinos are forced to shell out to maintain their customer bases.

Ask the host how much you need to bet to qualify for a suite. If you're already RFB, you'll have to bet a little more than is required for a regular room, unless you get lucky and are bumped up into the nicer digs. Deluxe two-bedroom suites with bars and jacuzzis will require considerably larger bets than even the mini-suites, and should only be played for by those with huge bankrolls.

Casino Rate

One indication of the low cost to the casinos of the room comp is that pit bosses have the authority to issue them. Another clear indicator of how easy it is for hotels to comp rooms is the ubiquitous "casino rate." Virtually any rated gambler, table games or slots, can get a casino rate at anywhere from a 35% to 70% savings off the normal rack rate. The casino department likes the casino rate, since it fills the joint with known players (low limit, but gamblers nonetheless). The hotel departments also appreciate it, since rooms that would otherwise be vacant are full of paying guests. The restaurants serve more food, the bars more booze. The valets park more cars and the bellmen pump more vinyl. The guests, too, are happy, because they get a hefty discount on the room.

Getting the casino rate is even more valuable during holidays and special events, when normal room rates are often tripled or worse. The casino rate in most places goes up proportionately, but you'll get preferential handling with reservations.

Note. Some casino rates are so easy to get you don't even have to be rated. Just call one of the smaller joints and talk to a shift boss or a host (not a pit boss or floorman). Tell him you gambled there on your last trip, but weren't rated and stayed somewhere else. Then ask what their casino-rate qualifications are. A lot of times you'll get lucky and get the discount just for the asking.

Late Check-Out

This is another one of the little-understood comp classics that is available to most players. Check-out in almost all Las Vegas hotels is at noon. If you've ever had the pleasure of queueing up with the masses and listening to them wail at the end of their weekend while another thousand or so are trying to check in, then you'll appreciate this tip.

Here's who normally gets what. Full RFB guests can call VIP Services anytime before noon to get a four-hour waiver; the real sportos can get eight hours extra in the room (or even another night if it's not busy) without additional charges. Room-only guests should call VIP Services before 10 am on check-out day (to give the housekeepers notice). They'll give you two extra hours with no sweat and four hours if the front desk isn't jammed with newcomers. But what about a little old casino-rate customer. Here's the move. Make sure to be playing blackjack around 11:55 am and call your floorman over. Tell him that you're (choose one) stuck, broke, on a roll, or earning your comps, and you need at least a couple more hours on the table. Ask him if he'll call VIP Services for you. He will. VIP Services will almost always agree. Remember, unless otherwise noted, VIP Services runs the joint.

Food Comps

Personally, I'd never want to be known as a nickel and dime chiseler. Since that's exactly what I am, too bad for me. Why am I a nickel and dimer? Sometimes it's for the money, but most times it's for the game. Even if you're playing penny-ante poker against your friends, you still want to win. So why not make it a challenge to go for every scrounge move in the book and save yourself some money in the process? No reason not to. And the best part is no one but you will know what you're up to. Except maybe the waitress or busboy, and you can buy them off real cheap.

As a professional value grubber, most of your grind scrimpings will occur with food and beverage. The tips that follow are especially effective if the casino is monitoring your comps (room only, RFL, etc.).

A Doggie Bag For All Occasions

If you've just nailed an off-premises no-holds-barred gourmet or coffee shop comp, there's no way you'll be able to eat everything the casino is willing to pay for. The answer is doggie bags full of never-touched food that you can take back to your room for a late-night snack. Of course, you shouldn't haul dangerous foods (seafood, sandwiches with mayonnaise, meats, milk-based desserts, or anything from the Circus Circus buffet) to your room unless you have a refrigerator on hand (most places will send up a mini-fridge for the asking), but there are plenty of other nice items you can weasel out of the waiters. You can put a lot of food in doggie bags. Read on.

Entrees

Chinese restaurants are best for walking out with entrees, because everyone who eats a comp meal in a Chinese restaurant orders too much food. If you have a refrigerator in the room, it's a snap. Go ahead and order all the appetizers and side dishes you want, and for the grand finale, tag 'em for the Peking duck. It averages about $40 for two and it's one of life's great late-night snacks. When they bring the duck to your table, try a few bites, and ask for a doggie bag. They'll gladly pack it up for you to take to your room.

Note. I've kept leftover duck in a room for more than six hours without a refrigerator with no ill effects, but then again, I also ate in the employee's cafeteria at the Riviera (affectionately known as "the Sump") for two years and didn't die, so my experience might not be the best to bet your health on.

Revenge Meal

If you get real unlucky and run into a boss who's a turd, hang tough. If he refuses you a comp, ask him how much longer you'll have to play. Then do it. It won't be more than another hour and your expected loss won't come close to what you're going to do to them once you sit down in the coffee shop. Nothing tastier than a revenge meal. Ask for a doggie bag and keep ordering until they cut you off. Hell, you could even treat Fido to a lobster. This also applies to the times when you lose. A revenge meal will always ease the pain.

A local friend who has taken scrounging to new lows goes into some of the places around town and orders three or four appetizers, soup, salad, a couple of side dishes, cocktails, wine, desserts, and the most expensive steaks on the menu. The thing is, he orders the steaks raw. Not rare. Raw! After his crew's eaten $50 worth of everything else they can stuff down their craws, they bag up the steaks and take them home to barbecue. It's shameless, but it works.

Buffets and Eat-Till-You-Drop Specials

Knowing how to get the best of a pitch-till-you-win spread is hardly limited to Las Vegans, but the practitioners here have taken unauthorized doggie bags to disreputable extremes. One chap wears nice dinner jackets and lines the interior pockets with sandwich bags. He makes two or three sorties to the peel-and-eat shrimp and cold-cut trays and loads up with about $25 worth of appetizers every time he nails a $6.95 buffet comp. A lady friend of mine always manages to have a nice Neiman Marcus bag sitting next to her, into which she shovels 10 pounds of meat at the prime rib buffets before she hits the door (I've seen it with my own wide eyes). She feeds it to her dogs. Talk about a doggie bag! Now, under normal circumstances, buffet etiquette requires that you take only what you're going to eat while you're there. But, if you're getting comped, you kinda, sorta, figure you're entitled to a little something extra.

Desserts

Go ahead and chow down on the surf and turf and order every appetizer and side dish you can stomach, making sure to leave no room for dessert. The trick here is to ask for two jumbo dessert specials at the same time you order your dinner. When the desserts arrive, groan and ask for a doggie bag, which the waitress will be glad to deliver. It's in her best interest to crank up the bill to jack up the tip. Food's on the house. Tip's on you.

If the restaurant uses a dessert cart, ask her nicely if she'd mind if you took the dessert to your room. Nine times out of ten she won't care in the least.

Now, before you go out on the town, take the goodies back up to your room and set them aside. When you return after a night of hard gambling, it's a nice little touch to have coffee and cake. You can call room service for the coffee and request that they send up a couple of forks. If the forks don't arrive, use the coffee spoons.

Another way to get in your floorman's good graces is to get the same outstanding desserts, package them up, and take them with you when you gamble. Give them to the boss to take home when she gets off. She'll be flattered you thought of her.

A Bad Meal

Anyone, anytime, no matter how posh the restaurant, can experience a bad meal. I even had some bad ribs once. If you've just ordered a $50 lunch and the food is bad, don't ever, under any circumstances, send it back. Why not? Have you ever seen the creatures that work back there? The best-case scenario is you'll get the same plate reheated with at least one foreign object plucked from the cook's body tucked in the food somewhere. At worst? I worked in a kitchen once—I'm not even going to tell you what's worst.

Your best recourse is to tell the waitress that the food isn't all that wonderful, make a joke about the danger of sending it back, and ask her if you can order something else. She'll almost always say okay.

If you've been unlucky enough to get a bad meal, don't ever mention it to the floorman who gave you the comp. It puts him on the defensive and may give him second thoughts about sending you back in there the next time you ask for something. Tell him it was wonderful and thank him for taking such good care of you. The next time it might be good.

Feeding Four on a Comp for Two

Almost all comps are written for two, and it's much harder to get a comp for four than it is for two. "But," you wail, "there are four of us! What do we do?" You could play long enough in two different areas of the casino and get two comps for two. But since you can't possibly eat everything you're allowed to order on a comp for two anyway, there's a nifty little shortcut that can save you the extra playing time. Here's how it works.

When you sit down, tell the waitress that you have a comp for two and order beverages for the four of you. Make sure to tell her to put the two extra beverages on a separate check. Then go over the menu and the four of you can decide how you'll share. When you place the order, give the waitress five bucks and ask her if it's okay for the other people to "taste" your food. I don't have to tell you how she'll answer. Now make sure to order plenty of appetizers so you'll have empty plates for your guests' portions of the comp (don't let the busboy remove them). Sound disgusting? Hey, this book's about getting the most for your money. If you want tomes on manners and etiquette, there're plenty of them out there. I'm just trying to save you some dough. If you are a Ms. Manners' fan, some of you can have appetizers, soup, and salads from your very own dishes, while the rest of you go for the entrees and desserts. Either way, you'll get plenty of food. Bon appetit!

How Far Can You Go?

If you're not a guest at the hotel (or they don't think you are), you can order everything you want without fear of reprisal. Very few places take floormen to task on extraordinarily high food comps if the person is not a guest of the hotel. Why should they? There's nothing they can do about it after you're gone, anyway. If you are a hotel guest, only eat what you really want, because a $100 breakfast counts against your account just as much as $100 in airfare. Moral: If you're going to be a pig, be a pig next door.

Getting the Most From Room Service

Most of us have never been able to afford full-contact room service. It's one of capitalism's great spectacles of gluttony, if done right. Imagine, hanging out in your underwear, remembering that fine free dinner and those two bottles of Pinot Noir and how tasty your number-one tamale looked by the time you were slugging down that Napoleon brandy just before you waddled up to the room.

Then you think, "Hmm. Bloody Marys with steak and eggs don't sound too bad right now." You think about it some more. "Let's see. If I was to order two steak and eggs at $12 each and about four bloody Marys for another $20, hell, that'd only be $48, and since I'm an ACES player, I'd only be paying $4.80 for the whole deal and, well, I'd be stupid not to." You pick up the phone, order, and hop into the shower, knowing that in a half hour you'll be receiving another gift from above.

The guy hits the door with the eats. You slip him a five and wake your friend. What a stud! Breakfast in bed again. She starts to think that maybe you're not as dumb as you look. And you're not.

Hey, I said we were talking gluttony here. You might personally want to tone it down just a trifle, but when you decide to make the jump to room service a part of your life, there are a few do's and don'ts to observe when considering the costs against your RFB account.

Don't Order Dom

Without ratting on myself too much, I will tell you my taste for the grape is much more sophisticated than my zest for designer grub. Even if you've got an unlimited RFB account or an exceptionally high equivalency and really want to go for it, don't order Dom Perignon. First of all, it's overrated. Secondly, it's overpriced. Thirdly, it's not even worth the tip, especially when there's much better stuff on the menu. As long as you're going to tear 'em a new one, be a sport and order the Cristal at $210-$250 a throw. It's the smoothest thing you'll ever drink from a glass—like swallowing fog—and worth every bit the measly tip you'll be giving up.

Order Cheap Caviar

I grew up in a land where pork chops were a finger food and gravy was a beverage. So I didn't really have the privilege of developing a refined taste for weird food from the continent that sensible folks back home fed to the pigs. But after all I'd heard about caviar and how much it costs, I figured I owed it to myself to learn how to like it if I really wanted to think I was a spiffy guy.

Here are the facts. Unless you were raised in some high-brow social-register third-generation blue-blood family with nine jillion extra dollars lying around, the difference between Beluga caviar and trout bait will probably be lost on you. It's good enough that you're getting salted fish eggs. For example, the Iranian and Russian tins go for about $200 an ounce, while you can pick up domestic sturgeon eggs for as little as $30 a throw. Why feel guilty about leaving a puny tip for a $200 appetizer you probably won't like anyway? If you don't have the seasoned palate to know the difference between the many varieties of unborn fish, this delectable foodstuff is best consumed while you nurture a bottle of Cristal to wash away the taste. On a bright note, it's small enough and goes down fast enough that you can eat it in bed, even if you're half-smashed, without getting any in your hair. If your gambling action doesn't warrant a $300 caviar-and-champagne late-evening room-service bill, go for the shrimp cocktail and smoked salmon plates with bottles of domestic white wine. Most casinos have semi-reasonable charges on these items. And *they* taste good.

Don't Eat Room-Service Lobster

Some of the megaresort guest rooms are more than a quarter mile from the room-service kitchen. They cook the crustaceans 10 or 20 minutes before they get to you and by the time they arrive, they're likely to be mushy, tough, cold, or a combination thereof. A couple of joints have tried cooking the lobsters on the way to the room, but that doesn't work either; they invariably show up overdone or rare. Think about eating rare lobster while you're trying to impress your new-found love. Ulp! Besides, lobster should be eaten in the ambience of a gourmet restaurant, not on the side of a bed.

Don't Overtip Room-Service Waiters

It's not like these guys have spent an hour and a half serving some spectacular flaming fantasia they've created just for you. They lug a cart to your room, pop a cork or two, set a table, and hit it. Hardly worth 15% of the already inflated prices, especially the booze and wine. A $10 tip is sufficient for a party of two and a $20 bill is all you should ever give these guys, even if they're outstanding. And if the waiter's a turd, stiff him. It's not like he gets to hang around the room and glare at you.

Be aware that a few casinos know that the room-service staffs get stiffed regularly, so they automatically tack on a 15% gratuity. Ordering up a couple hundred dollars' worth of food that you won't finish, or remember in the morning if you do, is not a real good percentage play. If they're going to slam you with the auto tip, it'll say so somewhere on the room-service menu. Read it carefully.

Never Leave Empty

If you're on a full RFB comp, never leave the hotel without taking home at least a couple bottles of booze or champagne. I've personally seen guys heist enough bottles to host a New Year's Eve party. How can you tell if you've gone too far? Don't worry, they'll let you know.

Off-Premises Comps

Since I've belabored the point, ad nauseam, of giving bosses comps from other casinos, I'll get right to the specifics of how to do it, with examples and everything.

Here's a beauty. Take a handful of black and green chips from a premium casino and go into one of the smaller joints around 7 am. Put the "foreign" chips on the table and ask if they're playable ("Do you take these?"). Every club in town will honor at least a few thousand dollars' worth of premium casino chips as long as the denominations don't exceed $100. You'll look like a live one and they'll do about anything to convince you to become their customer. Why? Because half the guys working in the little joints are scared witless about losing their cushy spots as soon as the layoffs come after the megaresorts gobble up all of their business. Then what? Then some poor sap will have to find a real job doing real work. And he'll probably have his Cadillac repossessed. And his wife will leave him for some 50-year-old earth child she met at an anti-nuke rally. Sound grim? That's how these people think. Bottom line? Smaller joints covet a good new player—you.

As always, your first bet should be your biggest. Make just a few "big bets" (in quotation marks because a big bet in a smaller joint at 7 am is hardly a big bet in a megaresort at midnight; refer to the "Choke Point Chart" in "The Mechanics of ACES"). Call the floorman over. Tell her you've never been in there before, but you've heard they have nice people and good food. She'll agree.

If you lose your first few bets, grimace and tell her you need to take a break. Ask her if maybe she could pick up breakfast for two as you point toward a bank of slots and tell her your wife's putting you in the poorhouse playing those damn dollar machines. You'll get the breakfast comp, but you won't have to use it right away.

If she offers you buffet tickets, point to your gut and tell her you're on a diet and would rather try the coffee shop. She'll probably go for it. If not, take the buffet. *Never* turn down a comp. If you do get the breakfast comp, who said you have to use it for breakfast? It's for a room, not a time. Use it for dinner, when the stuff you eat—steaks, prime rib, and seafood—cost at least twice as much, or take it back to your host hotel and lay it off on your favorite floorman. It'll be worth the effort before your trip is over.

If you start off winning, they'll start off sweating your action. A second, bigger boss (the one who expects to get fired any day now) will probably come in and watch you play. Laugh when you win and tell him how much you like his joint. Say something like, "How's the breakfast in here?" Most times, the boss will jump at the chance to buy you something—he might be scared, but he still wants you. If he doesn't immediately offer, ask him how to get credit there, making sure to mention that you put up a load of front money in the megaresort down the street. If you have a line of credit anywhere, in fact, tell him.

If he still doesn't crack, ask to speak to a host. Most of the little places will only have one and he may also act as the shift supervisor. If you can convince the host (by showing him money or applying for credit) that you're a potential mark, he'll be sure to buy you breakfast and with any luck at all, he'll probably invite you back for a nice dinner and a show. The hosts in these smaller joints are personable guys and they'll always lean in your favor if you're smooth. That's not to say slick, however. The more naive you act, the better off you are.

Once you've gotten the comp you want, quit. Remember, you're a salesman, and a good salesman never goes past the close. You've made the deal, so get up and cash out. Then you—or your favorite floorman—can come back and teach 'em a lesson in the restaurant.

Beverage Comps

You don't have to worry too much about the B when you're RFB. But what if you're RFL and just want to have a nice cocktail in the lounge, or a drink or bottle of wine in your room, even if you don't qualify for room service? Never fear, the answer's here.

Cocktails

Say it's time to quit gambling. You've put in your time and want to relax and savor a coffee and Sambuca at the piano bar. Or perhaps it's nice outdoors and you want to spend an hour or so by the pool sipping a pina colada. Maybe you're just dog-tired and want to go up to the room, but don't really want to cough up $7.50 for a nightcap. What do you do? Order the drink on the table. If you're through playing, it's no problem to wait outside the game or to stay in your seat while the waitress brings your libation. Nothing goes against your comp account and you've just saved a pretty good buck for waiting a couple of minutes, at most.

Another way to play it is to ask the floorman for a drink chit. Except in the worst grind joints downtown, any floorman can write you a comp for two drinks at the bar. Just ask. Try to make it at a convenient time for the boss. Get his attention about 15 minutes before you're ready to leave the table to give him time to get to it. If you can't give him sufficient notice, it might be better to get your drink from the waitress than from the boss.

Note. If you're ordering something fancy schmancy with a lot of different liquors in it, never order it at the bar (unless, of course, you've got a chit). On the table it's free. At the bar a Long Island ice tea or zombie will cost you up to $10.

Wine

If you're not full RFB, surprise! There is still a way to get bottles up to your room. When ordering a comped dinner, make sure to include an extra bottle of good red wine. During the course of the dinner the waiter will open all the bottles for your inspection. Select the bottle you want to take with you and after he opens it, tell him you want to let it breathe. Finish your meal while the wine catches its breath and then put the cork back in it and take it with you (along with the doggie bags) when you leave. The reason you want to order red wine is that it will keep in your room indefinitely. If you want to, you can even take it home.

The same technique can apply at a show. Order a couple of drinks, then tell the waitress you want a bottle of wine (or champagne). While the red wine will keep, the champagne won't, so only order it if you're going straight to your room.

Show Comps

In most joints, showroom comps are limited to the primo customers, RFL and up. Again, the computer has to show that you're entitled to it and a big boss will probably be involved in the comp decision. Showroom comps are a little tougher to analyze from a comp-wizard's perspective, because some show comps are soft comps. The hotel produces the show in house, so they can be liberal when giving away the ducats. Other shows, such as *Siegfried & Roy* at The Mirage, are hard comps, meaning the casino must pay, in hard dollars (either to another department or to the show's producers), for the entire ticket price. These are much harder to get than the in-housers.

Lounge comps are easier to come by, because the comp is only for drinks, not admissions. Most comedy clubs, on the other hand, are "four-walled," which means the entertainer (or producer) pays the hotel a fixed price for the room and makes his money on ticket sales and a percentage of the alcohol poured. Thus the casinos have to pay full admission to get their customers in the door, so these comps, too, are harder to come by. But ask anyway.

Line Passes

While many of the big showrooms have gone to assigned seating, lounges and some production shows still have invited guest lines. Line passes are considered relatively valuable—sort of a comp classic at a higher level. Almost any $25 player can get a line pass. After just a few hands, call a boss over and you'll get your ticket to move ahead of the masses. There is no monetary value placed on these passes, but it's a nice touch to be hustled past a couple hundred people waiting in a long line to see a show. Any floorman can issue you a line pass, and it doesn't go against your comp account.

Limos

Unless there's a huge week-long event happening in town, any RFB player can get a limo ride to and from the airport, but it has to be scheduled in advance. When you call to make your reservations (even if it's the first time: it's not automatic, but you might get lucky), ask VIP Services to schedule a limousine to pick you up. After you've played a session or two, call them again to schedule your ride back to McCarran Airport. If they want you to leave up to an hour earlier than you'd planned, go ahead. Win or lose, it's a great way to get out of Dodge. Best of all, in most places limo rides don't go against your comp account.

VIP Services or your host will let you know how far you can go with other free rides around Las Vegas.

Max's Rules of Limo Etiquette

With apologies to Emily Post, here's the real way to act when you're in a limo.

• Don't ask the driver to lug your baggage to the car. That's why God made skycaps.

• Don't offer to help load the bags in the trunk. That's how the driver makes you feel guilty enough to tip him.

• Never sit in the front (unless you have a party of seven or more). It makes you look like a goob.

• Always push the "privacy button," which closes the partition separating you from the driver. It's the only way to get the true limo experience. Don't worry about hurting the driver's feelings. After a few years of serving obnoxious gamblers, they don't have any.

• Nobody's watching. Pour yourself a quadruple and crack open the nuts.

• Drivers are on a tight schedule. If you ask them to take the "long way" so you can see the Strip and downtown, the tip should go up accordingly.

• If you're with a couple of buddies and want to yeehaw and woof at the girls out of the sunroof while you cruise down the Strip, yeehaw.

• You can heist the crystal glasses out of the limo, as long as you're checking into the hotel. Leave them on your ride to the airport.

• Always tip the driver $10, each way. It's cheaper than a taxi and nine times more fun. If you win big, still give him $10. You're supposed to show some discipline here.

Airfare And Walking Money

Airfare reimbursement is probably the best scam, er, method of recouping losses for comp counters. The procedure is straightforward. Take your ticket to a credit host and tell him you want to be reimbursed. If your rating is high enough and he sees that the casino's had a chance to beat your brains in (with credit or front money), he'll go for it.

There are several key elements to snagging airfare. Most of them depend on which casino you're playing in. Some casinos (Golden Nugget, Mirage, and others) demand that you stay in their hotels if you want them to reimburse your ticket money. Others (Caesars, Hilton, etc.) don't care where you stay, but insist that their expected win equals about $2,500 for the trip (it can be a $100 average bet for 20 hours or $2,000 a hand for 60 minutes—it doesn't matter) to get money back for tickets.

Airfare is tougher to score than the soft food or room comps and a lot of the criteria are different, because they're giving you hard cash, not the inflated value of a room or a service that they've pumped full of carbonation to make you think you're getting more than you really are.

Giving you dough for your tickets is the toughest thing a host comes up against, so it's important that you log plenty of hours with a sizable average bet. While the guidelines change from joint to joint, the ballpark criteria are something like this.

Hats & Horns Airfare Criteria

Airfare will be considered:
—on a trip to trip basis only, with a minimum of $10,000 credit line or front money.
—with at least 12 hours playing time. If a customer loses 75% of his total line or front money, playing time will be disregarded.
—only up to the value of the airline tickets.
—only if the customer is a registered guest of Hats & Horns.

Requirements		**Reimbursement**
Credit Line/ Front Money	**Average Bet**	**Maximum Airfare**
$ 10,000	$ 200	$ 500
20,000	400	1,000
50,000	1,000	2,500
100,000	2,500	5,000

Note: Total complimentary charges, including airfare, will not exceed 40% of a customer's earning potential for the current trip.

Casinos will give you, in cash, a maximum of 5% of your credit line or front money. Unlike soft comps, the joint won't give you, say, $3,000 in airfare even if you play 100 hours at $200 a hand (close to a $10,000 equivalency), but have only a $5,000 line. Why? Because no matter how much you play, they can't justify handing you $3,000 in cash when they only have a shot at $5,000 of your money. They will fork over that much in room and food to get you to stick around, but hard cash? Forget it. This is one of the primary reasons it's important that you show them how much they can beat you out of before you start to play. So, even if you happen to have $10,000 in your jeans but never reach into your pocket after your first $500 buy-in, you won't get that kind of money handed back to you. Put the money in the cage. Even if you only take one $500 marker against it, if you play the required hours, you'll get your airline tickets picked up.

The other way casinos will rebate airfare is to give you back up to 10% of your actual losses, regardless of how long you play, *if* you have a sufficient credit line or front-money deposit (most premium places require a shot at $10,000 or more) and lose a sizable portion of it. Remember "Hide Chips" and "Look Like a Loser"? I can't overemphasize how important a loser profile is if you're planning on playing short hours and picking up airfare before you leave.

If you're unclear on the casino's airfare reimbursement guidelines, ask the host. Most of the nice places have their criteria printed on cards that they'll hand you before you play.

For the professional comp counter, however, the best move goes like this. If you know you're coming to Las Vegas in, say, two months, buy your tickets at the lowest discount available, nonrefundable. Then, at the last minute, buy a first-class round-trip ticket from a travel agent (preferably one you know and are on good terms with).

When you get to Las Vegas, play in two different hotels. Stay in one that requires you to be a guest there in order to be reimbursed for your airfare. Play half the time in the second hotel and tell them you're either staying with a friend or at one of the business hotels (Alexis Park, St. Tropez, Marriott, etc.). After a long play at the hotel you're not staying in, show your host the expensive tickets and snivel, telling him how much you lost, and how you didn't even stay at his hotel, and you really like his place, and how the Hilton has always picked up your tickets, but now you'd rather play at his place, and how much you like him, and pleeeeease help me out here, I'm tapped and my wife's going to kill me and can you make reservations for my next trip.

If he says no, ask him how much he can give you. If you show a nice loss, he'll always give you something, unless you act like a total rodent. Then take that same first-class ticket to the joint you're staying at and tell your host there how you paid for all your own lunches, but you're tapped and cripes, you'd like to come back, but if you go home empty, you're gonna get killed and well, you never asked for him to extend your credit or anything and could he help you out just this one time? If he says no, pretend you didn't hear him. Make it an open-ended question and ask him how much he can give you again. If he holds fast, ask him to extend your credit line. This works especially well if your ticket is for only a few hundred, because extending credit is riskier for the host than giving you airfare (he has to justify all extensions if they're not paid on time). While your squirming may seem to be an obtuse form of blackmail, I prefer the much gentler term "airmail." If he still won't budge and he does offer you the extended credit, ask him how much longer you have to play to get him to pick up the ducats. If you have the time and the numbers are right (you can do your own math by now), take him up on it. You're still way ahead of the game.

Be polite, but persistent, and you'll likely get at least a portion of your high-cost first-class airfare picked up by both places. Then fly home on your budget ticket and cash in the first-class beauties. It's a lot of work, but it's a lot of money, too. Remember, this is war. It's a greed-on-greed situation. The classic cons always play on the greed of the mark; if the casino wasn't after you, you couldn't get them.

Sometimes walking money is the only way to get out the door with some of casino's cash, not to mention a little face. If you play in a joint you're not staying at and lose a lot, but the host says you have to be a guest in order to get airfare, ask him for walking money. Walking money is ostensibly a handout (courtesy) that enables you to get home if they believe you've played a lot and are completely tapped out.

When they give you walking money, the host literally walks you to the cage, fills out a voucher, and tells the cashier to fork over the dough. That's it. The walking money criterion is usually double that of airfare (which means you get half as much—usually $100 to $200, rarely up to $500). With the opportunities for mischief (no ID required, no controlled accounting, money paid in cash, etc.) among hosts, cashiers, and players, it's amazing that the auditors still allow walking money at all. But they do. So take advantage of it if you can.

Back to airfare, the best time to request airline ticket reimbursement is the night before you're ready to leave. That way, in case you haven't qualified, you can ask your host how much longer you have to play at your average bet. Then calculate your expected loss and determine if it's worth going for. If it is (and it usually will be), make the play.

Now you know how airfare works. How can you maximize your advantage using airfare? Drive. Huh? Yeah, drive, but come to town with a ticket or two in your pocket. Portray yourself as flying in and hit 'em up.

Note. Some clubs (such as Bally's and Hilton) put a stamp on the ticket alerting other casinos that your airfare has already been picked up by another hotel. Most casinos don't care if someone else has paid for the ticket or not, as long as your play warrants an airfare comp. However, if you plan on turning in your ticket for a refund from your travel agent, it may cause problems when you ask her to credit you for the unused ticket. It's very important that you have a good relationship with her to prevent any problems. If you don't do something for her every time she writes up a bogus ticket, your act is going to get old real fast.

Golf Comps

Golf comps are limited to hard-gambling locals and bona fide high rollers ($100 and up average bet) who're already RFB. If you can afford to bet the big bucks and like to tour the links, get ready for some awesome golf comps, including invites to free tournaments where the winners of the long-drive and closest-to-the-hole competitions sometimes get stuff they can actually use. Like money. Some of the other stuff I've never been able to figure out, like when they award the guy who hits the longest ball a new driver. (He just knocked one 320 yards down the middle and he needs a driver?)

These tourneys often afford you the opportunity to play a round or two with different celebrities. One day you might be teamed up with Boomer Esiason and the next day Jamie Farr could be driving your cart. Jamie Farr? You traveled 1,500 miles and they stick you with the cross-dresser from "Mash"? Hey, quit whining. You could have drawn Bobby Goldsboro. If you'd rather play with your chums on your own time, the joints'll take care of you, too.

How do you get a golf comp? Ask the casino what it'll take. When you scout the clubs, ask the host how much you need to play to get golf comps in addition to RFB. In some places, it doesn't cost a dime more in action, but you have to get your reservations in early, because most hotels don't own their own courses. Even if you're not sure that your play warrants the golf, ask a host to get you a tee time anyway, so you won't be shut out if you do get the comp.

You might have to bet a bit more to nail a golf comp, but it'll be a bargain compared to paying full-tilt greens fees. If you don't have to bet more, get the comp even if you don't play. What's a non-golfer going to do on a golf course? The same thing all the other hackers out there do. Slice the ball and cuss a lot. Or give it as a gift to a boss and watch your rating light up the computer terminal.

Shadow Creek

At the time it was unveiled, Shadow Creek was reputed to be the most expensive golf course ever built. The starter out there is one of the loneliest guys in town, because they only have about ten tee times a day and, except for company executives, the course averages less than a dozen golfers every morning.

How nice is it? Imagine Augusta National. With more flowers. And more water. And more trees. And gut-wrenching 100-foot drops. And wallabies. And exotic birds. And a custom cart with a built-in ice chest full of your favorite beverage. And a caddy who takes you to a private driving range and hands you a leather satchel full of brand new Titleists. And no tipping. None. Not the caddies, not the locker-room attendant, not the waiters, no one. And tee times staggered 30 minutes apart. Other than your foursome, you'll never see another golfer out on the course.

Is it a tough course? Nah. Not if you can toss a 230-yard tee shot above a chasm and drop the ball on an elevated green surrounded by gorgeous three-stroke misery. And that's one of the easy holes. Wait'll you get to the backside. The tougher it gets the prettier it gets until by the final three holes, you almost forget about the bets as you marvel at what man has wrought. Sold yet? Now all you gotta do is get out on the course.

How do you get on? You'll hear rumors that it's reserved for gamblers with lines of $100,000 and up, but that's not true. If you gamble at the Golden Nugget, Mirage, or Treasure Island at about $400 a hand for four hours a day, you have a chance. That's the minimum criteria, and you'll have to ask for it, but it's possible. If you do make it to the "Creek," it's an experience you'll never forget, and you'll be an instant mini-celebrity anywhere golf is played, because anyone associated with the sport knows about the course.

A final word about the Creek. When you're out there, you're liable to bump into Kenny Rogers or Michael Jordan or Julius Erving or Bruce Willis or Michael Jackson (just looking around), or one of the PGA's leading money winners. This is The Mirage's course and these are Steve Wynn's friends. They're out there because they want peace and privacy. They won't ask for your autograph. Don't ask for theirs.

Free Whiskey

You're asking the wrong guy to moralize about the evils of demon rum. I know the last thing this world needs is free booze, but it's here. For your sake, I probably shouldn't be letting you in on any of this, but as long as you're gonna go and make a fool of yourself, you might as well do it as cheaply as possible.

If you don't mind paying for alcohol (and I certainly wouldn't respect you in the morning if you did), there's no cheaper place in the U.S. than Las Vegas. You can find draft beers for 25¢ and premium imports for 75¢. You can pick up a mixed drink for about a buck in half the joints in town. And that's at the bars, when you're actually laying out your own money. By now you should be a master at scarfing up the good stuff, gratis, when you're at a blackjack table.

But let's say you are an accomplished comp wizard, you haven't quite learned to control your fondness for distilled spirits, and you've forgotten everything I've been telling you about managing your bankroll. So you're busted. It's still 24 hours before your plane leaves, and you're way over on an RFL account. You wake up on a Sunday morning about eight o'clock and you're feeling extra thirsty. You have twelve cents and the host has left a message that your comps have been cut off. Can you think of a better time to go on a bender? Here's how.

Head over to any mid-size sports book. Pick some losing tickets up off the floor and sit down. If you can't find any tossed tickets, just sit there ticketless. When a cocktail waitress comes by, order with authority. A double bloody Mary often shows confidence. When she brings it to you, apologize for being tapped out and thank her. If my math is correct (and it may not be, because, unlike many less-than-sincere authors, I practice what I preach and I'm writing this on a Sunday morning at 11 am), there are at least a half dozen easy spots downtown. If you're lucky, you'll get a double in every joint. That's a lot of hootch for one day. Make sure you're within staggering distance of your home hotel before you take your last few belts. While the Las Vegas cops are the most lenient in the world on drunks stumbling across the street, they're not about to let you get killed trying to do the foot weave in and out of busy Sunday traffic. Your best bet is to have the first pop in the joint you're staying at, and the last one too.

As an added bonus on Sunday mornings, you get to watch the ball games on 10-foot-wide screens. Some joints even give you free popcorn and hot dogs during football season. The easiest sports books to hustle free drinks are those with a local flavor: any place downtown, Palace Station, Gold Coast, Rio, Arizona Charlie's, Sam's Town, and the smaller Strip casinos. If you happen to fall into a sports book and no ball games are on, snag someone's *Daily Racing Form* and scribble up phony horse-racing odds while you wait for service.

So much for late mornings on the weekends. What if it's 2 am on a Tuesday and you're down to your last nickels? Mosey into the keno area and sit down. There'll be lots of losing tickets laying around. Pick one up and study it intently. When the waitress comes by, order a double. You'll get it. Once. Then it's time to move.

To the slots. Still got those nickels? Then you're still drinking. Scope out the slot department's cocktail waitress. See which way she's moving. Cut her off just as you're pretending to put a nickel down the tube. Order a double again. It'll take her about five minutes to get back with your drink. When she does, tell her she's your partner on the next pull (it's still the same nickel) and give it a tug. If it hits, so what? You should have lost anyway and now you get to order again. If it comes up lemons, so what again? It only cost you a nickel for a double. Once you've played out every available waitress in one joint, move on down the road. You'll run out of steam before you run out of beverages.

By the way, getting ignorant on someone else's tab is a lot more fun to do with a buddy, but a pretty cheesy way to go if you're trying to impress anyone who doesn't think *Animal House* was a classic. I know it sounds kind of desperate, but when I was back in college, these methods carried the Sigma Chi fraternity through some of the most fun weekends it ever had.

Note. Even comped players who are planning to watch a game should go to a sports book for the free brew and camaraderie. Believe it or not, the games are more exciting in a sports book than they are at the ballpark, because everybody in the room's got something riding, which keeps it interesting up to the final pitch, shot, pass, or run. Also, everybody's rooting for the same guy. Ben Franklin.

As always, if you smoke, ask for cigarettes, too. Some books comp them, some don't. If they bring you a pack and charge you, tell the cigarette girl that you're out of dough. She won't understand. So what? It's a good bet you're not the first guy she's seen run out of money and a dead mortal cinch you won't be the last.

If you have $10, you can go to almost any video poker bar in town and ask the bartender for a roll of quarters and a premium call drink. He'll comp you the drink and sell you the roll of quarters. Go to a change booth and cash the quarters in for another $10 bill, then head next door. This one has carried many an alkie through some desperate nights in Glitter Gulch.

Specialty Comps

While most of the comps you'll ever want are covered when you get RFB and airfare, there are some interesting accessory comps available if you bet enough or ask in the right spots. Almost nothing is exempt from comp criteria. I'll list a few to give you an idea of what you're up against.

Dolphins At The Mirage

Almost every rated player at The Mirage or Treasure Island (remember, it *is* part of The Mirage) can get a ticket for two to watch the Flippers frolic.

Rain Man Suite At Caesars

The rack rate for the two-story porno palace (complete with round beds, mirrored ceilings, sunken bar, and a jacuzzi overlooking the Strip) is $7,500 a night. That's a mess of equivalency. If it's not booked up, sometimes even $500 bettors can use it for a night. If it's a busy weekend, you'd best put up $100,000 to have a shot.

Thomas And Mack Skybox

If you want to go to a concert, watch a fight, or take in the National Finals Rodeo at the big UNLV arena while you slurp whiskey with casino owners in their private boxes, you'll need to bet $5,000 a hand. It doesn't cost that much to hang with the Pope.

Limo For The Night

For a house limo and private driver at your disposal, you'll have to bet at least $500 a hand in most joints.

Championship Fights

For the big heavyweight extravaganzas, it'll take a $400-$500 average bet to score ringsides. If the joint you're staying in is hosting the fight, almost all RFL players can get a ticket up in the nosebleed section (though the criteria for fight weekends will be higher than usual).

Off-Premises Golf At Desert Inn

They charge $150 to play there. It's nice, but it's not *that* nice. If you want your joint to pick up the full buck and a half, you'll have to be a $400-$500 bettor.

MGM Theme Park

If you're already set up for RFL or better, it's on the house with no extra play required. If you stumble in off the street, you'll have to get rated at $25 a hand for at least three hours.

Flights To Grand Canyon

You'll need more than a healthy disrespect for your personal safety to get on one of these puddle jumpers that tour the Colorado. It'll take about a $500 average to get your host to give you cash back for your death-defying outing over the canyon walls.

Use Comps You Want

There's a reason the host's area in one premium casino is called "the wailing wall." One of the most disgusting sounds you'll ever hear is the chorus of bleats coming from the losers who've emptied out their RFB accounts on amenities that didn't mean a thing to them, and suddenly get stiffed by the host when they expected cash for an airfare rebate. It goes something like this.

Barbie, a fledgling, awestruck secretary is waiting by the casino cage for Indiana Irv, her 48-year-old boss who snuck her out of town for a little extramarital R&R. She's beaming. This is her first trip to Vegas and he's treated her like a goddess. She sees him shuffle around the corner. She smiles. Their eyes meet.

"Did the Colts win?" she asks as she rubs his arm.

"Win?" he screams. "Yeah, they won! He makes a 52-yarder and we're up by ten already and I bet the under and blow a two-thousand-dollar two-teamer. Yeah, they won. But I lost."

Barbie gasps, "You lost two thousand dollars?" She pulls back and notices people staring, and starts to tremble.

Irv sees that Barbie's shaken. He's embarrassed. He cools down. "It's okay. It's only money. Right?" He grabs her hand and takes her toward the host's office. "I'm a big boy. Come on, let's go get my airfare. We've still got two hours before the plane leaves. Maybe I can get even playing some BJ."

Dudley Dapper is coming out of the office. Irv stops him. They shake hands. Irv tells him about the whipping he just took. Dudley shares in his sorrow as Irv hands him the two first-class tickets which set him back $980.

Dudley pulls up Irv's account and grimaces. He keeps looking at the screen as he gives him the bad news. "Can't do it, Irv."

"Can't do what?" Irv blurts.

"Pick up the airfare. You're already over. Look here." Dudley points to the computer screen.

Irv blows up. "I played eleven, twelve hours betting at least two hundred a hand and I just dropped two grand on the Colts right over there!" he roars as he points to the sports book. "And you picked it up last time I was here when I beat you out of four thousand. What's the problem?"

Dudley points to the screen again. "Here's the problem. It shows you played twelve hours at two-forty-eight a hand and. . ."

"And what?" Irv screams. "That ain't enough to give me nine hundred dollars worth of airfare?"

"Normally it is, but look at this," Dudley oozes as he tries to calm Irv down. "You took the penthouse suite, that's five-fifty a

Trip's Over . . .

When you're RFB and it's time to head home, you don't even have to check out, unless you have to retrieve the unused portion of a cash deposit. Just call VIP Services and tell a hostess when you want your limo to pick you up and what time you want the bellman at the room. Ask her if everything is covered (paid for). If it is, simply go on down with the bellman and load up in the limo. If there's a dispute, ask for your host and schedule a quick appointment with him. Then go down, settle up, and hit the road.

If you've put up a cash deposit for incidentals and have change coming, you'll have to go to VIP checkout to get it. Make sure you call first and tell them you're coming down so your tab and refund will be ready. Again, if there's a problem, they'll call a host over to resolve it.

You can stop by the cage for a final reconciliation of your markers (credit or deposit). If you owe money, you can cut them a check before you depart, or they'll send you a bill and you'll have up to 30 days to pay (depending on the arrangements night, your room service, meals, and two shows were over six hundred. Jesus, you're almost eight hundred over as it is. I'll pick that up, but. . ."

"The airfare?" Irv asks, hoping.

"The charges, Irv." Dudley hands Irv the tickets. "There's nothing I can do with these."

Irv's neck swells as he snatches the tickets from Dudley. "I'm never playing in this chintzy hotel again." He pokes Dudley in the chest. "You got that? Never!"

Barbie's stunned at Irv's behavior. She starts backing away.

Dudley tries to console him. "There's nothing I can do." He points to the computer again. "It's all right here."

Now Irv's completely lost. He's embarrassed himself in front of Barbie, he's out of jack, and he's got two hours before the limo takes them to the airport. He's been coming to Las Vegas with his wife for ten years and he's never had to pay airfare. Of course,

. . . Checking Out

you made with your host). If you're owed money (from your deposit), settle up now. If you have a large amount of cash coming back to you and don't want to carry it around, have the cashier convert it into a check.

It's always a good idea to pass by the pits on your way out and say goodbye to your favorite bosses if you have the time.

On a weekend, you should give yourself at least an hour and a half from the time you call VIP Services to when your plane departs. During the week an hour is usually sufficient.

If you expect a struggle wheedling airfare out of a host, give yourself an extra 30 minutes, especially on a busy weekend or holiday.

If you came in full RFB and never made a play, the best thing to do is leave your key in the room and take a taxi to the airport to avoid any embarassing moments with your host. The next time you come to Las Vegas, you'll have to show them some speed for a while.

he'd never needed the penthouse suite and three bottles of Dom in the jacuzzi when the wife was with him, either. He starts to whine to Dudley when another customer walks up with another set of airline tickets. Dudley turns away from Irv. Case closed.

Irv goes looking for Barbie. He can't find her. Why? She's in the restroom, staring in the mirror. When she was standing at the cage, listening to Irv grovel, for the first time she noticed his gut, his day-old beard, his wedding band, and the way his voice cracked when he was whimpering. Now she feels guilty for being with this toad and dreads the long plane ride home.

When she gets back to Indiana, she secretly sends out resumes and quietly leaves Irv's company within a month.

Meanwhile, before he catches the limo, Irv whips out his VISA card, gets hold of some cash, and blows it trying to get even. Now he has to figure out how to explain to his wife why his personal credit card has a charge of $1,040 from a cash machine in Las Vegas, when she thought he was at a sales seminar in Chicago. Yoiks!

The moral of the story is to use comps you care about. Irv and Barbie probably could have done nicely in a $150 mini-suite (which also has a jacuzzi), ordered two or three less appetizer plates from room service, held off on that third bottle of $100 wine at dinner, and he would have gotten his cash for the tickets and all would have been well. (Except for the 52-yard field goal, of course.)

Even though you may not play on Irv's level, you still have to be careful how you use your comps. Here are a couple of helpful hints.

• Stay in the least expensive room that you find comfortable. You'll use up $150-$300 a day on a suite, which leaves little or no equivalency for dinners, shows, or airfare. You're much better off getting the cheapest room available and saving your comps for the good stuff downstairs.

• Don't be a pig in the coffee shop of your host hotel. Make sure whatever you order from the menu is something you want to eat. When you just want a little taste of the shrimp appetizer or you want to experiment with something you've never had before, order it next door where it doesn't go against your comp account.

What They Don't Comp

When you check in, the casino will ask you to put up a credit card or $100 cash for "incidentals" even though you're getting comped. Incidentals include tips, phone calls, in-room movies, massages at the spa, and gift shop purchases. I've found it's a lot safer to put up the cash instead of a credit card. Here's why.

Most places now charge at least 50¢ for local calls and the standard rates for long distance. When you check out, you're presented with a bill that has all the numbers you called. If you don't check out and go right to the airport instead, they'll send the invoice to your home. If you spent the night calling escort services or dirty phone lines, or watching X-rated movies in your room, someone who shouldn't see the invoice might, and you won't get to come to Las Vegas anymore.

A lot of people short on cash try to sign off tips on their comped food and drink bills, particularly room service, hoping they can get away without paying. Unless you're a big loser and haven't asked for airfare, the house will make you pay up. If you did lose (or appeared to lose) and your tips exceed your cash deposit a bit, they'll sometimes waive the charges if you call your host first and tell him you'd like to come back, but you'd like him to fade your excesses. Be warned, however. Trying to lay off your tips will not endear you to anyone, and will make you look like a low-life flea.

Another amenity that isn't comped is in-room movies. The reason management doesn't want you vegetating in the room is obvious: it means you're not downstairs gambling and spending. For most joints, only the biggest high rollers' movies are picked up for that very reason. But what if you're lonely and that preview of those two blondes and the fettuccine piqued your artistic interest? Go ahead and order it. No one's watching but you. Remember, though, that's why you use cash for incidentals. If you've got items on the invoice that might embarrass you back home, always check out and tear up the paperwork. The VISA statement never shows up at your mom's place, telling her how you watched "Twin Pasta Porkers," and you'll still have her fooled into believing that you're an All-American guy.

Massages are another story. If you're a $200 bettor, don't run up huge bills, and it's at the hotel's own health club, they may pick it up. If they don't, even though it's illegal in Clark County for a female to give a male a massage, nobody back home will buy your story that all you got was a rubdown, pal. Pay with cash and save yourself a lot of anguish. However, if hometown grief isn't a concern, try to get it comped, anyway. This is one you might be able to slide by the bean counters.

Knowing Your Worth

You've done everything by the book to qualify for the freebies, but a surly floorman refuses to honor your comp request. What do you do? You know the casino's system, you know what you want, and you know it should be given to you, so you should never take "No" for an answer. First find the pit boss (the floorman's direct supervisor). Calmly explain how much you've been betting and for how long. If the floorman refutes you, insist that the pit boss query the dealers and other players on the game. Be polite, but be firm. If you don't get satisfaction from the pit boss, ask to speak to the shift boss. If he's snarly too, ask for the casino manager. These guys dedicate their lives to staying out of trouble, and the last thing they need is an aggrieved customer dropping in on the hotel president's office to tell him how shabbily his staff has treated you. Unless you're blatantly lying about what you bet, someone up the chain of command will recognize your worth to the casino and give you your just desserts (and entrees).

If all else fails, there's one last possibility. Insist that the shift boss or casino manager have surveillance (the eye in the sky) review your last couple of hours play. Three things can happen. First, the boss will think you're bluffing and order surveillance to confirm your bets—you win. Second, he'll capitulate and give you the comps without review—you win. Or third, you can visit the president and pitch your case for a video review—you win again.

If the hotel's been tightass with your comps and you're never coming back and they let you sign gift shop items to your room (most do), pull up the automatic billing on your television screen. If you've got, say, about $50 in incidentals, go downstairs and get another $100 worth of stuff. Then leave. My sources tell me that anything less than about $75 is forgiven over time.

Last and now least, the most popular incidental that hotels picked up in the past has vanished. Contrary to popular belief, hotels do not send hookers to high rollers' rooms. Las Vegas is becoming more and more family oriented, and a casino, no matter how big, would risk losing its gaming license if it supplied gamblers with women.

The Next Trip's Free–The Absolute Cheapest No-Risk Good-Time Weekend on the Planet

If you're on your ACES, after your first couple of stays at a hotel, a host will invite you back as a full RFB customer. That means the next time you show up, the house will spring for everything, no matter how much you play. Even if you're short on money, as long as you have enough for a couple tanks of gas and tips, all you have to do is call your friendly VIP representative and she'll set you up for the weekend.

If you want to do nothing more than eat room-service food, drink good wine, watch TV, and sit by the pool to work on your tan, it's okay. I've never seen the house take away a comp during a weekend stay—though some will threaten to. Anything longer than that and they'll start looking at your activity.

After you've tricked them into giving you a no-risk weekend romp, the next time you call VIP Services for reservations you'll be told your play will be evaluated during your next stay, and you'll be comped accordingly. No harm there. You've already got the best of them. You can either go to another joint or stay in the first one and play ACES to earn your next free vacation. After you've made a couple more seemingly bona fide plays there, guess what happens? They'll make you RFB again. Har!

There are so many casinos that if you play the free RFB weekend game right, one out of every three of your first 40 vacations will be risk free. If you find a casino that you want to play at forever, disregard.

7
In The System

Wendy Fools The Weezer– A Play In Three Acts

What does "In the System" mean? Reduced to its most basic level, it means that by being rated, your gambling activities are converted to electrons and squirted into computers so hosts and auditors can determine if you are worthy of their benevolence.

Gad, you're thinking, I'm going to be judged by the comp-gods on nothing more than glowing numbers on a display terminal? Yes, you are. It's up to you to make sure those phosphorescent images portray you in the best light possible.

To understand why all of the ACES moves you've learned are so important, let's take a look at Wendy Wizard. A self-made entrepreneur, she's been to the Hats and Horns five times and has developed a formidable array of comp-counting skills. She's just checked into the hotel for the weekend with her boyfriend, Billy Joe Beau. Now we'll follow her as she winds her way through the system and watch as she massages her pals (the floormen), soothes a friend (the host), and ultimately fools the number-one enemy of everyone on the casino floor (the dreaded auditor, Waldo Weezer).

The Players
(In Order of Appearance)

Wendy C. Wizard—*The accomplished nightclub owner from Texas who counts comps in order to score an RFB vacation.*

Billy Joe Beau—*Wendy's boyfriend who spends his days at the pool and his nights in the lounge.*

Carey Casinova—*The good boss who ignores Wendy for hours, except when he's hitting on her.*

Gary Greedhead—*The good boss who angles for booty and gives Wendy an inflated rating.*

Mary Mary Kay—*The good boss who tries to snare Wendy in her network marketing scheme and gives her anything she wants.*

Mr. Whiskey—*The fun boss who parties with Wendy.*

Ima Movinup—*The bad boss who sends Wendy packing with a bad rating.*

Salvatore Suavo—*The host who gives Wendy a break.*

Waldo Weezer—*The evil auditor who tries to bust both Wendy and Salvatore.*

And a cast of hundreds, including cocktail waitresses, dealers, pit clerks, room-service waiters, pool attendants, limo drivers, front-desk clerks, bellhops, sky caps, maitre d's, and more!

Note. All the floormen are characterized in "Know Your Floorman."

Act I - Scene 1

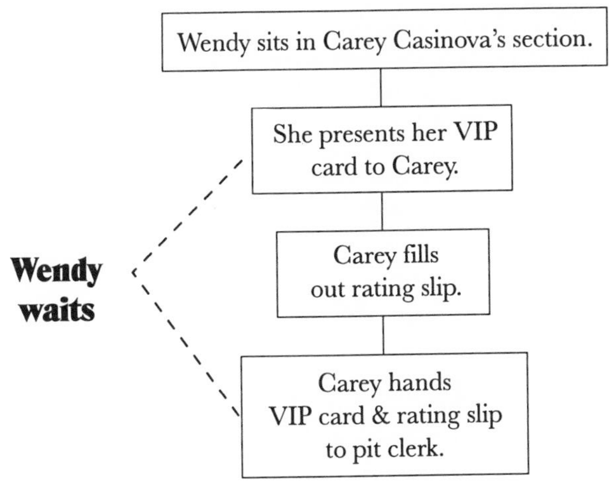

Wendy gives her VIP card to the floorman at 8:45 pm.

Floorman enters:

Wendy's VIP number,

dollar amount requested,

the pit she's playing in,

the game she's sitting at,

game type (double deck),

which seat she's sitting in,

the shift she's playing on (swing),

how many chips Wendy brought to the table ($200 black, $200 green).

HATS & HORNS

Player	VIP #	Available
Wendy Comp Wizard	*849749*	
1,000		
Time in	Time out	Markers
8:45 p		Chips
Pit *1*	Game *BJ-22*	Buy-in
Type *DD*	Seat *1* / Shift *S*	Money Plays
		Total
Average Bet	Comments *.2 B* *.2 G*	Out
Supervisor	Employee#	Win/Loss

Act I – Scene 2

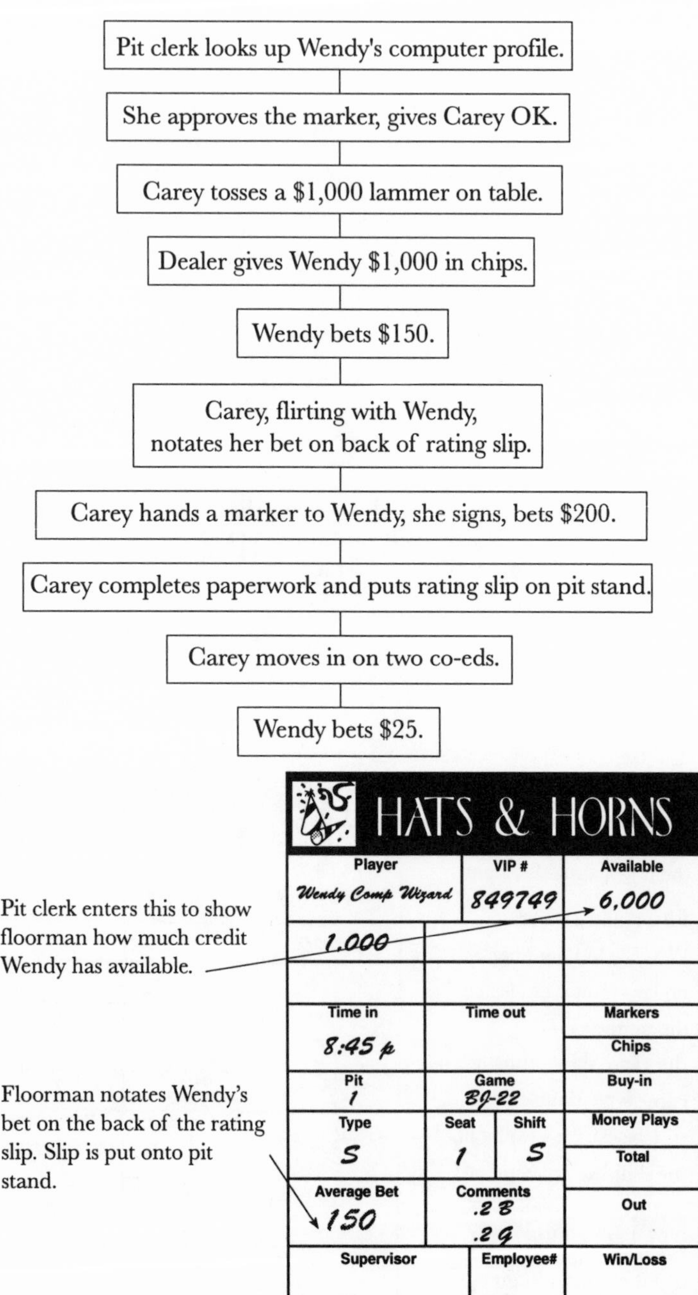

Pit clerk enters this to show floorman how much credit Wendy has available.

Floorman notates Wendy's bet on the back of the rating slip. Slip is put onto pit stand.

Act I – Scene 3

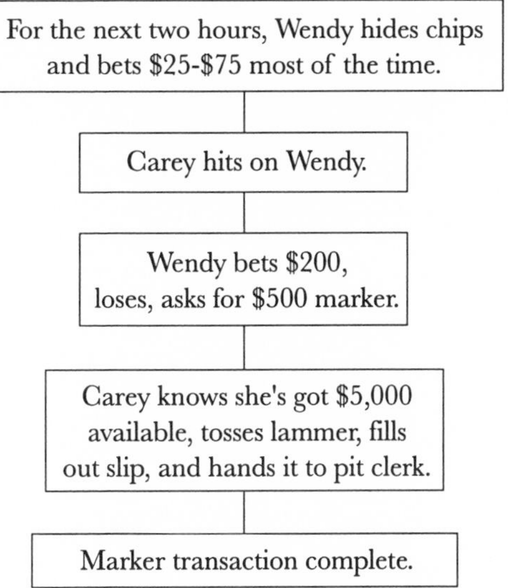

Wendy takes a $500 marker.

HATS & HORNS

Player	VIP #	Available
Wendy Comp Wizard	*849749*	*6,000*
1,000	*500*	
Time in: *8:45 p*	Time out	Markers / Chips
Pit: *1*	Game: *BJ-22*	Buy-in
Type: *DD*	Seat: *1* / Shift: *S*	Money Plays / Total
Average Bet: *150*	Comments: *.2 B .2 G*	Out
Supervisor	Employee#	Win/Loss

Act I – Scene 4

Wendy wins a couple of big bets.
She quits and hands dealer $1,000 in chips.

Dealer sets chips aside, notifies Carey.

Carey tells pit clerk: $1,000 "pick up."

Pit clerk gives Wendy's marker to Carey.

Carey gives marker to Wendy.

Wendy tears up marker, winks at Carey.

Carey sees that Wendy is out of chips and completes rating card.

Pit clerk enters rating card information into computer.

Wendy is "In the System" for this trip.

Carey circles Wendy's $1,000 marker as paid.

Wendy quits playing at 11:05 pm.

She had $500 *net* markers, $400 in chips lost.

Carey completes average bet; signs name, and employee number.

He circles Wendy's loss to let his boss know she's a live one.

HATS & HORNS

Player		VIP #	Available
Wendy Comp Wizard		849749	6,000
(1,000)	500		
Time in	Time out		Markers 500
8:45 p	11:05 p		Chips 400
Pit 1	Game BJ-22		Buy-in 0
Type DD	Seat 1	Shift S	Money Plays 0
			Total 900
Average Bet 150	Comments .2 B .2 G		Out 0
Supervisor C. Casinova	Employee# 44444		Win/Loss (900)

Act I – Scene 4 Notes

• While Carey Casinova was busy firing on all the other women in the pit, Wendy put more than $1,100 in her purse.

• The pit clerk entered the following information in the computer:

Hours played	2.33
Average bet	$150
Wendy's win/loss	[$900]

• The computer calculated:

Total betting handle	$20,970
House assumed edge	2.0%
House theoretical win	$419
Comp ratio	40%
Equivalency earned	$168

• Wendy earned $168 in comps and won $275.

Act II – Scene 1

Wendy takes and pays two markers.

She brought in no chips.

She leaves with no chips.

Graveyard

HATS & HORNS

Player	VIP #	Available
Wendy Comp Wizard	849749	5,500
1,000	1,000	
Time in: 8:00 a	Time out: 10:30 a	Markers: 0 / Chips: 0
Pit: 6	Game: BJ-5	Buy-in: 0
Type: DD	Seat: 6 / Shift: G	Money Plays: 0 / Total: 0
Average Bet: 100	Comments:	Out: 0
Supervisor: Gary Greedhead	Employee#: 55555	Win/Loss: 0

Act II - Scene 1 Notes

• Gary suspected that Wendy might be trying to fool him, but she brought him a tie on her last trip, so he didn't care. He gave her a $100 average bet.

• Wendy squirreled away $300 in greens, so she actually quit a winner and hightailed it to meet Billy Joe at the pool.

• The pit clerk entered the following information in the computer

Hours played	2.5
Average bet	$100
Wendy's win/loss	0

• The computer calculated the following information:

Total betting handle	$15,000
House assumed edge	2.0%
House theoretical win	$300
Comp ratio	40%
Equivalency earned	$120

• Wendy earned $120 in comps and won $300.

• Running total:

Time	4 hours 50 minutes
Win/loss	$575
Comps earned	$288

Act II - Scene 2

Wendy sits down in Mary Mary Kay's section.

Wendy hands Mary her VIP card, bets two blacks, and loses.

Wendy takes a $1,000 marker and bets $150.

Wendy chats with Mary, betting $100 a hand.

Mary breaks for 15 minutes, Wendy for 12.

Mary returns. Wendy bets $75 and loses five hands in a row.

Wendy takes a $500 marker and bets $25-$50 while Mary's busy.

Wendy asks Mary about network marketing, and bets $150.

Wendy wins a few, picks up her $1,000 marker and leaves empty.

Mary completes Wendy's rating slip and pit clerk posts it.

HATS & HORNS

Player	VIP #	Available
Wendy Comp Wizard	*849749*	*5,500*
1,000 (circled)	*500*	
Time in *3:20 p*	Time out *6:35 p*	Markers *500* Chips *200*
Pit *3*	Game *BJ-7*	Buy-in *0*
Type *S*	Seat *1* / Shift *D*	Money Plays *0* Total *700*
Average Bet *150*	Comments *.2 b*	Out *0*
Supervisor *Mary Mary Kay*	Employee# *77777*	Win/Loss *700* (circled)

Brings in two black chips.

Loses both black chips.

Act II - Scene 2 Notes

• Wendy chose a shoe game, because Mary was watching, and there was a slow dealer on a busy table.

• Mary likes Wendy. She gave her a $150 average bet.

• Wendy didn't squirrel away any chips.

• Pit clerk entered the following information in the computer:

Hours played	3.25
Average bet	$150
Wendy's win/loss	[$700]

• The computer calculated the following information:

Total betting handle	$29,250
House assumed edge	2.0%
House theoretical win	$585
Comp ratio	40%
Equivalency earned	$234

• Wendy earned $234 in comps and lost $700.

• Running total:

Time	8 hours 5 minutes
Win/Loss	[$125]
Comps earned	$522

Act II – Scene 3

Wendy sits down in Mr. Whiskey's section.

Wendy takes a $500 marker, bets $100 a hand, and loses it all.

Wendy takes another $500 marker and bets $50 when Mr. Whiskey is busy.

Wendy's losing. She takes two more $500 markers.

Mr. Whiskey breaks for 45-minutes. Ima Movinup relieves him.

Wendy bets $100 , then $150 to get even. She loses both bets.

Wendy quits. She leaves the table with $1,200 in chips.

Ima completes rating slip and pit clerk posts it.

HATS & HORNS

Player	VIP #	Available
Wendy Comp Wizard	849749	5,000
500	500	500
(500)		
Time in: 9:00 a	Time out: 10:45 p	Markers: 1,500 / Chips: 0
Pit: 6	Game: BJ-3	Buy-in: 0
Type: DD	Seat: 6 / Shift: G	Money Plays: 0 / Total: 0
Average Bet: 75	Comments:	Out: 1,200
Supervisor: Ima Movinup	Employee#: 66666	Win/Loss: (300)

Act II – Scene 3 Notes

• It was her last session, so she was conservative when she took her markers.

• Wendy quit because she likes to have fun and refuses to gamble on Ima's watch. Ima saw Wendy make two bets: one for $100 and one for $150. But she gave her a $75 rating.

• Wendy put $300 in her purse. She actually broke even. Ima put her down as a $300 loser.

• The pit clerk entered the following information in the computer:

Hours played	1.75
Average bet	$75
Wendy's win/loss	[$300]

• The computer calculated the following information:

Total betting handle	$7,875
House assumed edge	2.0%
House theoretical win	$158
Comp ratio	40%
Equivalency earned	$63

• Wendy earned $63 in comps and broke even.

• Running total:

Time	9 hours 50 minutes
Win/loss	[$125]
Comps earned	$585

• Wendy's vacation cost 20% of retail.

Computer Profile: Current Trip
for Hosts, Pit Bosses, and VIP Services

NAME:	Wendy C. Wizard	ID#: 275379		
ADDRESS:	2121 Lucky Lane	Borger, TX 79007		
PHONE:	702-555-1884			
BIRTHDAY:	10-09-47	SS#: 461-77-1121		
COMPANY:	The Bulldog Bar & Grille			
TITLE:	President			
PHONE:	800-244-2224			
BANK:	Borger Savings & Bad Loans			
ACCT. #:	XXXX-XX-XXXXX [1]			

TRIP HISTORY:	Current	01-29-94	09-14-93	06-02-93
CREDIT:	0	0	0	0
USED:	0	0	0	0
AVAILABLE:	0	0	0	0
DEPOSIT:	6,000 [2]	5,000	5,000	5,000
USED:	2,500 [3]	0	4,500	2,500
AVAILABLE:	3,500 [4]	5,000	500	2,500
TIME:	9.8 [5]	13.5	9.25	12.2
AVG. BET:	124 [6]	177	128	132
EQUIVALENCY:	585 [7]	1,002	568	773
COMPS USED:	785 [8]	1,244	988	933
DIFFERENCE:	[200] [9]	[242]	[420]	[160]
THEO. WIN [LOSS]:	1,462 [10]	2,504	1,421	1,932
ACTUAL WIN [LOSS]:	1,900 [11]	[1,000]	2,100	2,600
WIN/LOSS DIFF.:	438 [12]	[3,504]	679	668
FOUR HOUR CONV.:	152 [13]	199	148	134

COMMENTS: RFB [14]

1. Only collections has access to account number.
2. Wendy put $6,000 in casino cage.
3. Wendy quit playing with $2,500 in unredeemed markers.
4. Amount Wendy can pick up at cage before departure.
5. Total hours Wendy played.
6. Total of rated average bets divided by hours played.
7. Total comps earned.
8. Total comps used.
9. Comps earned less comps used; casino's perspective.
10. Casino's expected win.
11. Casino's actual win = Wendy's loss (so they think!)
12. Casino's expected win versus casino's actual win.
13. 9.8 hours x $124 ÷ 4 hours per day ÷ 2 days = $152
14. Shows Wendy was RFB when she checked in.

Act III

Wendy had planned to play another hour on her last session, but quit early when Ima showed up. She found Billy Joe in the lounge and they took in an early lunch. They went back to the room, stuffed a bottle of wine in the luggage, called to confirm that the limo was ready, and went downstairs to check out. While at the cage to pick up what remained of her cash deposit, she paid her respects to Salvatore Suavo, her favorite host. Sal was heading out to the golf course, so Wendy handed him a dozen Titleists, then asked if she'd be RFB next time in. Sal took a quick look at her computer profile and saw that she'd gone over her 40% equivalency by $200, but he also noticed that she'd lost $1,900 and had a reasonable four-hour conversion. So, what with her giving him the deluxe golf balls and all, he was a sport and told her she was welcome as his guest at the Hats and Horns any time.

Wendy bade him farewell and hopped in the limo with her beau. Billy Joe popped opened the sun roof and they enjoyed comped cocktails while cruising down the Strip as their RFB weekend came to an end.

Total cost? Wendy was out $125 in dealer tips and losses. Billy Joe picked up the airline tickets at $99 each and took care of the meal and show tips. It was a good deal for everyone. Or was it?

Epilogue

Not quite. Because Waldo Weezer, an I-know-everything-because-I-went-to-Wharton-and-you-didn't-and-numbers-don't-lie kind of guy, pursed his skinny lips and pulled up Wendy's lifetime computer profile to make sure that Sal didn't violate any of auditing's fail-safe edicts when he invited Wendy back for RFB. An IRS reject—judged too cold-blooded to work for the government—he beaded his beady eyes to see just what this Miss Wizard and her host were trying to put over on him. You see, not only does he distrust Wendy, he doesn't like this host. He doesn't like any hosts. Hosts play golf for free. He doesn't even know how to play. Hosts dine with guests in the gourmet room. Mr. Weezer, for all his exalted degrees, has to eat with the lowly floormen and dealers in the employee cafeteria. Hosts wear finely tailored suits. He shops at Sears. And hosts get to roam the entire property all day while he's stuck in a cubby hole that hardly reflects his (self) lofty status within the company. So it came as no surprise that he perused Wendy's computer profile with high hopes of finding a discrepancy that would put Mr. Suavo on the rack. What did he spot that will guarantee Sal unbearable torment? Nothing. Dang!

According to Wendy's lifetime record summary, which Mr. Weezer himself helped design and insisted on implementing to prevent player/host collusion, she lost more than $12,000 in six plays. Yes, he thought, her comps had significantly exceeded her equivalency, but Sal would argue that she's not a good blackjack player, that she's never asked for airfare, that all of her comps are soft comps, and that the bottom line is the casino makes money off of her. Mr. Weezer, unjustly stuck in his little world away from the real world, had to protect his little world and knew this was a battle he just wouldn't win. He begrudgingly gave Wendy's ongoing RFB status his holy stamp of approval and the host was spared. For now.

Computer Profile: Current Trip & Lifetime
for Auditors

NAME:	Wendy C. Wizard	ID#:	275379
ADDRESS:	2121 Lucky Lane	Borger, TX	79007
PHONE:	702-555-1884		
BIRTHDAY:	10-09-47	SS#:	461-77-1121
COMPANY:	The Bulldog Bar & Grille		
TITLE:	President		
PHONE:	800-244-2224		
BANK:	Borger Savings & Bad Loans		
ACCT. #:	121212-12-121		

TRIP HISTORY:	Current	LIFETIME	
CREDIT:	0	0	Total Trips = 6
USED:	0	0	
AVAILABLE:	0	0	
DEPOSIT:	6,000	31,000	
USED:	2,500	17,500	
AVAILABLE:	3,500	N/A	
TIME:	9.8	63.2	
AVG. BET:	124	133	
EQUIVALENCY:	585	4,035	
COMPS USED:	785	5,318	
DIFFERENCE:	[200]	[1,283][1]	
THEO. WIN [LOSS]:	1,462	10,087	
ACTUAL WIN [LOSS]:	1,900	12,600	
WIN/LOSS DIFF.:	438	2,513[2]	
FOUR HOUR CONV.:	152	140[3]	
COMMENTS:	RFB	Total Airfare = 0[4]	

1. Wendy's comps are $1,283 over her equivalency after 63 hours play. A tolerable variance.
2. Wendy's lifetime losses are $2,513 more than projected (She hides chips well). Numbers don't lie.
3. The four-hour conversion is based on all of Wendy's casino visits: three two-night stays and three three-night holiday weekends.
4. The key to Wendy's continued welcome is that she uses soft comps only.

8 Superstitions and Admonitions

The Great Myths

The great myths of all cultures and their underlying subcultures are usually a society's attempt to understand the unexplainable. They sprout from seeds of truth and are founded on a remarkable incident or sequence of incidents that have been repeated, altered, and embellished over time.

The gambling culture is no exception. It has its own rich lore, laden with universal myths, which almost all gamblers believe. The ones I've listed below are just a few examples of the useless drivel you'll be bombarded with while you ply your comp-wizard trade. You'll hear them near and far and they will befuddle you, exasperate you, and maybe even make you question the wisdom of *Comp City*. The upside is that once you understand that they are all wrong, they can work to your advantage.

Myth #1–Money-Management Systems Work

I've got a question for you. You're now an accomplished basic-strategy ACES blackjack player. You've won three big bets in a row while the boss is watching. She turns to another table. What do you do?

A. Bet the same. You're on a streak.
B. Bet more. You're on a streak.
C. Take one chip off the stack.
D. Bet the table minimum.

A. It's D. Unless you know something that has escaped Thorp, Griffin, Wilson, Wong and the other great mathematical and blackjack theoreticians, your "streak" means nothing. Blackjack mavens have computer-tested millions of hands utilizing every conceivable money-management model. In each and every instance, they have arrived at the same conclusion. Over time, your actual result will approximate the expected result, which is a product of the amount wagered times the house's built-in advantage. There is no system for betting your money that will overcome a negative expectation game. In other words, you will lose—money management or no money management.

The more you play blackjack, the more people will tell you of the times that they were "in the zone" and "knew" they were going to win. You'll be subjected to apocryphal stories about 21 players who won big using money management. It's all horseshit. Anyone who tries to peddle a system touting money management is at best ignorant and at worst a charlatan and a fraud.

Yes, you will have streaks, but you won't know when they're occurring because *all streaks are historical.* No one knows when he or she is "on" a streak or "in" a streak; you'll only know when you've "been in" a streak. This means that you should never vary your bet according to what happened in the past, because then you're making the erroneous assumption that past wins or losses somehow influence wins or losses in the future. As a comp counter, your only consideration is how much you should bet to get the goodies you want. Period.

The proof is simple. You're a logical person. Ask yourself: "At what point in a blackjack session does the *size* of my bet affect the odds so that the game is in my favor?" It never does.

Myth #2– Players Jumping In and Out of a Blackjack Game Upset the Sequence of the Cards

Let's dispel this myth in no uncertain terms. It makes absolutely no difference to your chances of winning or losing if another player comes into or out of a blackjack game. Sure, the future order of the cards is changed, but so what? You didn't know what it was in the first place. It's a stone cold fact: predisposed sequences of cards get "thrown off" equally good and bad when another player sits down on a game. However, by appearing to believe this myth, you can save a lot of money. Just sit out hands when these "card busters" come and go (remember "Play Slow"?). You can also skip a hand or two when your partner shows up and sits down.

Once in a while you'll encounter a player who will go so far as to ask you to wait until he loses a hand or the dealer shuffles before you make a bet. He'll explain that he's won a few hands in a row with the previous mix of players on the game and doesn't want the cards to change. If you come into a game and someone asks you to wait, tell him, "No problem," while you watch. If he wins, tell him you're glad you waited. It's a little better than even money that he'll lose. When that happens, smile and say, "I guess I should have sat down after all." He'll agree. Now you'll have a friend that you can compare hands with and slow the game down for the rest of the session.

Myth #3 It's Harder To Win at Blackjack With A Lousy Player at The Table

The way another person plays has absolutely no affect on whether you win or lose. It *will* affect how many hands you play. A blatantly bad blackjack player (who splits faces, doubles twelves, etc.) can empty a game faster than a red-wine-and-chili-dog fart, and if players leave the table you'll play more hands, which is bad. Most poor players aren't bad enough to run off the other players, though, and having a bad player on the game is actually a plus.

If you encounter an inept player, keep him on the game, making sure to take time to offer a few pointers. A "helpful" ACES player can slow the game down three rounds an hour just by conveying a little friendly advice, and up to five rounds an hour with a slow learner. My experience has been that men usually don't take advice too kindly, even if they don't have a clue about what they're doing. So you should be a little careful when trying to talk to them. Women novices, on the other hand, are usually open to all advice.

You can even bring your own bad player to the party. It's great sport to work with someone who has the rookie act perfected (females are best). If you are playing with a female partner, the less blackjack knowledge she appears to possess, the better it is for you. After you've played a couple of hands, have your covert partner sidle into a spot on the game. The first time she gets two face cards, have her split them. Before she gets her second bet out the other players will howl like they've just been prodded with hot pokers. Now she gets to ask why she shouldn't split tens. The whole table will be chock full of advice. After they've been so kind as to tell her how to play her own money, have her pull the money back and stand pat. It won't be long until all of the other "experts" on the game will be giving her constant advice, and she'll be able to slow the game down to reverse.

Whether you know the bad player or not, be sure to get maximum value from the situation. When you've finished your play, point to the player and make some comment to the boss such as, "Does this guy work for you?" as you shake your head and lament your extraordinary losses (trumped up, of course). He'll know what you mean, even though he doesn't understand that the poor guy's bad plays had absolutely no negative effect on you.

A related myth concerns the skill level of the player at the last seat (third base). Because the person sitting at third base acts last, just before the dealer, most blackjack players think that having an expert gambler there enhances their chances of winning. Obviously, they also feel that a poor player at third base costs them money. Again, another player's lack of skill has nothing to do with your own outcome. But to make sure that your partner's "bad" play gets the attention that it deserves, try to lock up third base for her.

Myth #4– If You Change Tables, You Can Change Your Luck

Yeah, right. Table hopping goes directly back to the streak theory that most suckers like to lean on when they're gambling. Not only does table hopping do nothing to change a streak of bad luck, it aggravates bosses who have to chase you around the pit and could, therefore, destroy your ratings.

On the subject of luck, a surprising number of bosses apply this myth to changing a player's good luck to bad. Let me tell you a story about something that happened at Lake Tahoe in the '80s that'll show you just how far the really superstitious in the gambling business will go to change a gambler's run of good fortune.

The shift manager was Bob the Bleeder, the kind of boss who believes that there are only two kinds of blackjack players: losers and cheaters. A drunk gambler had already tattooed his shift for about ten large. He turned to Lenny, a floorman who'd been watching the action for the past two hours. "Did you change the cards?" the Bleeder barked. Lenny nodded, "Yes."

"Did you change dealers?" Bob hissed. Lenny nodded, "Yes," again.

"Change them again!" Bob roared. Lenny took a dealer off a dead game and put her in. The blackjack player won three straight $500 bets. Bob turned to Lenny and glared. "Well?"

Lenny had just about had it with the Bleeder. "Well what?" he snapped.

"Do something!" Bob bellowed.

Lenny walked over to the table, pulled out the plastic paddle used to shove money into the drop box, turned it around, and stuck it back in its slot.

"There, that ought to do it," he said, as he smiled at the Bleeder.

The gambler won another $10,000 in the next five minutes. The Bleeder's sense of humor matched his tableside demeanor and Lenny found himself looking for work. On the bright side, Lenny is now an assistant shift boss at a premium Las Vegas resort and Bob is sweating the money for an Indian tribe in a converted barn somewhere in the Midwest.

The point is, and I can't emphasize it enough (although you might be getting tired of hearing it), *nothing you do that's non-mathematical will change the mathematics of the game.* Since you have an edge with ACES, you want as much playing time as possible credited toward your rating, so the less you hop around, the higher your ratings will be.

Now that you know you shouldn't hop around indiscriminately, there are a few good reasons for changing tables more than once during any single playing session. If you're unlucky enough to get a second rude dealer in a row, you'll want to make one more move, and it should be to another boss' area. Also, if you're on a game where another player is knocking the casino stiff, when a boss or two start hovering around and sweating the action, take a break or move to another game. It's a good bet someone will be gunning the big player and everyone else on the game, trying to detect collusion of some sort among the players and the dealer. And you won't want to be making ACES moves with that kind of heat.

If a dealer keeps making hands and beating everyone, the table will soon empty on its own. Since you don't ever want to play alone, this is a prime time to move. And it looks like a natural reaction to the bosses. You'll also want to leave a game, even if it's full, if a speed demon suddenly shows up to deal. These gunslingers are so fast that even if you weren't counting comps, you'd probably get dizzy trying to keep up and have to leave anyway.

Myth #5–
You Need a Sophisticated Card-Tracking System to Consistently Win at Blackjack

Nonsense. ACES is the most powerful long-term, no-heat, please-come-back-and-let-us-give-you-something-you-don't-deserve gambling method known to man.

Where Women Stand

Play The Cards You've Been Dealt

Most of the things I'm about to say aren't (necessarily) my own opinions, only an honest rendition of how the overwhelmingly male-dominated gambling industry has come to view and treat women.

Up until fifty years ago, only men participated in the business on either side of the tables. It wasn't until the 1940s that Raymond "Pappy" Smith broke tradition by hiring women to deal, and welcoming women to gamble, at his Harold's Club casino in Reno. Even so, half a century later the profile of the player most desired by the casino is male. In the eyes of the casino bosses, men are the real *gamblers*, who live for the moment, compelled to take a ride on a crash course where financial disaster looms around every corner (often to the dismay of the women with them). Bosses love men who have a gambling death wish, because they know the guy's bound to eventually blow everything he has, and if it's on their watch, they might even get a little credit when he goes down in flames.

Most bosses can't picture a woman crashing and burning. Women, they assume, play for fun, not out of an irrational need to risk money. Thus, the male bosses don't have much respect for women gamblers. This lack of respect, though personally annoying, presents a powerful opportunity for comp wizardry. Bosses don't feel there's a reason to fear or suspect women; it's up to you to reinforce, and take advantage of, that notion.

Getting comped is an art, a nurturing art. Women nurture. Ergo, women get more comps, especially from men. The power of the pen is a little-understood perk in the casino business. There's something downright sensual about being able to lavish meals and rooms upon those *you* deem deserving. Comps don't cost man-bosses a thing, and giving them away to the ladies makes them feel like big shots. That feeling of control and power, particularly for the guys who grew up hard, is addicting. As a woman, knowing this about man-bosses can take you a long way.

Egos and More Egos

The following are new moves to an old, old game. By now, your instincts and better judgment should automatically signal you *when* to play this game, and your comfort zone will let you know *if* you can pull it off with impunity. It might be a sad commentary on the human condition, but it should come as no surprise: by stroking a man-boss' ego, you'll have a definite advantage.

Playing it smart involves using some of the mechanics of ACES—with a feminine edge. For example, you can slow the game way down by calling a man-boss over any time you'd like some "expert advice" on how to play a hand. Of course, when you call him over, you'll have your biggest bet of the day out, and he'll remember that when he completes your rating.

Here's a shocker: men like women to notice them. When you sit down and ask him how long you need to play to get a comp for the coffee shop, be attentive. Let the conversation flow. That doesn't mean you need him to think you're on the make. Just let him know, in your own subtle way, that you think he's important. You'll be putting yourself in no real danger. Even if he has the time, freedom, and inclination to hit on you while he's working, he has to leave the property at the end of his shift. There's not a casino in town that will let a boss linger around the pit after he gets off work—for any reason. When he's finished, he's gone, and that's that. Then you can try it again on the next guy.

Of course, if you're playing cards with a man-partner, let him know what you're up to before you flirt with the man-boss, or you might draw a little fire yourself. If he's in on the deal, it can be fun for both of you as you watch the man-boss fawn. It's not too tough on the ego, either.

Laugh at the boss' jokes. Even if you've heard them a hundred times before, laugh again. It's always ego deflating for a man to tell a joke to a lady and have her say, "I heard that one." He's supposed to be the guy in the know. Let him think that. It doesn't cost you anything, and he'll be pleased when you chuckle, even though you're laughing for reasons he'll never be aware of.

Note. There's rarely any justification for you to play in a section with an unknown female boss. In addition to losing the advantages described above, women bosses are better at ferreting out the schemers and scammers. It's a fact. Women bosses are more conscientious, more suspicious, more territorial, and hawk their games instead of the cocktail waitresses.

Chauvinism

Twenty to thirty years ago, any attractive woman playing alone in Las Vegas was unjustly assumed by most everyone to be a hooker. If a single woman sat down to play a little blackjack and was friendly to a male customer on the game, it was his prerogative to discretely inquire if she was "workin'." Chauvinism still runs rampant, but the worst thing you're likely to encounter from the bosses (other than the ordinary stuff, like being stared at and occasionally being hit on) is that they'll refer to you as a "girl."

It's a fact of life in Las Vegas; no matter how old you are, most of the men, players and bosses alike, will still call you a "girl." I'm just letting you know up front, so you don't have a stroke when you sit down to play in one of the older clubs and hear some guy, who appears otherwise to be a gentleman, utter such gems as, "Jesus Christ, the cocktail girls are old in here."

You'll also, of course, have to be aware of the men you play with on the games. Many of them will be politely indifferent to you, intent on their cards and chips. Some will be friendly, and again you'll have to rely on your instincts to determine your response, but getting cozy can really slow down a game, especially if you can involve the dealer. The potential is there, however, for the odd man out to get nasty.

If another player is insulting you, it won't last long. Casinos are scared to death of harassment lawsuits. And, if they won't put up with harassment from a customer, they certainly aren't going to stand for it from a boss. If you do encounter any overt acts of harassment from a man-boss, and you've got the nerve for it, tell him you feel that he's harassing you, and you need to get away from the game, and you probably need some dinner to cool down, and you'd hate to say anything to his boss, so maybe he could make it a comp for four and you'll just forget the whole thing. Soooeee! You'll get the comp alright, no matter how many rules he has to break. All it takes is one sexual harassment incident in his employee file and he is virtually finished in the industry. Men, this move will not work with female floormen, so forget it.

Comp Counters Who Count Cards

Do you know how to count cards and win? If the answer is yes, then you, my friend, have the absolute nuts from this day forward. Think about it. If the bosses ignore you all night long, you can combine comp counting with card counting and win the equivalent of two bets an hour (one in money, one in stuff). If there's heat, cut your bet spread down to a level that's breakeven, and you'll still earn great comps. If you want deep cover, how's this? You can pound booze and never look at anyone else's cards all night long and still be an overall favorite because of the comps. Meanwhile, no one on that shift will ever suspect you're a counter, and you'll be welcome forever. This book was written to show basic-strategy-level blackjack players how to crush casinos by earning comps valued at ten times their gambling losses. Every tactic portrayed in *Comp City* can also be used by an accomplished card counter, and you won't even have to fade the losses.

Although I've played my share of winning blackjack, I don't pretend to be a world-class blackjack player on a level with the legendary counters who earn hundreds of thousands a year. But based on my extensive experience on both sides of the table, I believe I have some insight worth discussing here. Some of these tips you'll be familiar with and some may be new to you. A few of them threw me off when I was working the floor. If they're not already in your repertoire, incorporating them might gain you years of card-counting longevity.

Laying Cover

You know all about cover, while most bosses don't even know what it means. But that's not to imply that you should underestimate the enemy. A few bosses in every casino have read the books and a handful of them can actually play a winning game. Although their numbers are few, you should assume that at least one sharp boss lurks in every joint.

This is paramount. Don't take your money back when the dealer shuffles. You're giving up a little, but pulling the money back confirms all of the boss' worst suspicions, especially if the shuffle was prompted by your big bet.

Watching the Boss

If a boss catches you looking at him, smile and call him over. Ask him for something—a comp, directions, a recommendation for a show, anything—but don't ever let him see you divert your eyes away from his. It's a dead giveaway that you're up to something.

Tipping

Tip the dealers. You should budget at least 5% of your expected win for the dealers. If you're a big player with a high hourly return, it's almost imperative that you give the dealers at least 10% of your expectation. So what if your profit is reduced by a little blood money? I've had hundreds of conversations in pits about counters and 90% of the bosses believe that counters don't tip. Tipping will buy you years of playing time.

By the same token, if you're betting more than $100 a hand, tip the cocktail waitress $5, no matter what. The bosses will think that you're a sport and they know that counters are anything but.

Cover Bets

If a boss is watching, you want to look like a sucker. When you win a hand and he's watching, bet it up no matter what. If you lose, you can go up or down. (If the count's good, bet it up. If it's bad, bet it down.) A boss only has to see you do this two or three times in a session to be convinced that you're a negative-progression or money-management player, not a counter. It will reduce your expected win by a few bucks. But I see it as a valid expense of doing business. Unless you're the type who plays till you're barred, it's the only way to go. There are people in this country who play solo, live in penthouse casino suites, and make half a million dollars a year because they're not afraid to tip and lay cover. Some of these guys lay $500 in cover during a $1,000 session. Guess what the net result is here? $500 an hour—after hour, after hour, after hour.

Sucker Plays That Work

If you want to get a boss thinking you're a stone sucker, slam that first shot of whiskey and bet a quarter for yourself and a quarter for the dealer on the first hand.

Take insurance when you have a natural. You might even

insure your twenties when the boss is watching. Do it with conviction and without hesitation (you know you have to protect those good hands). It'll come up infrequently so it won't cost too much overall, but it leaves a lasting impression with the bosses. A move with similar value is not hitting a soft 18 against a nine, ten, or ace. The word is out on this play; hitting the 18 identifies you as a player in the know.

There are other plays. It's fun to use Stanford Wong's *Blackjack Count Analyzer* software program to discover those that cost you only a few dollars in expectation for hundreds of dollars worth of cover. If you're a comp counter first, and only use card counting to defray your over-the-table losses, these moves are inexpensive, indeed.

Appearance

I never trusted a guy who looked like he woke up just to play blackjack. Don't come in on graveyard shift between 4 and 7 am rubbing the sleep out of your eyes. No true degenerate gambler (which is what you want them to think you are) ever had to set an alarm clock to tell him when it was time to play. Most graveyard bosses are on the lookout for the ghouls nesting upstairs who descend on the tables before sunrise. If you're playing the graveyard shift, stay up all night or make your plays later in the morning when you can wake up naturally.

Don't drink mineral water. Don't ask me why, but an inordinate number of counters drink mineral water. Get juice, coffee, tea, Dr. Pepper, but stay away from the bottled waters. As far as the bosses are concerned, anyone sitting in a casino drinking anything that smacks of health is not to be trusted.

Conduct

Introduce yourself to the boss and give him your VIP card. Talk to him. A lot. If you want to enlist a co-conspirator for the weekend, buy your favorite floorman a $25 three-teamer for Sunday's games (Monday if you're staying that long). The boss will be your buddy for the next couple of days. If you win big, yuck it up. Until you've established a pattern of winning (five or more sessions), if your cover is good enough, there's no way they'll throw you out of the casino for counting. When they like you, some bosses will even warn you if the heat is on upstairs.

Hiding Chips

As a pro, you know you're doing well if you win an average of one big bet an hour. All you have to do is *hide* one big bet an hour and you'll be doing great in terms of preserving your welcome. Unless you're playing head up, where the boss can determine exactly how many chips are missing from the rack, you can swing with up to two bets an hour and you'll look like a loser forever. Most places are reluctant to bar "losers," unless they're blatant scufflers.

Buying In

If you're a cash player, don't ever buy in with a lot of currency. Don't buy in for $500 and make $15 bets, for example; gamblers don't do it that way. If your eventual big bets will be $100, buy in for $100 and start by playing quarters. Win or lose, you'll be able to move your bets into your normal spread within a few minutes. If you're losing, it looks natural for you to come out of your pocket, especially when you want to bet big. If you're winning, it looks like you're making a parlay play—also very natural. If you bet $5 for the dealer and $25 for yourself early on, you'll look real easy!

When you come out of pocket, let the money play. I haven't seen five counters in my life who let money play (unless they were trying to get around Regulation 6-A).

Drinking

Buy an O'Douls or a Sharps at the bar. Pour it in a glass. Take it to the table with you. When the waitress comes by, ask for a shot of whiskey, making sure the boss hears you. Slug it down when the boss is watching. Then chug the O'Douls. The next time the waitress comes by, order a real beer and sip it slowly. Time for a break. Take the beer and get rid of it. Buy another fake beer, pour it into a glass, mosey back to the table, and chug it while you're talking to the boss. Order another real beer. Then you sip again. When it's a quarter gone (half an hour or so), order another cold one. By now you'll have to go to the bathroom again and, yep, go get some more fake stuff. In a two-hour session you'll consume the equivalent of a drink and a half and look like you're getting smashed. It works.

Wonging

Start your play with the best of it. Wong into a rich shoe and make those important big bets when you have a big edge. If you're good, you can back count the game next to you (make sure you're in a position to watch the other layout) and pop into that one when it gets juicy. Just let the boss know you're moving.

Getting Rid of Bosses

If a boss is hawking your game, get in his face. Be nice, but bombard him with requests. Ask him for reservations for the show. He'll have to do it, even if he doesn't want to. If he comes back to your game, ask him for reservations for dinner. If he comes back again, ask him for a comp for the coffee shop. Keep this up long enough and he'll stay as far away from your game as he can get. The problem is, he'll also get mad, which will probably have an adverse effect your rating. If you are playing primarily for the comps, you'll have to tolerate a boss' scrutiny.

Safety Tips

This section is directed toward those souls who, just like me, seem to have no trouble finding trouble. One of life's irrefutable truths is that it's a whole lot easier and cheaper to get *into* trouble than it is to get out of it. Armed with these timeless tips about common traps that have snared more than their share in Glitter Gulch, you can save yourself a little money and a lot of grief.

Wedding Chapels

Do you know why divorces cost so much? Because they're worth it. More than 152,000 people fell in love and got married in Las Vegas last year. Love? Well, maybe not, not when you consider the ease of getting married here (no blood test, no waiting period) and of losing control. To some people, Las Vegas' magic spell looks a lot like love.

Getting married in Las Vegas is as cheap as it is easy and informal. You can get married here in a jogging suit, bikini, or a $5,000 gown, and believe it or not, without getting out of the car.

So what's the safety tip? I'll sum it up in one word. Don't! Don't ever decide to get married *after* you get to this town. Unless you *both* decide to get married while you're still sane and sober back home and *then* hop in a plane and come out here to ratify your life together in one of our temples of love, you'll be one sorry sucker come morning.

Sure, you thought he was some kind of hero after he smacked the blackjack tables for $8,500 and got the honeymoon suite, but how good do you think he's going to look tomorrow after you both wake up hungover and he tells you he's lost back most of the score? (He's probably lying—check his wallet when he's in the shower.)

All right, so you're going to ignore my expert advice and do it anyway. The Marriage Bureau downtown is open from 8 am to midnight on weekdays and 24 hours Friday through Sunday. Fork over 35 bucks and you're ready to tie the Gordian knot. God, this is a cruel town. Now it's on to a chapel to pop for another $50-$10,000, with a standard $35 toke for the ministers who make the Jimmies (Swaggert and Baker) seem downright sincere.

If you're on a budget and can't afford a chapel and are still looking to sanctify your "love," walk across the street from the License Bureau to the Commissioner of Civil Marriages (open the same hours), where a deputy bureaucrat will, without sermon or fanfare, pronounce you man and wife for $35 bucks. (If you ask me, it ought to cost about $50,000 to get married and divorces should be free. You don't suppose the attorneys have anything to do with putting this deal together, do you?)

"Okay, Max," you say. "Enough of the sermonizing. We're getting married anyway. What's the best deal?"

The best deal is to get it comped. A lot of the casinos have wedding chapels and if you're RFB, you can get the whole sucker handed to you on a flowered platter. Unless you're a big, big player (at least $500 a hand), they won't pay for incidentals, such as photographs ($50 and up), flowers ($50 and up), tips, and limos, but they will give you the room and it's convenient to exchange vows right in your hotel, especially if some friends have joined the celebration.

If you go to a chapel, they'll rip you apart with the live organ music, videotapes of the wedding, renting tuxedos and gowns, buying rings, cakes, garters, and all the trimmings. If you show any speed at all it'll cost you at least $500-$700 to get married away from the casino. Take a comp and keep the money—you're going to need it.

Most wedding chapels require at least a one-hour lead time. If she's in labor and you want to make it legal on the way to the delivery room, you can save a lot of money and time at the Little White Chapel, Las Vegas' own drive-thru wedding window. Push a button and a minister sticks his head out the driveway window and starts preaching while the wedding march blares over outdoor speakers. Make sure you turn down your radio or you might miss it. I don't think burgers and fries come with the ceremony, but for the money they probably should, though the burgers might make the experience a taste too formal.

Jewelry

Just for grins, check out the prices in the casino's jewelry shop after you check in, when you're sober and still semi-rational. You'll see that a Seiko watch, for example, costs about twice as much in the friendly hotel shops as it does at the Zales back home. How do these gift shops get away with selling the stuff for twice retail? By relying on two time-tested human traits: guilt and vanity. If you've been real bad, sneaking away to Las Vegas, leaving your lover behind, and having the best time ever since reaching the age of consent, and if you've got any kind of heart at all, you'll probably feel a tad remorseful about going AWOL. And if you happen to have a pocketful of chips and a snoot full of booze while you're waiting for the limo to take you home, you'll be glad to pay double for something she probably doesn't want anyway. Don't go in there. You're supposed to be a percentage player by now. If you want to make a heads-up play, take her a slug of hundred dollar bills. That's *always* appropriate.

So much for the guilt trip. What if you've just snagged some sweetie on a game? She happens to drag you by the shopping arcade on the way up to the room and stops in front of the jewelry stand, just to "window shop." Don't let your ego get the best of you during this trying time by showing off and tossing your hard-earned green on the counter. The only thing to do to get out of that one (*and* continue up to the room after) is *lie*. Tell her you'll bring her back to shop in the morning. Don't worry. It's a long time till morning, and by then the bloom might be long off the rose.

Escort Services

I doubt that it's true, but there's a rumor floating around Las Vegas that an escort actually escorted a guy somewhere years ago. If she did, she probably got hoorayed out of town, so I won't include her in my long-distance evaluation of the trade. There are 20 full pages of ads for these soiled doves in the Yellow Pages, but you'll have to look under "Entertainers" now. If the Yellow Page ads don't meet your fancy, any one of the scuzballs standing outside the nice hotels will be glad to hand you four-color flyers of these male and female "dancers" complete with phone numbers. It's none of my business what you do to get yourself through the night, but there are obvious, and subtle, dangers inherent with the escort trade. Be advised.

• The legal brothels 60 miles from Las Vegas conduct weekly checks for the wide array of sexually transmitted diseases now available to the unprotected. Because they require all clients to use protection, there has (reportedly) never been a case of a licensed working prostitute having AIDS at one of the legal establishments (although occasionally applicants have been rejected for employment after being screened and found to be HIV positive). Since the "entertainers" are unregulated, no such protection exists. Bad odds here, folks. If you're determined to do something dirty on your trip to southern Nevada, travel about 60 miles to Nye County. It could save your life.

• If you'd still like companionship in your room, it works like this. You call up the girl's number from the Yellow Pages or a sex rag. You give your name, room number, and preference of entertainer. Then Bambi or Cherry or Sugar gives you a call to discuss price. The going rate is about $150 for a "dance." Totally nude. If you want something more (and you wouldn't have called if you didn't, because you can watch totally nude dancers at 10% of the price in several local dives), you'll have to negotiate the "tip" face to face. Sort of. The going rate for "extras" is about $100-$1,000, depending on how drunk, stupid, or desperate you are.

• When your little love muffin shows up, don't tell her how

much money you have, because pretty soon that's how much money she'll have.

• Don't ever go to sleep while she's still there. If you do, when you wake up you'll be lucky to find your shoes and underwear.

Hookers

The rules for entertainers apply to hookers, with some notable exceptions.

• The blatant hookers are usually more honest.

• If the hooker is working the bar, she may have a pass from someone in management (never the owners), which means she probably won't rob you once she gets to the room.

• You can negotiate with a hooker before you go upstairs and then leave the rest of your money in the casino's safe deposit box.

• If you pick her up on the street, you're putting yourself in immediate danger of being mugged, dosed, VD'd, or worse.

• It's a felony for an AIDS-infected hooker to solicit or engage in prostitution. So she's committing a felony. Big deal. You're still vulnerable to the virus and although one little tryst might or might not do the trick, that's one lottery you really don't want to play.

Trick Rollers

You'll at least have a vague idea of what you're getting yourself into when you hire a hooker or entertainer to come to your room. There's a much more dangerous breed out there, known as trick rollers. Often posing as school teachers, accountants, or lonely girls on a weekend's runner in Las Vegas, they're usually pleasantly attractive (but never dressed like hookers) and somewhat aloof when you first meet. Then, after an hour or so of hearing your witty rejoinders and banter with dealers and bartenders, she'll slowly become attracted to you. After another half hour (and a couple more drinks), she'll wait for you to suggest that you go up to your room. When you do, she'll slip you a mickey (elephant tranquilizers) that'll knock you cold. Then she'll rifle through your belongings and take everything you have. You get to wake up 12 hours later (if you haven't been fed an overdose) with the worst hangover in the history of revelry. Then you'll have to call your wife and make up some lie about getting mugged in the hallway. And finally, you'll have to decide if you want to go through the legal circus. Gulp.

The tough thing about trick rollers is that they're hard to spot. Luckily, there's one sure warning sign that can keep you on your toes and away from these vile creatures of the night. If she's cute and she thinks you're slick, then something's wrong. I mean, c'mon! What nice girl in her right mind would want to go up to the room with (choose one) a bald headed, overweight, drunk, married man; a young egomaniac with the morals of a goat; or an old geezer who's probably good for at least three minutes before the pacemaker goes off. You can't win. Go watch a dirty movie in your room and save yourself a lot of heartbreak.

Sex-Tease Clubs

A new style of club has popped up around town over the last five years. They're known to locals as "sex-tease clubs" (they call *themselves* "singles clubs").

A bunch of damn-near naked women hang out by the front door, licking their chops when a sucker comes around to strike up a conversation. They'll point to a glass booth where a big ugly guy is collecting admissions and paying off cabbies who deliver the marks for a kickback. The cover charge is anywhere from $10 to $50, depending on how well-heeled and dumb you look. The girls are extra friendly, so you pay. Now you go in and talk to a beefy bartender who negotiates a deal for you. He'll sell you a bottle of champagne (nonalcoholic, which they don't tell you) for the reasonable price of, oh, $1,000 (and unlike Sea World, Mr. Family Man, they *do* take American Express). For that you're promised a "party" with a couple of the girls, your choice from the bevy of beauties lounging by the door, in a private room. When you ask what you get for your party, he'll say something like, "You're at least 21, aren't you?" and you'll grin and mumble something snappy like, "Uh huh." Then he'll tell you you can do anything you want.

The little trollops take you in the back and pop the bubbly and sip it with you. When you suggest that they get naked and do disgusting things to you, they promise unspeakable pleasures to come—after another couple of $1,000 bottles. When push literally comes to shove, the girls tell you that prostitution is illegal in Las Vegas and all they can do is share your drinks. Now you get angry and start screaming. This brings the body builders who have black belts in bone breaking; they throw you out the back door and if you're lucky you won't get thumped in the process. Meanwhile, they pocket your thousands, which you could have parlayed into several $10,000 Las Vegas vacations with a respectable lady from your local haunts. Feeling stupid yet?

This scam has been going on for years and the local cops and Chamber of Commerce have a very hard time closing these clubs down. For now, they flourish, so stay away.

One way to recognize a sex-tease club is to ask for a scotch or a bourbon, or a beer. That they can't serve alcohol is a dead giveaway, because most of the legitimate topless places have liquor licenses, but the ripoff joints can't get them. Another clue is that the guys taking the money are always big and mean. If you're with a couple of buddies and reasonably sober, these clubs are fun to visit just to get a peek at the suckers being scammed. Once they start to put the arm on you, tell them you've only got a couple bucks left and they'll be glad to quickly show you to the door.

Metro Police

When you're walking off your 5,000-calorie free meals, you'll probably see guys wearing yellow shirts and black helmets riding around together on bicycles. Although it may be 3 am and they look like choir boys, they aren't. They're cops. There's no question that they're the most liberal cops in America when it comes to letting you walk around with open bottles and glasses of booze, and they truly are masters at dealing with drunks on foot. But don't ever let their friendly demeanor fool you into thinking that they won't hurt you. At any given time, thousands of tourists are strolling the Strip and most of them are carrying cash. I have spent hundreds of hours walking between the casinos and I've never seen anyone get mugged on the Strip or downtown on Fremont Street. Why? Simple. You just don't mess with Las Vegas cops and the professional bad guys know it.

If you challenge one of Las Vegas' finest to fisticuffs or even "dis" one in front of his fellow bike soldiers, he'll stomp the crap out of you, hog tie you, and toss you in jail before you can squeal "Miranda." And if you continue to make trouble, it'll probably get worse.

Unreasonable force? Maybe, but I like being able to walk the streets at midnight with a couple of thousand in my pocket. If you're out on the Strip or downtown and screw up and they're on your case, be humble and show them the respect they demand and they'll do anything within reason to sort out the problem before running you in. If you take one step over that imaginary line and challenge them, you're in deep trouble.

Security Guards

A much more dangerous breed of gun-toting cowboys is the wannabe cops, casino security guards. Former football players, fighters, military men, and NRA extremists who couldn't get past police department psycho screenings, the only way they can justify their pay is by finding someone doing something wrong. It could be you, so be careful, especially when you're drunk. While the new-age joints train their guards in advanced customer-handling techniques, some of the older places still take great pleasure in sending human hamburger to the emergency rooms.

For example. Binion's Horseshoe's guards make the cops look like wimps. You can raise hell in there, you can win a million dollars in there, you can spill drinks in there, you can puke on the table in there, but don't ever get on the muscle in there. Not with the dealers, not with the customers, not with the bosses, and *especially* not with the guards. If they ask you to leave, say, "Yes sir," and hit it. Immediately. For more than 40 years, the Binions have prided themselves on dispensing swift western justice, so don't push your luck. If you want to fight in Las Vegas, go to the gym.

Cheating

Entire books have been written on how to cheat casinos and how to catch the cheaters when they do. The good cheats use moves that aren't written in any books. This is advice for you, an amateur gambler and professional comp counter. Don't even think about cheating.

What, me cheat, you say? Let's suppose you have a $25 bet out, you're sitting in the last spot, and you're dealt a blackjack. Some lout on the other end of the table is giving the dealer a hard time and she's not paying any attention to you. So, with a couple of beers to cloud your mind, you put another chip on your bet.

What's the worst thing that could happen?

The worst thing that could happen is that the dealer, a boss, the eye in the sky, or another player sees you. If any one of them notifies the casino manager about it, the bosses will run back the videotape of the game. If they verify that you "capped" the bet, they'll haul you into the back room. There, you'll wait for Gaming Control Board cops to show up and arrest you for cheating at gambling, a felony. If you don't have a record, you'll get off with a fine and probation, but you'll have a crime of moral turpitude against you the rest of your life. Try to get any kind of professional license with that hanging on you, pal. Forget it.

But won't they give you a break if they know that you're a good guy with too many beers in you? No, they won't give you a break. They don't have a choice. If they even suspect anyone has cheated, for any amount, and don't tell the Gaming Control agents, they can lose their gaming license, which means they're out of business. In early 1993, a 22-year-old kid about ready to graduate from college in Arizona capped a bet for $25 in a major resort on the Strip and was arrested. The case is still in legal limbo, but you can bet he and his parents are wishing today that he'd never made that stupid move. Is it worth an extra $25? Not even close. It's something you should only try if you want to compare the difference between room-service early-morning steak-and-eggs to a county-jail bologna-and-white-bread breakfast.

Note. If you want to take your comp hustling to new levels and learn how to count cards, don't be afraid of what casinos will do to you. Case law has determined that card counting is not cheating, only taking advantage of the casino's policies and procedures. Go ahead and count, but be warned. Card counting is a grueling hard-fought grind that's best left to those with little opportunity to make money at a legitimate job.

Chip Switch

It's an old move, but if you're new to Las Vegas, it'll be new to you. You'll see someone standing outside a casino. He'll act drunk. He'll hold out a handful of chips and tell you he was thrown out and can't go back in to cash out. He'll hand you a few hundred dollars worth of chips and offer to discount them if you'll buy them off of him. Don't do it. They could be counterfeit. If they're not, you missed a bargain. If they are and you try to cash them, you're in for one of the most interesting experiences of your life, because you'll get to test the validity of everything I've already told you about the horrors of Las Vegas cops, security guards, Gaming Control Board agents, and the wonders of Wonder Bread.

There aren't as many chip switchers as there used to be when casinos that changed hands would sell the old chips for souvenirs for about 25¢ each. The best sucker play I ever heard of happened with a group of college guys from UNLV. The Thunderbird Hotel had just changed hands. One kid, who's now the director of marketing for a big-time casino, had a father who was a big boss at the old Thunderbird. His dad kept a couple of boxes of the old green and black chips in his closet as souvenirs. The kid found them. He knew they weren't any good at the T-Bird anymore, but he had an idea.

He rented a room at the Desert Inn. Then he walked down the Strip to the Thunderbird where he met up with three of his chums. They all got in a taxi and told the driver to take them back to the DI. The kid went on to tell the driver that they'd just won over $7,000 and showed him the chips. The driver was impressed. When he got to the DI he handed the driver a legitimate $25 chip from the new Thunderbird and told him he wanted some girls up to the room. Now, in the old days, every cab driver on the Strip knew a bell captain with a stable of working girls. The driver parked his cab and went right up to the DI's bell captain, an old running mate. The standard deal then was 40% for the bell captain and 60% for the girls. The driver and bell captain agreed to split his share and the calls were made.

In about 30 minutes four call girls came to the renegade's door. The boys showed the nice girls the chips and offered them $1,000 apiece for a deluxe tag-team four-on-four love-fest. Of course the ladies agreed and the love-o-rama was on. According to the stories, and I've heard them from three of the guys involved, it was two hours of non-stop, we're-gonna-go-to-hell-for-doing-this debauchery. When they were finished, they gave each of the ladies a $500 tip and told them they'd like to see them the next night, too.

Talk about happy hookers! They went downstairs and jumped in the friendly driver's taxi and raced to the Thunderbird, only to find that the chips were bogus. I've heard that the scene at the cage that night was probably more entertaining than the romp the girls had engaged in earlier (but I doubt it).

Needless to say, the collegians who rented the room dashed out the back door as soon as the hookers went downstairs and lived to tell the tale. On a grimmer note, the hookers blamed the bell captain and never worked for him again. He thought it was the taxi driver's fault and they haven't spoken for the past 25 years.

Chip Hustlers

Let's say you're playing black chips and you go on a big-time lucky streak. You'll get real popular real fast when your stash starts growing. Crafty women will somehow discover you. How they find you, I'll never know. But they will.

The most common move a chip hustler uses on you is to make a couple of bets for herself and somehow go broke after she's ordered a drink. She'll wink and blink and laugh and scratch and ogle your chips. If you're as easy as most guys, you'll make a little bet or two for her while she waits for her cocktail. When she wins, she'll thank you and maybe give you a little arm rub. Then she'll bet again. As soon as you look away or concentrate on your cards, she'll plop a chip or two into her purse. I've seen the real pros do this for hours, always appearing to be out of their own chips, while their purses bulge with yours. Before the night is done, you'll be out of jack and she'll be at the cage cashing out a couple thousand in greens.

If you've made buddies with the bosses, they'll usually stop the hustlers from moving in on you. On the other hand, if they don't like you, they might even give a chip hustler a call and let her know you're there.

Lobster Traps

These are the BIG-lobster places. When you walk in the door, a waiter greets you with a big grin. Why the ear-to-ear? He's about to bankrupt you on your meal! All the menu says (in bold) is market price for the tasty-looking morsels. A closer inspection of the six-point type reveals that they cost anywhere from $18 to $22 *a pound.* And, the smallest they have is a three-pounder.

The smiling waiter puts timeshare salesmen to shame. He'll

power-close your party of four on a 15-pound beauty, and if you don't go for it, he'll make you feel like a tightwad. Tightwad? Gee, that's only $330, plus wine (which isn't cheap), for a steroidal crustacean. And tasty? If you think bulked-up NFL linemen are tough, try nibbling on this mutant that has a bigger tail than your date.

Bottom line? If you want lobster, get a good one—and get it comped.

Pawn Shops

Las Vegas has more pawn brokers per square foot than any other town in America. While they do admittedly provide a way for the wayward to get instant money, they are best avoided. They make the casino cash machines look like good deals. Pawn brokers give you about a third of what something's worth and then tack on a $5 service charge and 6% interest a *month* (that's 72% a year) to get your own stuff back.

When you walk into one of these instant loan joints, it goes like this. You show them a family heirloom or the watch your father gave you for graduation. They ask how much you want to borrow. You ask how much they'll give you. They never crack, so you finally tell them how much you'll take. They tell you if they'll give it to you. When the deal is done, you've settled for half of what you wanted.

They hope you never come back, because in four months they can sell your keepsake to another mark for up to 75% of its original value. In order to dissuade you from coming back with your pawn ticket, they print it on pink tissue paper that'll dissolve in a light rain or a heavy sweat. You don't suppose they know their borrowers are going gambling, do you? Nice guys, huh?

Years ago the pawnshops weren't regulated as tightly as now and they'd charge up to 10% a month on what they'd loaned you. But now they're limited to the 6% monthly charge. Plus the service fee of five bucks, even if the loan is for a paltry $10.

If you happen to fall on hard times and have to resort to using a pawn shop to replenish your gambling stake, but then get lucky enough to make a little money back, be sure to pick up your pawned stuff right away. You might think that you're coming back to town in a month or two, but things happen. If you don't get back within 120 days, some slob with a pocketful of twenties who always wanted a watch like yours is certain to buy it, even if your name is engraved on the back.

Avoiding Criminals

Las Vegas has a lot of crime. Every city does. Like other cities, most of the violent crimes happen in the grimy, older sections of town. It is extremely rare for someone to get mugged or raped near the Strip, but the edges of downtown are a different matter. If you're anywhere on Fremont, Ogden, or Carson streets between 4th and Main (Plaza, California, Golden Gate, Horseshoe, Fremont, Golden Nugget, Four Queens, Fitzgeralds, Lady Luck, etc.) or the surrounding area, you're pretty safe as long as you don't walk around with money sticking out of your ears. Wander two blocks away, especially north or east, and you will run into the sleazy flophouses and week-to-week hotels where the dregs of Las Vegas lurk, waiting for a prize like you to come along. I'm not saying don't go down there, but if you do you might meet some ugly people with bad intentions.

Cover Your Tracks

More than a few men have brought their wives to Las Vegas and wound up with a hooker in the room while the wife's downstairs enjoying a show or playing the slots. Talk about a high-risk town! Let me tell you what can happen. Elmore and Shirley check in about 5 p.m. They go down to dinner and then gamble a while. Now, Shirley, a 55-year-old brunette, wants to see Liza, but Elmore hates Liza (or so she thinks). Elmore slips Shirley a couple hundred, escorts her to the showroom, and tells her he's going to gamble. And gamble he does. He dashes to the bar, discovers an extra-friendly 26-year-old six-foot redhead, and hustles her up to the room. He slips *her* a couple hundred, pulls back the covers, and she earns her keep in about ten minutes. He quickly remakes the bed and they dash out of the room and everything's jake. Until Elmore and Shirley come back to the room a few hours later. She pulls back the bedspread and spots these tiny little red curly hairs all over the sheets. She levels a fish-eye on Elmore. He gives it the old "yabba dabba doo!" while he's trying to figure a way to get out of the grease. Never anybody's slouch at fingering someone else, he gets on the horn and calls the front desk, demanding another room and berating the maids. If he's lucky Shirley doesn't snap to what he's been up to and his heart holds out during the twenty minutes they wait for housekeeping to show up and explain that the bed *was* made up with fresh linen before they got there. His only hope now is to leave the hotel in a huff and go somewhere where the sheets are "clean." At best he's put a damper on the weekend and at worst Shirley will wind up with his computer business and the house. The moral? I told you before I'm not a moralizer and I'm not about to tell you how to conduct your life, but I will give you one of life's great practical hints: don't leave enemy short hairs in your bed, boys.

9

For Locals Only

Take 'Em Out and Keep 'Em Happy

Las Vegas. Like me, you live here. You may have come for the career opportunities, the inexpensive housing, or to retire in the sun, but there's a chance that you also picked Vegas because of the nightlife, the good food, the shows, and the gambling.

Your missus likes to party too, but lately she's been on your case. "We never go out any more," she laments. But you can't afford to go out every night, can you? Yeah, you can. Starting now.

Every night you can take your partner out to eat. Every night. I don't know about the rest of you guys, but things run a whole lot smoother around my camp when she ain't doing the cooking.

Say your spouse lacks just a tad's worth of talent in the kitchen. This book can save your marriage. Have you ever tried to kindly tell your wife that you're not too fond of something she just spent two hours whipping up? Talk about gambling with no upside! You're way better off gagging down her tuna surprise or finding an excuse not to come home for dinner than you are advising her that her culinary creations could use a little help.

Be a sport. Take her out. You get what you want, she gets what she wants, and the only ones not getting what they want are the casinos. But they won't even know it.

Company's coming? They are now. We all live with it. You've been here eleven months and you've been visited by six old friends and cousins that you hadn't seen in ten years. Somehow they find you. They think everyone here goes out every night. Guess what? You can. And you can look like a big shot at the same time—you're buying. Of course, you can politely hint that they pick up the tip or you can introduce them to the "guess-the-number" game.

There's a danger here, though. When they go home, they're bound to tell some mutual friends and soon you'll be going out with your old buddies at least once a month. It's happened to me, it'll happen to you.

Another Risk To The Good Life

This might not apply to you and if it doesn't, I'm happy for you, but sometimes one partner will get nervous when the other partner gambles for a comp. And if you lose a couple of hundred the first time out, your mate might never let you try it again. To avoid this possibility, you might want to play some blackjack first, on your own, then tell your partner about the comp after it's already in hand. Any explanation will do: a guy at work got it for you, or you won it in a paycheck promotion. Of course, that'd be lying. To your spouse? Although I've never personally been involved in such a thing and I don't recommend it, I've heard that it happens. After a while, when your wife or husband starts to become accustomed to the good life, you can come clean.

Binion's Minions

Let's get right down to it. What you really want to know is how to get all these free eats I'm talking about. How much money will it take to get started and how much will it cost you in the long run?

You've heard the old Las Vegas adage, "It's cheaper to eat out than it is to eat at home." Believe it, it's true. Binion's Horseshoe, for example, loses about $3 on every $2 steak dinner it sells in the coffee shop. It's good food with good service. How do they do it? Look at the line of folks waiting to chow down, then go back to the casino and try to find a seat on the low-limit blackjack games. You'll tip your hat to Benny (the deceased patriarch) and Jack (Benny's son, who runs the joint now and hasn't let the bean counters take over) for making the Horseshoe such a wonderful food haven.

Okay, you can eat for two bucks, so why would you ever want to risk your hard-earned money to get a comp there? If you've only got a few bucks in your jeans, you probably shouldn't, it's that easy. But, and this is a big but, if you have a decent job or a reasonable retirement income, and you play the game right, you can have the same great meal for two (including tobacco and four drinks) for about 7% (or what the state sales tax would be) of what it would cost you retail. Here's how you do it.

Show up just before the count (6:15-6:30 pm, depending on the pit). Find a table with two empty spots and sit down with your playing partner. Buy in for $300-$400 and give your partner $50 in chips. Your partner should bet no more than $5 a hand. Make your own first bet $25 and order drinks (preferably high-priced call brands) and tobacco for the two of you. You're already way ahead.

When the boss sees the count team coming, he'll ignore you. Bet $5. The count in his area will take about five minutes. Keep betting five bucks. When he gets to your game, bet the $25 again. It'll take about one bet. In a few minutes, his relief will show up. He'll point out the players in his area. When he turns over the helm to his reliever, bet $25 on both spots and call the new boss over. Ask for a dinner comp for two in the coffee shop. When the boss goes to write the comp, stop playing; if the cocktail waitress is handy, order a couple of glasses of red wine for you and your partner to take to dinner. After he gives you the comp, collect your drink and hightail it to the coffee shop. If it's the 10-ounce $2 steak special you're after, you'll have to wait until 10 pm to take advantage, but it's available until 5:45 am. Check out the math in the chart below. It proves that it's never better (unless you're damn-near tapped out) to pay the paltry two bucks for the special.

Binion's Horseshoe Coffee Shop Comp For Two

Expected Loss

20 hands @ $5 x -0.2% house advantage	[20¢]
6 hands @ $25 x -0.2% house advantage	[30¢]
Total expected loss	[50¢]

Comp Value

2 premium cocktails	$ 2.00
2 glasses red wine	$ 2.00
2 tobaccos	$ 5.00
2 specials with trimmings	$ 4.00
2 desserts	$ 3.00
2 beverages	$ 2.00
Total comp value	$18.00
Total expected loss	[$ .50]
Net comp gain	$17.50

The return on your expected loss is an astounding 3,500% for fifteen minutes work!

If you get lucky and the boss offers you an open comp, you can also order a bottle of wine with your dinner and a big-time 16-ounce T-bone or other great slabs and run your dinner tab into the high $50s.

You won't have to time the count if you've scouted out the place in advance and know when a boss in a busy section is scheduled to be relieved. If you bump into a boss that's tough to crack, run the play again in another area. At worst, you'll wind up playing for an hour or so and may end up with expected losses of up to $5, but you'll still chow like a champ for five bucks.

Beyond Binion's

Now you know how to take advantage of Binion's, but what about all the other great stuff around Las Vegas? Can comp wizardry work for that too? You bet. What will it cost? Damn near nothing, if you play it right.

Let's take a family of four. Excluding vacations and the like, we'll assume the parents go out once a week. How much can you save by being a comp counter? Read on.

Dinner at a mid-priced restaurant with a little wine will run you about $15 a head. After tip, you're talking about $35 every time you eat out. Do that 52 times a year and you're looking at an annual dining-out budget of $1,820.

Now what if you use that $1,800 for a comp-counting stake? If the two of you play blackjack at $15 a hand for an hour each (to earn dinner) at about a .4% casino edge, your combined expected loss is $7.20 every time you play. If you did this week after week instead of whipping out the credit card at some local restaurant, you'd save yourselves $22.80 every time you ate out—and that includes forking over a $5 tip. That's a $1,185-a-year savings. Not enough to buy a new car, but certainly enough to take an extra week at the beach with the kids every year. And that's with no ACES maneuvering; you're really betting $15 a hand for 60 hands.

Sound good? It gets better. If you're on your ACES, it'll look like you're betting that same $15 a hand, but you'll really be averaging half of that, between breaks and timely tiny bets. So your expected losses will be reduced to only $3.60 a night plus a $5 tip, and your savings will amount to $1,350 a year. All told, your weekly dining-out sprees will cost you $450 instead of $1,800.

You can also manage to take the kids with you (see "Feeding

Four on a Comp for Two"), but what to do with them while you play is always a problem. If you leave them in the video arcade, your losses will probably be greater than the cost of the meal. The best bet is to gamble at the Gold Coast or Sam's Town, where they have free daycare—along with the free food from your comp.

So much for the family folk. What about the rest of you who don't have kids at home? The savings can be astronomical if you decide you want to eat out every day. Now, I realize that eating coffee-shop fare every night can get pretty dull, so let's change the format a little here. Say two of you will be eating out once a day. The mix includes lunches, coffee-shop dinners, buffets, and one gourmet meal a week.

Weekly Dining-Out Expense
Retail

3 lunches @ $10 each x 2	$ 60
3 coffee shop/buffet @ $15 each x 2	$ 90
1 gourmet meal @ $50 x 2	$ 100
Total Weekly Budget	$ 250
Total Annual Budget	$13,000

Sticking with our assumption that you have to play an hour each at an average bet of $15 to get the lunch, buffet, and coffee-shop comps, with a .4% game that comes to an expected loss of $50 a week. The gourmet meals require much larger bets or a lot more playing time; let's use an average of $75 a hand (each) for two hours. (The $75 is an average based on a mix of low-, middle-, and high-end gourmet rooms.) On the plus side, most of the places with decent gourmet rooms have better rules, so we'll go with an average house advantage of only .3%. The gourmet meal will cost the two of you about $55.

Here's what you'll be paying. It looks like a lot, but it's a whole lot less than you'd be paying if you weren't a comp wizard.

Weekly Dining-Out Expense With Simple Comp Counting

6 Buffet/Coffee Shop/Lunch	$ 50
1 Gourmet Dinner	$ 55
Total Weekly	$ 105
Total Annual	$ 5,500
Total if you paid retail	$13,000
Total savings	$ 7,500

That *is* enough to buy a new car, or lease a Cadillac, and that's what you get just for showing up. If you happen to arrive with ACES knowledge in your hip pocket, you can really tear 'em a new one. Take a look at the difference in expected weekly losses for a basic strategy player versus an ACES player. Playing 60 hands an hour with an actual average bet of $7.50 (apiece) at a .4% game, your expected loss for the six buffets and coffee shop lunches comes to $25. The gourmet meal (120 hands x $40 actual average bet each at .3%) will cost you about $30 in expected losses. That's $55 a week, $2,900 a year, for a grand savings of $10,100.

Weekly Dining-Out Expense With ACES Play

Buffet/Coffee Shop/Lunch	$ 25
Gourmet Dinner	$ 30
Total Weekly	$ 55
Total Annual	$ 2,900
Total if you paid retail	$13,000
Total savings	$10,100

Now you can put the kids in a private boarding school and still be able to enjoy the benefits of comp counting.

If you really want to step up your play, you can make a run on the gourmet rooms at Caesars Palace or The Mirage, but now you'll have to play for a couple of hours at big numbers and they'll still probably limit you on wine and booze. I don't blame them. The Palace Court at Caesars has an extraordinary wine list and certain bottles cost more than a meal for four at other gourmet rooms in town. If you do ask for a comp at Caesars, tell them it's okay to put a limit on how much you spend. If you don't, your chances for the comp are greatly diminished, because they know you can really hurt them.

It's important to understand that most gourmet comps are only issued if the numbers in the computer justify it. That's fine. You'll still have the best of it if you only play basic strategy, but it's a must to be on your ACES if you want to pound them in proper fashion.

Scouting Casinos

The drill is different for locals. If you plan to snag a comp once a week or so (as opposed to every day), you'll want to set your sights a little higher quality-wise. You'll still count comps according to the general concepts explained earlier in the book, but you'll practice your craft every week, rather than a few times a year. Look for casinos with good blackjack rules, liberal comp policies, and a good buffet or coffee shop. After a month or two, you'll have a system worked out for a few favorite places.

Keep a log of the good joints and good bosses. If you run into a bad situation once in a while—bad boss, bad rules, bad food—don't go back. You won't have to. The Las Vegas comp universe is enormous.

If you plan to eat out once a day, comp counting will turn into an avocation or even a part-time job. Your entire modus operandi will be different. You'll frequent these joints every day of your life. Who needs notes? In short order, you'll fall into a rhythm and become fast friends with a lot of the local fauna you're out there hustling comps from. You'll get to know dozens of bosses on a first-name basis and will eventually become part of a Las Vegas subculture of professional comp wizards. One thing you'll want to avoid is another wizard who's just tagged a floorman. Give the boss a little air before you attack him if you see one of your brethren making his move just before you're about to strike.

Finally, try getting into the habit of taking a walking tour of downtown or the Strip every time you go out to play. You'll not only be walking off your free eats, you'll get to case a few other joints every time you make a play.

Special Pointers For Locals

Dress Nicely

Appearance is more important for locals than visitors, because you have an overall impression to create and maintain. This is particularly true if you're playing downtown. They see so many people with bad teeth and B.O. that seeing you should be a welcome sight. Never wear a Grateful Dead T-shirt. Muscle shirts, jogging shorts, thongs, and pre-shredded Levis turn most bosses off. Clean casual attire will often get you the benefit of the doubt. If you must wear a cap, make it a golf cap. Don't wear baseball caps (usually the sign of a poker flea, cheapskate, or someone with dirty hair) or any kind of ornamentation that makes them think you work on cars or in construction. Please, I'm not making judgments here or trying to label you, but they do.

Local's Joints

Strangely, most Las Vegans who frequent locals' joints away from the Strip or downtown (Gold Coast, Palace Station, Arizona Charlie's, Jerry's Nugget, Sam's Town, etc.) don't have a clue about how to get a comp. They go to these places for the relaxed atmosphere, cheap food, and "loose" slots. These joints are usually very generous with their comps because they don't get hit on much. Show them some action and you could quickly become a premium local player.

Buying In

Always buy in for at least $100. That way the dealer will have to get the boss' attention when you arrive. When he looks your way, smile and greet him by name. For buffet and coffee shop comps, you can buy in for up to $300, but not too much more, or the boss'll wonder why a $15 player needs so many chips.

Automatic Comps

Cultivate your floormen. Unlike a tourist who comes and goes, you're going to become part of these people's lives, especially in the choice joints. If they've got you pegged as a good sort, the comps become automatic.

Double Comps

You can sometimes get a low-end comp twice in the same play. The way it works is to get a comp from the first boss, then wait for him to go on a lunch break. If another dealer comes on the game about a half hour later (who won't know anything about you), you can ask the relief boss for a comp, too. All he can say is no. If two of you are playing, one can ask the regular boss and one can ask his relief.

A corollary. Most of the comps you'll be asking for are available from your floorman. If you ask for a comp for more than two people, a bigger boss is often brought in to make the decision. You're much better off asking for two comps for two from two different bosses than one comp for four, even if you deserve it (which I hope you don't).

If You're A Winner

If you're a regular and make a big win, get up and tell the boss you won enough to buy your own meal. Act a little bit guilty. He'll probably offer to pick up the tab anyway.

Tipping

Don't be a stiff. Don't begrudge tokes for cocktail waitresses or dealers. Think of it as an investment in the longevity of your welcome. If you only play 10 or 20 minutes with each dealer, they won't expect a tip, but if you have a nice win, a buck or two won't hurt, especially if you're planning on playing in that particular pit again.

Special Occasions

If you become well known at a place or two, it's not out of line for you to ask for an occasional special comp, such as a room for a couple of nights or a show. Be sure to ask for something when you know that business will be slow and they'll be giving away unused inventory anyway. It's a good idea to ask a week or two in advance of the occasion, and always call to confirm that it's been taken care of. This will make you a big hit with visitors.

Gifts

If you have a few bosses who go out of their way to take care of you, remember them during the holidays. If you have a favorite dealer or two, take care of them too.

Others

The same concepts that were explained in "Bracing for ACES" and "Mechanics of ACES" apply to locals, too. Take as many breaks as you can get away with. Try to look like a local loser—get the bosses to commiserate about your sports, keno, or bingo losses. (They live the life too; you're all part of the same fraternity.) Don't forget to hide chips. You want the bosses to think you're a sucker. A nice sucker, a local sucker, but still a sucker. After a month or two, playing slow gets to be a snap, because you'll recognize the situations where you can take breaks, or hop on a table full of socializers.

Party in the Room

The last and best comp for locals is the one-night (RFB) stand. How's this sound? You tell your lover you're taking her to a gourmet dinner. You dine for a couple of hours and then catch a midnight superstar show. She thinks it's time to go home. Not so fast. As you cruise by the elevator, you usher her in and push the button for one of the top floors. When you get to the top, you pull out a key and open the door to a beautiful room overlooking the Strip. Then it's champagne in the room, a little sleep, breakfast in bed, a couple of bottles from room service to take home, a late check out, and you're back at your place having spent $25 in tips—$50 if you go wild in the gourmet room and you're a real sport.

Here's how to do it. Call a host and tell him you're a cash blackjack player. Go through the scouting drill—"How much do I have to bet for a room, gourmet meal, and show?" With a little research, you'll find there's an RFB night for almost any budget. In some downtown joints, it'll be as little as $50 a hand for four hours. At the mid-level Strip joints it'll be about $100 a hand. And in the most exclusive premium casinos with elegant dining and world-class shows, they'll want you to bet as much as $250. In every instance you'll get a great deal if you play your cards right.

When you're ready, head for the blackjack tables, buy in for a thousand or two, ask to get rated, and play till you've fulfilled the requirement. Then contact the pit boss. He'll put you in the system and make all your reservations. Next you check in. If, for some reason, you're hesitant about claiming you're a local, simply say you're from L.A. (or Phoenix or San Diego). When you check into the hotel, hand the clerk a VISA, and nobody will be the wiser. But don't worry about having a Las Vegas address: you won't be the first local to engage in a little Romance 101 at a Strip hotel.

And now you're RFB for the night. You get to sign your meals, drinks, and show to the room, then check out without owing a dime. You're living the life of the ACES comp wizard—all a ten-minute drive from home.

10
Haul of Fame

Every one of the following methods of comp weaseling has been used in Las Vegas. Some will bring a tear to your eye (especially if you own a casino). The names have been changed to protect the....well, they're really not all that innocent....but I changed 'em anyway, because most of these characters are friends of mine and they're still at it.

Sammy Schecklemeister

Sammy buys coach airline tickets for himself and his wife three months in advance of his trip. Two days before he departs, he calls the airlines until he finds one that's close to being sold out on their Vegas routes. Why? Because that's when they cost the most. Then he orders two round-trip, first-class airfares and pays cash. He flies coach on the original tickets, plays eight hours at $500 a hand in two joints where he has $25,000 in credit, and gets reimbursed for the first-class beauties at the end of his play in Vegas *at both hotels*. He cashes in the unused first-class tickets when he gets home and scores over $3,000 in cash (or ten times his expected loss and he's not even an ACES player) every time he takes a trip to Nevada.

Sammy Schecklemeister

Total playing time:	16 Hours
Average bet:	$500
House edge	0.3%
Sammy's expected loss	[$1,440]
Sammy's Gain	
RFB	$ 840
Airfare	$2,500
Total comps	$3,340
Less cost	[$1,440]
Net Gain	**$1,900 ***

* *Sammy's gain is all cash.*

Lucy Lunchbucket

Lucy was a 350-pound chain smoker. She had the shift-changes down to a science at three downtown Las Vegas casinos famous for their cheap food and liberal comp policies. Just before the change of shifts, she'd buy in for $50, bet $1 on a single-deck blackjack game, and order a pack of cigarettes and an orange juice. When the shifts changed ten minutes later, she'd change tables and ask the new cocktail waitress for another pack of $2.50 cigarettes and a refill on the juice, then bet $5 a hand for three hands before she'd asking the floorman for a buffet ticket. She played 30 minutes every morning with an expected loss of 18¢ for $5 worth of cigarettes, $2 worth of juice, and a $3.99, 6,000-calorie brunch, which carried her to the next change of shifts, where she'd pull the same maneuver again. She beat the same clubs out of $21.98 in nicotine and high-cholesterol food every day for five years until the inevitable happened.

One mournful night while grazing at the Polynesian Buffet in her muumuu. Lucy couldn't hold herself back and started wolf-ing down a jumbo scoop of the $12 a pound lox while pushing through the serving line, heading toward the Tub 'o Tapioca, her favorite evening confection. A big chunk of salmon caught in her throat and she panicked. She keeled over next to the dessert stand, had a massive coronary, and died as close to heaven as she was ever likely to get.

Lucy "made" $7,783 a year on a paltry bankroll of less than $1,000. In any other city, Lucy couldn't have lived like this for thirty times the same $1,000 (although she might have lived a bit longer). Is Las Vegas great or what?

Lucy Lunchbucket

Total playing time	1800 Hours *(5 years @ one hour a day)*
Average bet	$2
House edge	0.3%
Lucy's expected loss	[$648]

(In many downtown casinos, buffet comps are given to almost all known $5-$15 players. No allocation is ever made for tobacco and drinks served on the table. As the table below illustrates, over time, it can mean a lot.)

Lucy's Gain

Tobacco *(4 packs a day for 5 years. Whew!)*	$18,000
Juice	$ 7,200
Food	$14,364
Total comps	$39,564
Less cost	[$ 648]
Net Gain	**$38,916**

Sherry Slithermore

Sherry has been in the hotel for three days. She tells Freida the floorman that she's heard about the Goochi Poochi restaurant upstairs that only people with $100,000 lines can get into. Freida pooh poohs her and says anyone can eat there, it's just expensive. "How much does someone have to lose?" asks Sherry. Freida goes on to tell her that it's not how much you win or lose, it's how much you bet and how many hours you play, etc. "Do you think I might qualify?" asks Sherry. Freida pulls up Sherry's file on the computer. It's close. Sherry's been nice, she hasn't used any room comps (yet), and she even brought Freida a pastry from the breakfast Freida comped for her on Saturday morning. So Freida calls her pit boss and recommends that Sherry's party of four get a full comp in the Goochi room, explaining that Sherry had only used $12 on her breakfast comp the day before and $3 of that was for a pastry for her. The pit boss goes for it and calls in the unlimited comp. Sherry thanks them both, plays a few more hands, says her goodbyes and leaves. Pretty standard stuff.

Until she sashays over to the VIP desk and asks a host, Harvey Handsome, if he would comp her rooms. He looks her up in the computer. No comps show because *comps don't show until they're used.* It's marginal, but Sherry isn't pushy. She wants to come back in five weeks, and the computer shows she should have lost about $1,200. Still, it's a tough call to pick up a $200 suite for three nights. Sherry turns on the charm and tells her new friend Harvey that she doesn't have a host yet and she really likes him and maybe he could be her host in the future. Harvey's annual review is about to come up and he could do a lot worse than having Sherry as a new customer in his book. He goes for it. She thanks him and asks if she can have a late check out time, "Oh, maybe about 6 pm."

"Sure," says Harvey, already a close friend. "It's Sunday night, the hotel's only running about 70%. What does it hurt?" Harv (it's Harv now) gives her a wink. Sherry thanks him and goes up to her room to rest up for the chow-down slated for later in the evening.

She straps on her best strapless gown, checks out of her free suite, and takes her three traveling companions to Goochi Poochi to put on the dog. She hands the captain her comp slip. They open with a bottle of Cristal champagne ($165) and two appetizers each (at $12 a pop). Then they proceed with a no-holds-barred, tag-team, food fest. They order soup, tableside salads, four chef's surprises, an extra lobster tail or two, and a couple bottles of wine.

Flaming desserts are a must and before the smoke clears from dinner, drinks, and coffee, they've scarfed down $330 worth of food, sucked down $315 worth of champagne and French wine, and slurped up another $80 in cognac. Their performance makes the waiter, who's in on the conspiracy, downright misty-eyed as he helps them pump up the bill as far as they can in anticipation of his 15% gratuity. By custom, Sherry's dinner guests offer to pay the tip. Always the lady and not wanting to make a fuss in such fine surroundings, of course she demurs. They finish their espressos and mosey downstairs where a limo is waiting to whisk them to the airport.

Sherry Slithermore	
Total playing time	8 Hours
Average bet	$125
House edge	0.3%
Sherry's expected loss	[$180]
Sherry's Gain	
Room	$ 600
Other *(drinks on table, etc.)*	$ 100
Dinner	$ 725
Total comps	$1,425
Less cost	[$ 180]
Net Gain	**$ 1,245**

Andy Amblin

Andy Amblin can sell bullshit to a congressman. He's that good. Being the type that makes new friends real easy, he'll slide into a game, sit next to a green- or black-chip player, bet $25 for himself, strike up a conversation, and find out if the gambler is a guest of the hotel and/or being rated. If he isn't, Andy will whip out his own VIP card, call over the floorman, hand him the card, point to the green-chip bettor's chips and say, "We're on the same card.

It's my money and I'm teaching him how to play." He'll get credit for the other guy's play (double, triple, up to five times Andy's average bet) and earn comps for losers that he doesn't book. This one's worked for years and will continue to work, because many bosses are too lazy or grumpy to introduce themselves to players they don't know and will look for any excuse to keep from doing any extra paper work.

Andy Amblin

Total playing time	8 Hours
Average bet	$25
House edge	0.3%
Andy's expected loss	[$36]
Andy's Gain	
Room	$200
Other	$ 50
F&B	$400
Total comps	$650
Less cost	[$ 36]
Net Gain	**$614**

Gerome the Gnome

The Gnome is a loser, a big loser, at a big-time casino. Just look at his rating slips. In its zeal to keep Gerome as a favored customer, a premium casino lets him assign his comps to other people; they don't care as long as his comps don't exceed his equivalency.

What they don't know is that Gerome gave up high-stakes gambling a long time ago when he took over as the owner of an advertising trade-out business in downtown L.A. Now he's got five floormen in the casino wired into a complex scam, in which anytime an unrated player or non-house guest sits down and loses, Gerome gets the credit for the loss and the time played.

It works like this. Steve Stranger loses five grand and Buster the Boss writes up a ticket for Gerome, saying he played two hours at $2,000 a hand and lost the dough. Then casino marketing gives Gerome $1,600 in comps, which he *sells* to other barter folks around Los Angeles at 60% of retail. That's for anything the hotel offers. Room, food, shows, the works.

Why do the bosses go out on a limb for the Gnome? Because he cuts them in for 20% of the profits. Everybody makes out and the casino's comp/play ratio is still in line. Someday Gerome will wind up in prison on this one and a bunch of casino executives will lose their work cards, but for now, it's gotta be in the haul.

(Stats unavailable until statute of limitations expires.)

Charlene Swiss

Cheesy Charlie (that's what her friends called her) liked to stay up late. She liked to drink. She also liked to eat out. Nice combo when you live in Las Vegas. Charlie had it down. She'd hit the casino about 3:40 am and scout out the pits, making sure to pick a blackjack table about ready to close with only a straggler or two playing on it. She'd buy in for $20 and watch the floorman groan, knowing his chances for missing E.O. (Early Out) and having to do O.T. (Overtime) just went up five-fold. She'd play a couple of hands at the table minimum and smile at the boss. "I'm starved. Could you maybe pick up breakfast for me?" "Sure," the boss would quickly agree, knowing his chances of beating the clock just took off again. "How many?" he'd ask. Cheesy Charlie would shrug and say, "Oh, four, but just for the coffee shop." The boss would wince and say, "I can do it for two."

At that point Cheesie Charlie would fish out another $20 and say, "Oh, that's okay, maybe I can win breakfast for my friends," while she bet two hands at the table minimum. Immediately, the boss would write her the ticket and hand it to her with a smile. She'd tuck it in her purse until the other players got up from the game. Then she'd pull it out and peruse it. "Can I get some drinks on that too?" she'd ask, knowing that by now she could have gotten this guy to recommend that the hotel send a limo to take her home. "Yeah, sure," he'd mumble as he grabbed the ticket and told the dealer to pull up the lid and close the game. "You *are* quitting *now*, right?" Charlene would smile, inspect the ticket to make sure it was correct, then give her friends the high sign.

They'd all stampede to the coffee shop, order shrimp cocktails, New York steaks and eggs, three bloody Marys, and two pastries each. They'd score a major comp coup by running up a $108 tab, just because a floorman making $150 for an eight-hour shift wanted to go home twelve minutes early.

Cheesy Charlie's still in action and, thankfully, so are scores of bosses who can't wait to close games so they can hit the bars for a quick one before heading home.

Cheesie Charlie

Total playing time	15 minutes
Average bet	$5
House edge	0.3%
Charlie's expected loss	[23¢]
Charlie's Gain	
Tobacco	$ 2.50
(Always gets a pack for a friend)	
Drink (on table)	$ 2.50
Breakfast for 4	$108.00
Total comps	$113.00
Less cost *(includes $15 tip*)*	[$ 15.23]
Net Gain	**$ 97.77**

**She may be cheesy, but she's a sport.*

Jack the Grinder

Jack ran a collection agency. He was also a professional heckler, always ragging someone, somewhere, about what they ate, drank, wore, drove, or dated. His incessant harangues left him with few friends and even fewer scruples. He discovered the magic of comps way back in the '60s and took the art of squeezing every nickel out of everyone he knows to new lows. Although hardly aware that he was getting the best of it, and often thinking he was getting screwed by the casinos, the Grinder invented many of the methods the less genteel of us use against casinos today. The first thing he'd do upon checking into a room was call the front desk and insist that he had no towels, soap, or shampoo. The front desk would send housekeeping up and sure enough, nothing would be there. It was in Jack's suitcase already. When the maid apologized, he'd give her a dollar tip and tell her to make things right. While she was straightening his room, he'd sneak out into the hall with a small bag and empty her cart of the hand-milled soaps and designer shampoos. Then he'd loot the toilet paper and Kleenex from the room before dashing down to the coffee shop, where he'd swipe all the sweeteners off the table and ask for more before he ordered.

His best move was in the limo back to the airport. He'd stash empty bottles in his carry-on bag, and push the privacy button to make sure the driver couldn't watch him in action. Then he'd empty every decanter of booze into the bottles, while opening the drawers beneath the seats and taking all the nuts, chips, bottle openers, sodas, and crystal glasses he could get his hands on before they reached the airport. The way he saw it, they wouldn't have put the stuff in the limo if they didn't want him to have it. Wrong? I'm not here to judge, only to tell you what lengths some folks will go to get maximum comp value.

Net gain? A lot. But it didn't have anything to do with playing blackjack.

George the Gorge

George the Gorge liked to gamble in the local joints and, being a long-time Vegas kind of guy, he knew the value of flash cash. He'd buy in for $2,000 on a full double-deck game in a locals' joint when he knew there was only one hand left before the dealer shuffled up. His first bet would be $200. A boss would introduce himself and George would immediately ask for a comp while the dealer shuffled. The boss would give him a coffee shop comp for four, unlimited. George would play three more hands while the boss wrote out the slip, then get up, win or lose, and saunter to the Theme Room where his wife and two friends were already waiting outside the pit. George flashed his comp slip and the hostess would seat them in front of 60 disgruntled people who'd been standing in line 45 minutes. The party was ready to begin.

George and his guests opened with double martinis around the table. They bravely ordered the Lobster Cantonese entree as an appetizer, charged through full steak dinners, then finished with deluxe cake and ice cream. Including the coffee, wine, and post-dinner cocktails, the tab came to $93.85.

George the Gorge

Total playing time	4 minutes
Average bet	$200
House edge	0.5%
George's expected loss	[$4] *

* *With enormous swings.*

George's Gain

Tobacco	$ 2.50
(Always gets a pack for a friend)	
Drink (on table)	$ 2.50
Dinner for 4	$ 93.85
Total comps	$ 98.85
Less cost *(includes $15 tip)*	[$ 19.00]
Net Gain	**$ 79.85**

Ernie Expense Account

Ernie goes to Las Vegas twice a year for conventions. He's a hired gun salesman who pays his own freight and gets reimbursed by whatever company he's representing—if he makes enough sales to justify the expenses—so he's got a few more moves than the average engineer. He misses every meeting and plays blackjack for about 50 hours during the convention. When the trade show is winding down, he goes downstairs, checks out of the hotel, pays with his personal credit card, and gets receipts for everything.

Then he finds a host and asks why he wasn't comped or why they didn't pick up his airfare. The host pulls up his account, sees that Ernie hasn't used any of his $1,800 equivalency, and promptly gives him cash for his airline ticket, and credits his VISA for the full charge amount.

Miraculously, he meets scores of other businessmen playing hooky from the meetings, and manages to sell them lots of products. When he gets back home, he has hefty receipts (including airline tickets) and plenty of sales orders, so the company pays him full bore for his expenses and gives him a nice commission to boot.

Ernie Expense Account

Total playing time	50 Hours
Average bet	$75
House edge	0.3%
Ernie's expected loss	[$675]
Ernie's Gain	
Room, food, beverage *(casino)*	$ 600
Room, food, beverage *(company)*	$ 600
Tobacco	$ 50
Drinks *(on table)*	$ 200
Airfare reimbursement *(casino)*	$ 440
Airfare reimbursement *(company)*	$ 440
Total back	$2,330
Less cost	[$ 675]
Net Gain	**$1,655 ***

**This is pure cash back to Ernie.*

Joann Jackrabbit

Joann sat on a crowded blackjack table late in the evening at a joint that had a dangerous buffet, but a magnificent coffee shop, betting a couple bucks a hand. She waited until the boss took a break and then bet $5. She asked the new boss for a comp to the breakfast buffet, always the easiest to get. It was automatic. The next morning, she sat down again just as one boss was going off duty and asked the incoming boss if the comp could be changed to the coffee shop. The boss agreed. So, Joann bet $5 in two spots, one for her and one for her husband, who was now on the game, to see if they could make it for two. No problem. Joann had taken a comp worth a trifling $4.99 breakfast and parlayed it into a coffee shop dinner comp worth $50.

Joann Jackrabbit

Total playing time	30 minutes
Average bet	$3
House edge	0.3%
Joann's expected loss	[27¢]
Joann's Gain	
Tobacco	$ 2.50
(Always gets a pack for a friend)	
Drinks (on table)	$ 5.00
Dinner for 2	$ 50.00
Total comps	$ 57.50
Less cost *(includes $7.50 tip)*	[$ 7.77]
Net Gain	**$ 49.73**

Danny Doubledip

Danny knows how to get off-premises comps. Each trip he gets in the system of a different premium casino. At the new joint, he asks a floorman to tell him exactly how much he has to play for a coffee-shop comp for two. If it's an hour or so, he plays an extra 30 minutes to make sure he's built up $30-$40 in his comp account. The floorman completes the rating slip and writes the comp ticket.

Danny comes back in about four hours, when he knows his

rating has been entered into marketing's computer. He walks up to another floorman, hands him his VIP card, and asks for a coffee-shop comp for two. The second floorman looks him up in the computer, sees he's qualified, and issues the comp.

He goes to another pit. He gets another comp for two. Now he's got comps for six people and nothing shows against his account in the computer, because comps don't show until they're used. He calls up his buddies at the host hotel. They come over and hit the coffee shop together, running up a $150 bill on an expected loss of $13.50.

Danny Doubledip

Total playing time	90 minutes
Average bet	$50
House edge	0.3%
Danny's expected loss	[$13.50]
Danny's Gain	
Tobacco *(Always gets two packs)*	$ 5.00
Drinks *(on table)*	$ 5.00
Dinner for 6	$ 150.00
Total comps	$ 160.00
Less cost *(includes $20 tip)*	[$ 33.50]
Net Gain	**$ 126.50**

Beth the Bruiser

Beth was the widow of a former high-stakes personal-injury attorney who also had a serious gambling jones. He blew over $30,000 on the dice table in a premium casino one night, had a stroke, and croaked. Beth soon became the bane of all hosts and bosses in the hotel. Everybody wished she'd been the one who dropped dead, but they had to treat her nice anyway, because her beloved Herman had left her a small percentage of stock in the hotel and she would call the president every time she didn't get something she wanted. One time, to his everlasting dismay, the president sat Beth down and told her she didn't warrant the comps she was asking for, based on her $25 average bets. Beth said all right and checked out in a huff. He thought he was through with her. He was wrong.

She sued him and the casino and served up the papers at the annual stockholder's meeting claiming malfeasance, misfeasance, nonfeasance, and every other kind of unfeasance she could think of. If you've never been to a publicly traded company's annual meeting, you might not understand. But let me tell you, the board wasn't happy to see her. They didn't want to see her again. After the meeting, they quickly settled with her and from then on, Beth the Bruiser got just about anything she wanted, as long as it was only moderately unreasonable. I know it's hard to believe, but Beth hailed from New York City.

Net gain? Beth's been brutalizing this company for years. If you want to figure it out, you'll need a securities attorney, CPA, casino host, and a real strong stomach.

The Lingo

Now that you're ready to play a brand new game in a brand new world, you need to learn a brand new lingo. You'll have to leave your stuffy old (pre-ACES) self back home while you learn how to speak the speak, even if it does sound like wise-guy trash talkin'. Hey, that's what it is. Did you ever see a caper flick that didn't have its own lingo? And everybody that's in on the caper uses the same buzz words. Those who don't know the jargon are the obvious outsiders. You're on the inside now.

Imagine jumping into a rockin'-and-rollin' blackjack game and watching the lady next to you move her bets up and down in rhythm with yours. Talk about magic! Wait till you say something sexy like "equivalency" and watch her squirm. Oh, you rake, you. And ladies, how are you gonna feel when that handsome dog sits down next to you, asks for a marker, and you whisper, "Do you think I've got a hundred dollar E.P.?" And he says, "I'd give you twice that right now. Your comp or mine? " Oh yes, it's going to be grand. It's going to be glorious! It's going to be free.

After just a few minutes of tossing comp-counter riff around the table, you'll know if you're among the anointed who have chosen comp wizardry as their new blood sport for the '90s.

But please. Comp wizard and ACES lingo is for our ears only and should never be repeated within earshot of the Philistines.

ACES (Advanced Comp Equivalency Strategy)—A sophisticated comp-earning system which yields luxury vacations for 10¢ on the dollar.

ACES player—A professional comp wizard. A long-term winner.

action—The total of all bets. Also known as "handle."

actual result—The amount of money lost or won as a result of gambling.

airfare (complimentary)—Typically 5% of the customer's credit line or front money, or up to 10% of a gambler's losses.

average bet (actual)—The precise average bet, as determined and known by the comp wizard.

average bet (apparent)—The often imprecise average of a gambler's bets, assigned by a floorman and forwarded to casino marketing for complimentary evaluation purposes. Actual average bet should always be less than apparent average bet.

bar—When a casino bans someone from the premises. Also known as "86."

barber pole—A bet made using several different colored chips.

basic strategy—The optimal way to play blackjack without counting cards.

black chip—A $100 casino chip.

bleeder—A boss who agonizes when a gambler wins (see "sweat").

boxman—The boss who sits at the center of a dice table and supervises buy-ins, markers, chip conversions, and all other dealer activities.

cage—The casino cashier's area where all chip, cash, and credit transactions take place.

casino marketing—"Back-of-the-house" department responsible for, among other things, determining comp criteria.

check—Chip.

color up—To convert lower-denomination chips into larger denominations.

comp counter—Anyone with a direct and specific understanding of how to profit from the comp system.

complimentary—Free room, food, beverage, or miscellaneous items that a casino offers players to entice them to gamble. Also known as "comp," "freebie," "RFB."

complimentary play—When a player makes a token laydown in order not to embarrass a host, pit boss, or floorman who has just issued an unearned comp.

comp wizard—Anyone who has a consciousness of comps and makes an effort to acquire them.

comp wizardry—The ultimate alchemy of the '90s, where players turn their bankroll, charm, and wiles into free stuff.

day shift—The second shift of the day in a casino. Typically runs from noon to 8:00 pm.

dead hand—A blackjack hand terminated because of a dealer mistake that results in no action for the house or player.

difference—Player equivalency minus comps used. The amount a gambler has available in his comp account for additional comps.

double-deck blackjack—Blackjack played with two decks.

drop—The money tendered at the tables for gambling.

earning potential—The amount the casino thinks it can win from a gambler, based on time played, average bet per hand, and the casino advantage (generally around 2% of the apparent average bet on a blackjack game). Also known as "E.P." and "theoretical win."

equivalency—The gross amount of comp value earned during a particular vacation.

equivalency ratio—The percentage of a player's earning potential that the casino is willing to allocate in comp privileges. Typically between 35% and 50% of the earning potential.

expected result—The expected loss or win based on casino or player advantage and total amount wagered. Also known as "expected value" (see "actual result").

face-down blackjack—A multi-deck game dealt from a shoe in which the players handle the cards.

face-up blackjack—A multi-deck game dealt from a shoe in which players do not handle the cards.

false drop—An artificially inflated drop, generally created when players churn cash, chips, or markers.

first base—The first seat, starting from the dealer's left, at a blackjack table.

flat bet—Consecutive wagers of the same size.

floorman—A table-games supervisor, one step below a pit boss.

four-hour conversion—The standardized ratio casino marketing uses to determine a player's value as a comp customer.

front money—Money placed on deposit in the cage, which is drawn out on the gaming tables in the form of chips.

George—A good tipper.

Grand Wizard of Comps—Max Rubin.

graveyard shift—The first shift of the day in a casino. Typically runs from 4:00 am to 12:00 noon.

green chip—A $25 chip. Also known as a "quarter."

grind store—A casino that caters to low-limit players.

hard comp—A comp which the casino has to pay cash for.

head-up game—In blackjack, a single player against the dealer.

heat—The close monitoring of a game by the bosses, especially if they suspect subterfuge.

heaty—A game that has two or more bosses watching it closely.

host—Casino marketing representative responsible for approving high-end comps and airfare reimbursements.

house edge—The casino's mathematical advantage over the gambler on a given wager.

incidentals—Items that most casinos will not comp, including in-room movies, telephone bills, gift-shop purchases, tips, and massages.

in the system—Any gambler who is or has been listed in the casino's electronic data base to be evaluated for purposes of determining comps.

junket—A group gambling excursion.

laydown—A bet or a series of bets. When a player buys into a game and gambles he is said to be making a laydown.

layout—The felt covering on a gambling table.

marker—Any debt or debit instrument the casino uses to issue chips on a game.

marker down—When a credit instrument is paid off.

masking bets—Timely mixing of bets to deceive a floorman into giving a player an inflated average bet.

mini-junket—An abbreviated junket; usually one or two days.

money management—An extraneous and generally useless gambling consideration.

nickel—A $5 chip. Also known as a "red."

off-premises comp—A comp earned with a short play at a casino you're not staying in. Off-premises comps are ideal for lunches or dinners where you plan on running up a big bill. They are also excellent floorman barter.

on tilt—When a player starts making non-rational decisions, generally following a run of misfortune.

pit—The casino area where the table games are located.

pit boss—A casino supervisor who monitors table games and oversees floormen.

possible result—The universe of gambling possibilities. Usually considered when assessing risk.

power of the pen—The authority given to a casino executive to issue comps.

premium (casino)—A state-of-the-art casino which caters to high-end play.

rated player—Any gambler whose play is monitored for the purpose of issuing comps (see "in the system").

rating—A gambler's "time played and average bet" determined and logged by a floorman.

rating slip—The form a floorman fills out to complete a player's rating.

redeem—To pay off a marker or a cash-deposit voucher on the table or at the cashier's cage.

rundown—A player's current credit activity, supplied by one boss to another or one casino to another.

runner—A non-stop, several-day drinking, gambling, and food fest.

scouting casinos—Surveying casinos, either by phone or in person, to determine the best comp-counting conditions.

single-deck blackjack—Blackjack played with one deck in which the players pick up their cards. The comp wizard's favorite game.

slot club—The vehicle by which gamblers are awarded comps in accordance with slot-machine play.

soft comp—A comp which a casino provides in rooms, food, shows, limo rides, etc., which has built-in departmental profit margins.

spree—A vacation package incorporating a reimbursement program by which low-level comps are awarded in direct proportion to play.

steamer—A gambler who increases his bets in an effort to recover losses.

stiff—Someone who doesn't tip.

stroker—Someone who creates unnecessary work for a floorman.

sucker—Anyone who plays table games, slots, or video poker and fails to play intelligently and maximize every comp opportunity.

sweat—When a floorman intently watches or worries about player activity on a game, particularly when the players are winning (see "heat").

sweatshop—A casino which treats its staff and winning gamblers like criminals.

swings—The ebb and flow of gambling wins and losses.

swing shift—The last shift of the day in a casino. Typically runs from 8:00 pm to 4:00 am.

table games—Casino games that require dealers.

tapped out—When a gambler loses all of his money and can't get any more.

third base—The last seat, starting from the dealer's left, on a blackjack table.

tracking—A casino's particular method of observing and evaluating a rated player's action.

toke—A tip.

token—A tip. Or a facsimile silver dollar used in slots and on table games.

VIP Services—Arm of casino marketing department that arranges comped customer services.

walking money—Money issued to a rated player who's tapped out (never exceeds 5% of a player's losses).

whiner—Anyone who grouses and complains to hosts and bosses about losses, comp policies, and casino conditions.

Wonging—Jumping into a blackjack game in progress when it's advantageous to the player (a card-counting technique).

Appendix

Player's Hourly Expected Loss

Playing Basic Strategy Blackjack Vs. Games With Casino Advantage Ranging From 0.1% to 0.8%

Average		Casino Advantage						
Bet	**Handle**	**0.1%**	**0.2%**	**0.3%**	**0.4%**	**0.5%**	**0.6%**	**0.8%**
$15	$900	1	2	3	4	5	5	7
$25	$1,500	2	3	5	6	8	9	12
$50	$3,000	3	6	9	12	15	18	24
$75	$4,500	5	9	14	18	23	27	36
$100	$6,000	6	12	18	24	30	36	48
$125	$7,500	8	15	23	30	38	45	60
$150	$9,000	9	18	27	36	45	54	72
$175	$10,500	11	21	32	42	53	63	84
$200	$12,000	12	24	36	48	60	72	96
$225	$13,500	14	27	41	54	68	81	108
$250	$15,000	15	30	45	60	75	90	120
$300	$18,000	18	36	54	72	90	108	144
$400	$24,000	24	48	72	96	120	144	192
$500	$30,000	30	60	90	120	150	180	240

Determine the casino advantage at blackjack based on number of decks and rules. Determine how much you will wager per hand. Find intersecting point in chart to determine your expected loss per hour. Example: casino advantage equals 0.3%, your average bet is $250 per hand, expected loss equals $45 per hour.

Casino Scouting Checklist

Room, Food, and Beverage

Casino ______________________________

Phone ______________________________

Ask for room reservations.
Request: weekend room rate ______ weekend suite rate ______

Transfer to a table-games host.
Ask how much you have to gamble at blackjack to earn:

Room Only	Average bet ______ X ______	hours per day
RFB	Average bet ______ X ______	hours per day
Airfare	Average bet ______ X ______	hours per day

Transfer to 21 pit.
Ask for their blackjack rules.
Refer to "Variables" chart (p.34) to determine the house advantage.
Advantage______

Complete this formula to calculate your **expected loss** for **room only; room, food, and beverage;** and **airfare**.

Hours required (2 days)	______	X
Average Bet	______	X
Hands per hour (60)	______	=
Total betting handle	______	X
House Advantage	______	=
Expected Loss	______	

Casino Scouting Checklist

Low-Limit and Local Gamblers

Casino____

Phone____

Ask for room reservations.
Request: weekend room rate______

Transfer to a table-games host.
Ask how much you have to gamble at blackjack to earn:

Room Only	Average bet ______	X______	hours per day
Casino Rate	Average bet ______	X______	hours per day

Transfer to 21 pit.
Ask for their blackjack rules.
Refer to "Variables" chart (p.34) to determine the house advantage.
Advantage______

Ask how much you have to gamble to get these comps for two:

Buffet (if available)	Average bet ______	X______	hours per day
Coffee Shop	Average bet ______	X______	hours per day
Gourmet Dinner	Average bet ______	X______	hours per day
Show	Average bet ______	X______	hours per day

Complete this formula to calculate your **expected loss** for **room only; food;** and **show.**

Hours required	______	X
Average Bet	______	X
Hands per hour (60)	______	=
Total betting handle	______	X
House Advantage	______	=
Expected Loss	______	

Scouting Flowchart

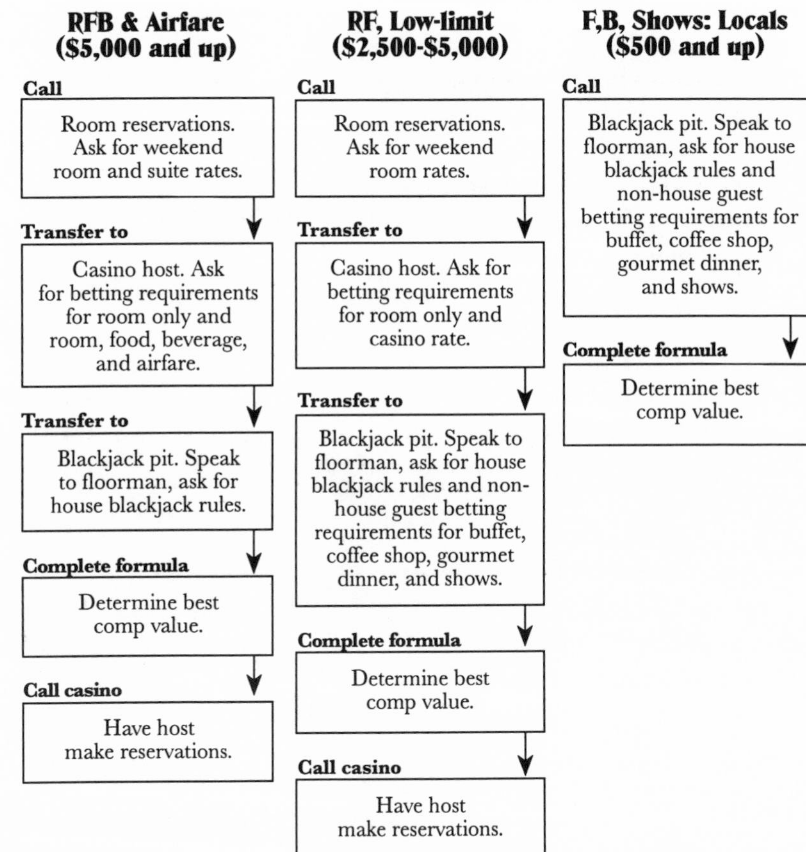

Vital Statistics

Aladdin	(1-800-634-3424)	736-0111
Arizona Charlie's	(1-800-342-2695)	258-5200
Bally's	(1-800-634-3434)	739-4111
Barbary Coast	(1-800-634-6755)	737-7111
Binion's Horseshoe	(1-800-237-6537)	382-1600
Boardwalk	(1-800-635-4581)	735-1167
Bourbon Street	(1-800-634-6956)	737-7200
Caesars Palace	(1-800-634-6661)	731-7110
California	(1-800-634-6255)	385-1222
Casino Royale		737-3500
Circus Circus	(1-800-634-3450)	734-0410
Continental	(1-800-634-6641)	737-5555
Debbie Reynold's	(1-800-633-1777)	734-0711
Desert Inn	(1-800-634-6906)	733-4444
El Cortez	(1-800-634-6703)	385-5200
Excalibur	(1-800-937-7777)	597-7777
Fitzgeralds	(1-800-274-5825)	388-2400
Flamingo Hilton	(1-800-732-2111)	733-3111
Four Queens	(1-800-634-6045)	385-4011
Fremont	(1-800-634-6182)	385-3232
Frontier	(1-800-634-6966)	794-8200
Gold Coast	(1-800-331-5334)	367-7111
Gold Spike	(1-800-634-6703)	384-8444
Golden Gate	(1-800-426-0521)	382-6300
Golden Nugget	(1-800-634-3454)	385-7111
Hacienda	(1-800-634-6713)	739-8911
Harrah's	(1-800-634-6765)	369-5000
Imperial Palace	(1-800-634-6441)	731-3311
King 8	(1-800-634-3488)	736-8988
Klondike		739-9351
Lady Luck	(1-800-523-9582)	477-3000
Las Vegas Club	(1-800-634-6532)	385-1664
Las Vegas Hilton	(1-800-732-7117)	732-5111
Little Caesars		734-2827
Longhorn		435-9170
Luxor	(1-800-288-1000)	262-4000
MGM Grand	(1-800-929-1111)	891-1111
Maxim	(1-800-634-6987)	731-4300
Mirage	(1-800-627-6667)	791-7111
Nevada Palace	(1-800-634-6283)	458-8810
O'Shea's		792-0777
Palace Station	(1-800-634-3101)	367-2411
Pioneer		386-5000
Plaza	(1-800-634-6575)	386-2110
Rio	(1-800-888-1808)	252-7777
Riviera	(1-800-634-6753)	734-5110
Royal	(1-800-634-6118)	735-6117
Sahara	(1-800-634-6666)	737-2111
Sam's Town	(1-800-634-6371)	456-7777
Sands	(1-800-634-6901)	733-5000
San Remo	(1-800-522-7366)	739-9000
Santa Fe	(1-800-872-6823)	658-4900
Showboat	(1-800-826-2800)	385-9123
Silver City		732-4152
Slots a Fun		734-0410
Stardust	(1-800-634-6757)	732-6111
Town Hall	(1-800-634-6541)	732-1499
Treasure Island	(1-800-944-7444)	894-7444
Tropicana	(1-800-468-9494)	739-2222
Vacation Village	(1-800-338-0608)	897-1700
Vegas World	(1-800-634-6277)	382-2000
Western	(1-800-634-6703)	384-4620
Westward Ho	(1-800-634-6651)	731-2900

Complete Basic Strategy for Single and Multiple Deck Blackjack

Hit-Stand

	2	3	4	5	6	7	8	9	T	A
12	H	H	S	S	S	H	H	H	H	H
13	S	S	S	S	S	H	H	H	H	H
14	S	S	S	S	S	H	H	H	H	H
15	S	S	S	S	S	H	H	H	H	H
16	S	S	S	S	S	H	H	H	H	H
17	S	S	S	S	S	S	S	S	S	S

Hard Dougle

	2	3	4	5	6	7	8	9	T	A
11	D	D	D	D	D	D	D	D	D	D/H
10	D	D	D	D	D	D	D	D	H	H
9	D/H	D	D	D	D	H	H	H	H	H
8	H	H	H	D/H	D/H	H	H	H	H	H

Soft Double

	2	3	4	5	6	7	8	9	T	A
A9	.... ALWAYS STAND									
A8	S	S	S	S	D/S	S	S	S	S	
A7	S	D	D	D	D	S	S	H	H	S*/H
A6	D/H	D	D	D	D	H	H	H	H	H
A5	H	H	D	D	D	H	H	H	H	H
A4	H	H	D	D	D	H	H	H	H	H
A3	H	H	D/H	D	D	H	H	H	H	H
A2	H	H	D/H	D	D	H	H	H	H	H

Split Pairs

	2	3	4	5	6	7	8	9	T	A
22	H	P/H	P	P	P	P	H	H	H	H
33	H	H	P	P	P	P	H	H	H	H
44	.... NEVER SPLIT									
55	.... NEVER SPLIT									
66	P/H	P	P	P	P	H	H	H	H	H
77	P	P	P	P	P	P	H	H	S/H	H
88	.... ALWAYS SPLIT									
99	P	P	P	P	P	S	P	P	S	S
TT	.... NEVER SPLIT									
AA	.... ALWAYS SPLIT									

NEVER TAKE INSURANCE

* Hit (A,7) vs. ace if dealer hits soft 17.

KEY: H= Hit S=Stand P=Split Pair D=Double Down

How to Use Complete Basic Strategy Chart

(previous page)

The combinations down the left hand side of the chart represent your hand. The numbers across the top represent the dealer's up card. Example: You hold (A,4) and the dealer shows a 6, the proper play is to double down. Where there is a slash (i.e., D/H), the first play is versus a single deck and the second is versus multiple decks. The most important tables are Hit-Stand and Hard Double. They are also easiest to learn.

Basic Strategy for Favorable Blackjack Options

Pair Splitting vs. Single and Multiple Decks (Double After Split Allowed)

You Hold		Single	Multiple
2,2	split vs. dealer's	2-7	2-7
3,3	split vs. dealer's	2-8	2-7
4,4	split vs. dealer's	4-6	5 & 6
5,5	never split		
6,6	split vs. dealer's	2-7	2-6
7,7	split vs. dealer's	2-8	2-7
8,8	always split		
9,9	split vs. dealer's	2-9 (except 7)	
T,T	never split		
A,A	always split		

Surrender (late)

You Hold	Single	Multiple
16 (except 8,8)	10,A	9,10,A
15	10*	10*

**Also A if dealer hits soft 17.*

Resplitting Aces

always resplit

Four-Hour Conversion

Hosts and VIP Services representatives often refer to something called the "four-hour conversion." This is a method they use to determine what their expected win is if you don't happen to wager a fixed amount every hand for exactly four hours a day (nobody does). Since hosts are required to base their comp decisions on fairly rigid guidelines, the four-hour conversion gives them a benchmark that they can refer to quickly to determine if you qualify for what you want. Take a look at this table and you'll see what I mean. Assume the house requires a $100 four-hour conversion for you to qualify for RFB.

Player	**A**	**B**	**C**
Hours Played per Day	8	4	2
Times Average Bet	$50	$100	$200
Equals Gross Conversion	$400	$400	$400
Divided By Four Hours	4	4	4
Equals Four Hour Conversion	$100	$100	$100

Even though these players have different bet levels, each has the same $100 four-hour conversion because the total action works out to be the same for each—$24,000. Players betting less have to risk their money for longer periods to reach the same level. In this case, even though player A can only afford to bet $50 a hand, by simply betting twice as long he can still qualify for the same comps that Player B gets. Player C, on the other hand, may be a $200 bettor, but if he only plays two hours a day, he's worth no more to the casino than players A or B.

The key to utilizing the four-hour conversion to your benefit is to understand three things. First, players are required to provide a pre-determined amount of total action to get comps, but how you reach that amount can be variable. Second, four-hour conversions reflect how much you must gamble to earn *one day's* worth of high-level comps. And third, players are not required to play four hours each day to earn high-level comps. You can fulfill your comp requirements for an entire vacation in a single day, or spread it out over the length of your stay.

The four-hour conversion's real value to the player is its flexibility, with implications for both bankroll and time. For example, if the four-hour conversion for a room is $50 per night, and you have a limited comp-counting bankroll, say $2,500, you can play eight hours per day at $25 a hand to qualify. Betting less for longer periods of time smooths the swings in your winnings and losses. Or, if the four-hour conversion for RFB is $150 for three nights, you can bet $450 a hand for four hours on your last night and still earn your comps.

Because of the four-hour conversion, any bankroll of $2,500 or more can qualify for virtually any comp if you're willing to play long enough.

One more look. Let's say you want to spend five nights RFB, and the four-hour conversion is $125. You can:

	Total Playing Time
• Play ten hours each day at $50 a hand.	50 hours
• Play four hours each day at $125 a hand.	20 hours
• Play two hours each day at $250 a hand.	10 hours
• Play one hour each day at $500 a hand.	5 hours
• Play one hour only at $2,500 a hand.	1 hour

(All five of these options result in $150,000 in betting action.)

The ramifications for ACES players are enormous. Say you have a good boss who consistently upgrades your average bet by 100%, you're staying for three nights, and need a four-hour conversion of $100. You'd need to bet $100 a hand for 12 hours officially, but unofficially $100 a hand for only six hours will suffice (since the boss is cranking your average bet up to $200).

Additional Tips

• Put enough money in the cage, in either credit or cash deposits, for the casino to feel justified in giving you high-level comps. This is not to say that you actually risk the money.

• Four-hour conversions do not apply in casinos that don't have computer generated tracking systems.

• Most premium casinos will not computer-rate anybody betting less than $25 a hand.

Resources

If you read *Comp City* cover to cover, you know more about comps than most bosses do. If you want to surpass the marketing and accounting whizzes with your gambling knowledge, I suggest you add at least some of these titles to your library. All of these products are available from Huntington Press, 1-800-244-2224.

Blackjack

Books

Theory of Blackjack, by Peter Griffin, $9.95, Huntington Press
Basic Blackjack, by Stanford Wong, $14.95, Pi Yee Press
Blackjack Secrets, by Stanford Wong, $14.95, Pi Yee Press
Professional Blackjack, by Stanford Wong, $19.95, Pi Yee Press
Blackbelt in Blackjack, by Arnold Snyder, $12.95, RGE Press

Software

Blackjack Analyzer (IBM), by Stanford Wong, $29.95, Pi Yee Press
Blackjack Count Analyzer (IBM), by Stanford Wong, $79.95, Pi Yee Press
Blackjack Trainer (Mac), $75, ConJelCo

Newsletters

Las Vegas Advisor, Anthony Curtis, 12 issues, $45, Huntington Press

Video Poker

Books

Winning Strategies for Video Poker, by Lenny Frome, $15.95, Compu-Flyers
Professional Video Poker, by Stanford Wong, $14.95, Pi Yee Press

Software

Stanford Wong Video Poker (IBM), $29.95, Villa Crespo Software

Slot Clubs/Video Poker

Bargain City—Booking, Betting, and Beating The New Las Vegas, by Anthony Curtis, $11.95, Huntington Press

Guide/History

Las Vegas, by Deke Castleman, $14.95, Compass American Guides

Bankroll Index

This "Bankroll Index" will help you determine what size bankroll you need to pursue the comps described throughout this book. Example: If you have a gambling stake of $750, reference the pages listed in the row titled "$501-$1,000." You might also find information relative to your situation by referencing pages listed under bankrolls of lesser amounts.

Index

L

M

N

O

P

R

S

T

V

W

Get on the Huntington Press Mailing List!

Huntington Press is a specialty publisher of gambling and casino-related books and products. If you've purchased *Comp City* from a source other than Huntington Press, call the toll-free number below to have your name placed on a preferred customer list. You'll receive pre-publication notification and discount offers on new Huntington Press books, special reports, and products. A pre-publication purchase assures you of being the first to receive a new book, often at a substantial discount from bookstore prices.

To have a Huntington Press catalogue mailed to you, call:

1-800-244-2224

9 am-5 pm, PST, Monday-Friday

Huntington Press
5280 S. Valley View Blvd., Suite B-8
Las Vegas, Nevada 89118